D1380852

NIGHT FALLS ON ARDNAMURCHAN

BY THE SAME AUTHOR:

Poetry

POETRY INTRODUCTION TWO
(*Faber & Faber*)

FROM THE WILDERNESS

WAKING THE DEAD

NIGHT FALLS ON ARDNAMURCHAN

The Twilight of a Crofting Family

by

ALASDAIR MACLEAN

LONDON
VICTOR GOLLANCZ LTD
1984

First published in Great Britain June 1984
by Victor Gollancz Ltd,
14 Henrietta Street, London WC2E 8QJ
Second impression July 1984
Third impression December 1984

© Alasdair Maclean 1984

ACKNOWLEDGEMENT

The passage on pp. 203–4 from *The Rocks Remain* by Gavin Maxwell, first
published by Longmans, Green in 1963, is copyright © Gavin Maxwell,
1963 and is reprinted by permission of Penguin Books Ltd and E. P. Dutton
Inc. Poem XIV from *More Poems* by A. E. Housman is reprinted on pp.
222–3 by permission of The Society of Authors as the literary representative
of the Estate of A. E. Housman, and Jonathan Cape Ltd, publishers of A. E.
Housman's *Collected Poems*. The poem on p. 213 from the Irish of Egan O
Rahilly, translated by James Stephens, is reprinted by permission of The
Society of Authors on behalf of the copyright owner, Mrs Iris Wise. The
three stanzas on p. 200 are from 'Daisy' by Francis Thompson. Five lines
from 'Wild Peaches' by Elinor Wylie are from *Collected Poems of Elinor
Wylie*, 1921, reprinted by permission of the publisher, Alfred A. Knopf,
copyright renewed 1949 by William Rose Benet.
The publisher acknowledges subsidy from the Scottish Arts Council
towards the publication of this volume.

British Library Cataloguing in Publication Data

Maclean, Alasdair, *19---*
    Night falls on Ardnamurchan.
    1. Farm life—Scotland—Ardnamurchan
    Peninsula   2. Crofters—Scotland—
    Ardnamurchan Peninsula   3. Ardnamurchan
    Peninsula (Scotland)—Social life and customs
    I. Title
    941.11'85   S522.G7

ISBN 0-575-03460-2

Photoset in Great Britain by
Rowland Phototypesetting Ltd, Bury St Edmunds, Suffolk
and printed by St Edmundsbury Press
Bury St Edmunds, Suffolk

To the memory of my parents

Open thy mouth for the dumb, in the cause of all such as are appointed to destruction.

Proverbs

ACKNOWLEDGEMENT

I am grateful to the following people who helped me at various times and in various ways during the writing of this book: Stewart Conn, Livia Gollancz, Bruce Hunter, Ronald and Baldina MacDonald, Ian and Mary McLeod, Mrs Peggy Rose and Bill and Margaret Stevenson. Particularly I wish to express my thanks to the Scottish Arts Council for their financial help which enabled me to finish the book.

I am especially indebted to my sister, Jessie, for her unsurpassed local knowledge, so generously shared with me.

Parts of the text were broadcast on BBC Radio, in 1982, under the series title 'Ardnamurchan Journal'.

                                                                    A.M.

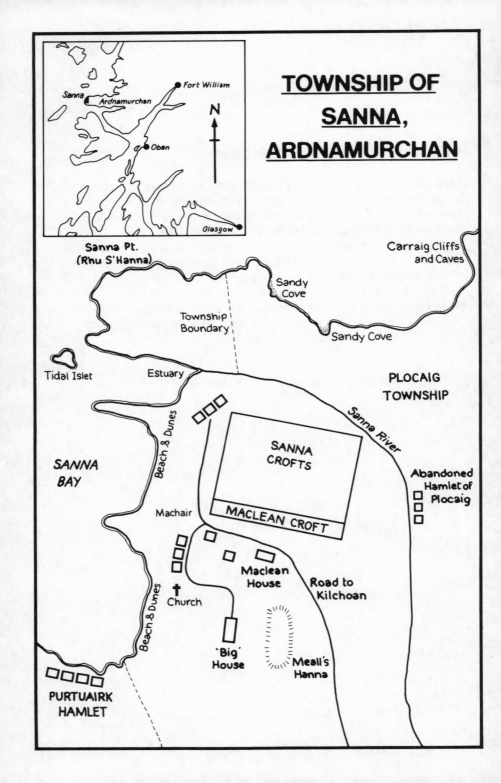

TOWNSHIP OF SANNA, ARDNAMURCHAN

Fort William

Sanna
Ardnamurchan

N

Oban

Glasgow

Sanna Pt.
(Rhu S'Hanna)

Carraig Cliffs
and Caves

Sandy
Cove

Township
Boundary

Sandy Cove

PLOCAIG
TOWNSHIP

Tidal Islet

Estuary

SANNA
BAY

Beach & Dunes

SANNA
CROFTS

Sanna River

Abandoned
Hamlet of
Plocaig

Machair

MACLEAN CROFT

Maclean
House

Road to
Kilchoan

Church

Beach & Dunes

'Big'
House

Meall's
Hanna

PURTUAIRK
HAMLET

CONTENTS

PHOTOGRAPHS

NIGHT FALLS ON ARDNAMURCHAN

[The road into Sanna under snow: the Maclean house is the first on the left]

PROLOGUE

[Carraig Cliff: Father in foreground]

PROLOGUE

IT MAY BE my misfortune that I end this work and come to the small luxury of preface and acknowledgements only to find books about the countryside issuing from the presses in their hundreds. Indeed they flourish rather more greenly than their subject matter. It is a new irony. Instead of the Year of the Tree we have the Year of the Book of the Tree. Forests are laid waste to arouse the public against the laying waste of forests.

I can only plead that the field was somewhat less crowded ten long years ago when I first began to think about this book and to make tentative notes for it. Nor, as far as that goes, did I sit down in cold blood to compose upon a certain topic. I wrote out of compulsion and with more of sadness and anger than glee. What follows this preface is a debt of conscience owed to certain gravestones in the remote townships of Western Ardnamurchan: in Kilmory, whose round little cemetery was old when the Reformation was young; in Kilchoan, where the churchyard has overflowed and a new square of acid hillside has been staked out for posterity to sweeten; in forgotten and half-forgotten places like Tornamona under Ben Hiant, the enchanted mountain, where the crofts were so improved by reforming landlords that no man now can say where they began and where they ended. These were my ancestors. It is regrettable, no doubt, that my subject is too much in vogue but to me and my purposes it is not very material.

Another sad truth is that books about the countryside preach largely to the converted; they are bought by the sort of people who buy books about the countryside. That, indeed, is the audience they are aimed at. And these people are not, in general, people who already live and have their being in rural surroundings; neither are they passionately committed to the city. Instead, they are a sort of in-between class whose souls yearn for the outdoors even as their bodies crowd the pavements. They are sufferers, that is to say, from a kind of spiritual schizophrenia peculiar to our urban civilization.

I do not know what the solution is to this problem, either for writer or reader. Certainly we owe the countryside rather less to those who are vigorous in its defence—usually, to their very great credit, members of that same in-between group—than to our confirmed city-dwellers, for if the latter did not pack contentedly into their hives there would be scarce a pasture from Land's End to John o' Groats that was not muddied to extinction. Yea, our very mountains would be flattened.

That is irony number two. If we who write on country affairs were to go outside our chosen audience we should have to act as forbidders instead of encouragers. 'Dear city-dweller,' we should have to say, 'do not on any account come into the country,' thinking the while, 'for if you do there will certainly be none left for us to write about.' I have the longing that all writers have for new ears to pour my words into, yet if there were the least danger of my being heard by the unconverted I should in all conscience have to stop what I was doing, for my own sake and for the sake of all who love as I love.

One can at any rate say confidently that books about crofting are less common than the field guides and the good life kind of thing that now and then deservedly and blessedly make the bestseller lists. One would have to add, however, that by and large they are also less worthwhile. It is true that two—at least—very fine works of crofting scholarship have come on the market in recent years: Philip Gaskell's *Morvern Transformed* and James Hunter's *The Making of the Crofting Community*. These are shining exceptions. The others that have appeared are mostly highly-coloured and semi-fictional attempts to cash in on the supposed naïvety and comicality of Highlanders and the saddest thing about them is that they achieve most of their success—often considerable—in Scotland, where they ought most to be despised.

Mockery of Highlanders, in the guise of comedy, has a long and dishonest tradition in print. Stage Irish has nothing on it. If I had a gallon of paraffin and a match for every book I have come across in which the people of the Highlands, whose standard in English even yet is probably rather higher than what obtains in the rest of Britain, are made to sound like substandard cretins bartering for trade goods in a kind of Hebridean pidgin, I could light such a fire as by God's grace would never be put out in Scotland.

Changing attitudes to the Highlands and those who live there could be made the subject of a fat volume. There is enough on record for it. Indeed those changes, if plotted on a graph, might well serve as a mental health chart for the rest of the nation. What Highlanders have thought of the lives and beliefs of those around them is somewhat less well documented. I often wonder, for instance, as I drive north through Luss and Tarbet, what the Highlanders made of Loch Lomond when they began their great exodus in the middle decades of the last century, when the potatoes failed and the landlords throve and they trekked down to Glasgow in search of a living with the memory of their own tarns and fiords still fresh upon them. How puzzled they must have been! Here, interminably foisted on all who would listen, was a watery substitute for Scotland whose pre-eminence could only be accounted for in terms of bulk and availability. It was the nearest sizeable piece of—not Highland landscape, certainly, though it was thought to be that by those who knew no better; non-Lowland perhaps—it was the nearest such to the industrial belt of the south and that is where the symbols for export are manufactured. What an eye-opener it must have been to them, what a chillingly prophetic glimpse of Lowland provincialism and chauvinism! How—and the dismay must have grown—could something so unexceptional have brought even to the half-life which is all, mostly, they possess, the endless stream of paintings and photographs generated by it? How could it have come to stand for all the pain of exile, gathering to itself so much of borrowed loveliness that it was celebrated round the globe? It compared but poorly with ten thousand truly Highland lochs yet there it lay in its usurping and potent length—and indeed there it lies still, all Landseer and Lauder, a mere tourist bus ride out from Glasgow and you can do it in an afternoon.

They do not yet sing 'Loch Lomond' in the ceilidhs of the Hebrides but they are in grave danger of swallowing the ethos behind it, and the consequences of that may well be fatal.

Or what price Glasgow itself as an indicator? Glaswegians, when I was small, took their holiday pleasures in the resorts of their own Firth of Clyde. They are quintessentially children of the bright lights, neon tube babies, and now that their home-based electrical industry has been largely eclipsed they seek dazzle elsewhere, in Blackpool or Benidorm. The Rainbow Road that leads up Scotland's west coast has never meant aught to them except insofar as it channelled them a steady flow of those supreme figures of Glasgow amusement and contempt, the Highlanders, (my father amongst them), with their shiny blue serge suits, their trousers hoisted high, their trilbies, their comical accents. It would have astonished and chagrined them to learn that the amusement and contempt were reciprocal, that to the Highlanders they merely scurried along the darksome alleys of what they fondly imagined was a self-sufficient paradise. Had they been at all interested they might have discovered that the fabled Rainbow Road, like all roads, had two directions to it with a different sort of crock at either end, and that what impelled the hapless newcomers to their midst was not the intrinsic merit of Glasgow but the tarnished glitter of its wage packets.

Glasgow is not for me.
I do not see the need for such a crowd,
all jumping and biting like fleas in a great blanket.
How long is it since I met myself?

The people lock their faces every morning
before they go to work,
for fear, I think, of having a good look stolen.
Who knows where the key is?

Here nothing grows but memory and that crookedly.
That sitting-rock by the ford on the way to Plocaig
—I can feel its roughness on the back of my legs.
Our folk had a name for it. What was it?

I was a good man with a spade once.
The houses are too high;
the streets too narrow.
Who could dig himself out of so deep a ditch?

I'd give all I own: my good name,
the linings of my pockets, that kiss you gave me
when I left (you'd replace it surely),
if I could go home once more to Ardnamurchan.

So sang, once, a Gaelic poet with the travel sickness on him. They give you pills nowadays and where there is no pain there is no poetry. Glasgow permeates the Highlands now, from its language to its political parties. The fisherman in Stornoway chats to tourists not in the soft, pure English of his grandfather but in something that approximates more and more nearly to the dialect of Clydeside. Straws in the wind, no doubt.

I catch myself speaking as if I were fully cognizant of my subject and how I have dealt with it. In truth I am not. Certainly I write about myself in these pages as much as I tell the story of my crofting father and the way of his world. In fact, I started out with some pretensions towards producing an area guide book, though even then I knew that it was likely to be both personal and idiosyncratic. My focus narrowed as the years passed and as my awareness grew that my lack of inclination for such a task was equalled only by my lack of ability. In the end I discarded most of my earlier notion and concentrated on one family in one tiny hamlet. It is left to me to hope that in being so particular I have been general as well.

I can at least inform the reader that my book is built around extracts from two journals, my father's and my own, both set (mostly) in the same small village but featuring rather different ways of life and having very different aims and methods. About the circumstances in which each journal was kept and about the plan followed in using it I shall have more to say later. Father was a working crofter, if that is not too much like saying of someone that he was a fare-collecting bus conductor, and his portion of the book constitutes a factual and totally unadorned account of his daily round, an *aide mémoire* for his own benefit as much as anything. His record of crofting life forms the backbone of the book.

Following the extracts from his journal I have included selections from my own daily notes. These sometimes gloss Father in a more extended and looser way, a more indirect way, than the immediate glosses I have given him. Sometimes, too, they reflect on his life and work and sometimes diverge totally into my own concerns. To the extent that I was a crofter it was intermittently and never considering it my chief of occupations. I was a part-time assistant to my father and, briefly after he died, a later and lesser follower. Mainly I thought myself a writer, a poet, and the records I kept necessarily suggested my quite different business. I have tried to prevent the more strictly literary part of my life and thought from overwhelming the rest of my material, reckoning a tale of poetry and its production too narrow a specialization in this day and age for the general reader. But that aspect of things was naturally insistent for me and I have let it intrude on a number of occasions. Were I to present any other picture of myself I should be guilty of serious falsification.

What matters is that there should emerge from these pages something of the rise and fall of a crofting hamlet in a remote and little-known region of these islands, and that this should be displayed through an account of the life and hard times of my father, who was the last man to practise the art of crofting in that hamlet. If, parallel with this account and rounding it off, there should also appear a little of myself, who watched that life and that death and who, perhaps, survived it, I trust the reader will not think it too great an imposition. My literary work, indeed, grows out of that background, or did so when I kept my Ardnamurchan journal, and even where I may appear to depart most radically from the matter in hand a link of some kind could generally be found, for all that it might take a course in psychoanalysis to trace its windings. The reader should picture me as an antiphonal chorus to Father and make what allowance he can when I show myself too much the soloist.

I have dawdled, then, or detoured, whenever I felt inclined and even once or twice when I did not, the latter that my reader might have a chance to get his breath back after some gallop, (or master his astonishment or his resentment), while his author gathered wit and muscle for a fresh assault upon the senses. I have trod on as many toes as I might conveniently reach and have found no shortage of suitably corned and bunioned subjects, some of them Scottish, I am very pleased to say, and not a few Highland.

I do not quite absolutely vouch for dates or facts and when once or twice, or three or four times, I have had to choose between refusing an anecdote because of its suspect authenticity and including it for its illustrative power I have plumped solidly for the latter course. I am an interpreter who presents a version rather than a word for word translation. In my sort of writing the parable is mightier than the history; it is the difference between metaphor and ordinary description.

I hope, in brief, that my book is entirely true as a poet reckons truth; certainly, trying to make it so has been my chief consideration. But as to how much confidence the reader should place in even that reduced—or inflated—claim, he must decide for himself. Poets are fond, perhaps overly fond, of such arrogation, for of course it is an inflated claim in their eyes, but a close look at their working methods may reveal no more in the way of ethical concern than is required by the juggling of a page of words to fit a kind of template carried in the mind. (The closer the fit the greater the poet.) Their truth might better be described as accuracy and their accuracy defined as a by-product of poetic engineering, with the advertising of it a mere afterthought, a fortuitous profit-taking.

If this book could be summed up at all it would be as my struggle to understand myself and my background. Perhaps I had better leave it at that for the present, letting the text speak for itself and the reader judge for himself. Where more detailed explanation is required for a particular passage it will, I trust, be found in the body of the book.

So, no apologies. I have written entirely to please myself and enlighten myself. If I perform the same service for any reader I shall be proud of that. If not, I shall have myself to blame.

SANNA, ARDNAMURCHAN—
KIRKCALDY, FIFE
1973–1982

INTRODUCTION I
Father and Son

WE HARDLY CONCEIVE of our parents as human. There are in-numerable actions, there are whole areas of life and thought, that we do not care to see connected with them, that we scarcely allow ourselves, far less others, to connect with them. These two figures are our father and mother, we say: actors permanently burdened with the parts we have written for them, however unwillingly they may tread our boards, however dreadfully miscast they may be. Or were they not so appallingly mortal one might describe them as minor household deities, handed down in the family and worshipped conventionally rather than through any great belief in their fading powers. They may not step aside into ordinariness, into normality or frailty, from the narrow track we have appointed to them. In our minds, in our memories, they trudge forward always, wrinkling as they come. It is the only direction permitted them, for all the time, of course, we are pulling them after us. It is we who trudge.

I feel, as I settle down to write about my father, that the most difficult imaginative feat that could be required of us is to recreate our parents as children or even as young men and women. It is so difficult that few of us ever attempt it, if indeed—so unthinkable is it—it occurs to us at all. And not a little of the small tragedy of family life—those sensitivities towards others whose edge we have allowed deliberately to grow dull in the interests of our own comfort, those faintly dingy compromises that we half-regret when some circumstance forces us briefly to acknowledge the bitterness of our days—not a little of all this is precisely due to just such an incapacity in our love, to just such a blank spot in the picture of our dear ones that we have so fondly and so blindly constructed.

My father died in 1973, in the tiny hamlet of Sanna in Western Ardnamurchan. He died in his own home, a Mark Two version of the Highland cottage of his parents that, seventy-five years previously and a hundred yards distant, had seen his birth. In material terms it was not very much of a progress.

Between his dates he did much that was typical of the times he lived in and the class he was born into, though it would nowadays be considered unusual or more likely would be forbidden altogether. Thus: after six years at our one-room school he went to sea at fourteen, adding two years to his age. He joined the Royal Naval Volunteer Reserve during the First World War and saw service at the Dardanelles. When the war ended he came ashore, married and settled in Glasgow, where such work as was then available in Scotland was most likely to be. He fathered four children, a boy and a girl older than me, a boy younger. He and my mother endured poverty so severe that my elder brother had to be permanently fostered by my paternal grandparents, my crofting grandparents here in Ardnamurchan, who were no better off but could at least count on a fairly regular supply of potatoes and fish. Once, when I was seven. I had to join my brother for a year.

Eventually Father obtained a post with the Clyde Navigation Trust, the body that ran the Greater Glasgow docks system. He became a Deputy Harbour Master, which sounds impressive but was actually the bottom rung of the ladder and simply an inflated title for a berthing master. It was a uniformed job that always provided more in the way of prestige and steadiness than large salaries. Poor we remained.

Due to Father's complete lack of push, coupled with his unwillingness to flatter or connive, he was passed over for promotion on several occasions. In the early 1950s he retired, somewhat prematurely, and came back to Ardnamurchan to operate the family croft, which my grandparents were getting too old to look after. Poverty accompanied him north and this lasted till a state pension at sixty-five brought some slight ease. He died five months after my mother, of a coronary, they said, but of being worn out and heartbroken, say I.

A shilling life will give you all the facts—and tell you precious little about the naked man who stands trembling behind them. My father was a complex, moody, introverted person, though capable of great natural charm. Indeed he had a patent sincerity about him, a complete lack of affectation, that ensured his being liked everywhere. Though generally somewhat reserved, preferring the company of his family or his own company to any other, he could surprise one in this respect. Quite often—while travelling, for instance—he would approach some likely-looking stranger and strike up a conversation (a thing I would never do). He was a handsome, tall, well-built man, attractive to women and fond of their presence when the mood took him; something of a gallant, indeed, though in a rather gauche and utterly innocent way.

Normally timid and unassertive outside the house (unless roused), he was very much the master within. I remember him, during my childhood, as being someone whom one approached on tiptoe. He was thin-skinned in the extreme, lightning-quick to feel hurt and to take offence and much given to monumental huffs. These almost always lasted a day or two and sometimes a good bit longer than that. Though he often, and violently, lost his temper and at least once, to my knowledge, fetched my mother a good thump, (to be fair, it was a quarrel and she had thrown a shoe at him first; the only such physical occasion that I recall), he never once raised his hand to the children. His outbursts of temper, unlike his huffs, were soon over and he was quick to seek reconciliation. I suspect that his anger may have frightened him a little. I know that it frightened me a lot. Indeed such a marked effect did it have on me that I have retained a great fear of angry people to this day. I am sure, however, that he was all too aware of his faults, even if, like most of us, unable to do much about them.

I have often wondered since, quite unresentfully, what the effect is of such a moody and unpredictable father on a sensitive young child (for I must suppose myself to have been one). I should imagine the consequences to be incalculable. Still I would not change my upbringing. For I think, too, that a happy, well-adjusted father would have his own effect, equal if different, and who could be sure of his proving to be in every way a greater good?

Life is life and, interpose what steel we care to, yet will our breasts be bare to some of its arrows, childish flesh and adult equally pocked. It is all taken into account, I dare say, in the plan. The perfect armour would breed within its darkness the perfect monster.

Father was rigidly straightforward in all his business, a man whose integrity was a by-word and whose good name was important to him. He worked hard to support his family and turned over his wage packet every week to Mother (when he had one) without demur. He smoked but did not gamble, and only rarely drank. He cobbled my brothers' shoes and mine when we were boys and cut our hair (though I would guess, as I study early snapshots of myself, that his shoemaking may have been more proficient than his barbering). He mended watches and built and repaired wireless sets, often for relatives or neighbours but always for love and never for money. He did a lot of competent carpentry around the house. He was a keen amateur photographer, doing his own printing and developing, good technically, if only rarely and freakishly compositionally. He was virtually tone-deaf and almost totally lacking in artistic good taste.

I do not remember that he ever played with us children, I mean in the sense of getting down on the floor with us and joining in our make-believe. On the other hand he never tried to dictate the course of our lives or called us to account. Simply, we were left to get on with it.

Whether such easy-going lack of direction was altogether quite wise I do not know. I can only say that, were it given to me to return to those days with a godlike hand, I should tremble to alter a single minute. I have become what I have become, for good or ill, and I have never really wanted to be anyone else or other than I am. I do think sometimes—and increasingly, perhaps, as I grow older and as the burden of being a writer grows with me—that I should like to be a happier person. But if I were, almost certainly I should not find myself carrying that burden and should have no need to wish it away. The argument is circular. I have contracted a marriage with the dark side of my being, the poetry side. We have come to suit over the years, as married couples come to suit who are not so much lovers of one another as addicts. We could not now tear ourselves apart without bloodshed, and if we did what would become of us?

Father certainly took us for regular walks and, when I became a little older, sometimes went cycling with me. Cycling was yet another of his enthusiasms. Perhaps I make him sound too brilliant an all-rounder. It was not so, or not wholly so. He was not as unusual then as he would be now. Merely, life was so different in those far-off pre-war days, different to an extent, I am sure, incomprehensible to anyone who did not experience it. People *did* so much more, were so much more an interacting part

of their world. Technology was on a human scale and interesting.
Everything about one seemed fresher and everyone more alive.
Even the drab streets of the Depression had a vitality now quite
gone, a vitality bearing no resemblance to the spurious and
random energies of today.

I believe that Father was a man constantly gnawed at by
insecurity and forever walled in behind his own inhibitions,
incapable of relaxing or unbending to any noticeable extent.
Only with animals was he completely at ease, for only animals
would never snub him or hurt him.

And even that, it occurs to me as I write, was not invariably
true. I remember, for instance, one or two dogs of ours that were
acquired or reared to be special to Father but that in the event
fastened themselves promiscuously to whoever in the family
happened to be available. They would prefer going for a walk
with me or fetching the cows with my sister to following in the
footsteps of their supposed master. Or they would accompany
Father to peat moss or fishing rock, then trot home rather than
spend several hours waiting there while he concluded his business. The truth, of course, was that our dogs were undisciplined
and spoiled. Each newcomer to their midst rapidly learned to
prefer play to work and amusement to boredom.

Father would grumble a little at being thus deprived of his
chosen companion and plainly there were times when it hurt.
What! To be incapable of attaching even a dog! No doubt it was but
another turn of the screw to him, one more example of his own
inadequacy and of the conspiratorial unfairness of the world.

(Ah, to find among the teeming millions the perfect companion! To be loved for oneself alone, wholly and exclusively,
without cessation or stint! It is a sweet dream—and a sour waking
taste in the mouth.)

Father was an intelligent, well-read man. He remained astonishingly tolerant of the modern world, interested in all that went
on and, despite the remoteness of Ardnamurchan and its entire
lack of cultural resources, trying always to keep abreast. Space
travel, for instance, fascinated him. In our garden with me, one
evening near the end, he gazed up at the moon and marvelled that
men should be walking around on it even as we watched. How
pleased he was, he told me, to have lived to see that. Towards the
end of his life, too, he resumed study of the Spanish he had loved
as a young man sailing to ports like Valencia and Cadiz. About

the same time he taught himself to use an old typewriter I gave him and from then on typed all his correspondence. To the last he remained capable of surprising one. In the year of his death he asked me one day what I thought of Reich and we discussed that great, if sometimes very silly, man about whom he proved rather more knowledgeable than I.

Only gradually and much too late have I come to grasp the extent of my father. I am sure that he loved us all very deeply. If I have seemed to deal harshly with him or in an overly-clinical fashion I must here and now attempt to redress the balance by acknowledging that I have inherited most of his faults and not nearly enough of his virtues.

I had been casting around for a way in which I might round off this portrait of my father and myself in terms perhaps less conventional, less schematic, than those above. When I came across the phrase 'the old banger' in his journal I knew I had found what I was looking for.

A 'banger', it may now be necessary to explain, was a slang term of the sixties for an old and decrepit car. Father, typically, took an interest in our changing tongue and was fond of being as up to date and as youthful as his restricted circumstances allowed. His keenness, unfortunately, sometimes outweighed his knowledge and overcame his caution. Slang is no passport for innocents, being by definition an attempt to exclude them. Half an understanding, a partial capacity, are never enough with language. An ability to pronounce 'shibboleth' merely gets you past the frontier guards; to survive in the interior you must also know, with great precision and delicacy, what the word means and how to use it.

Lacking such information, Father was sometimes self-betrayed. I remember a period when he took an inordinate fancy to the verb 'to frig', another slang term of the banger era and, of course, one that began life as a euphemism for the Anglo-Saxon 'to fuck'. Needless to say, he was quite unaware of its origin. In language context is all. The expression which goes unnoticed amid the worldliness of the city may well sound startling in a quiet Highland village, especially in the mouth of a reserved and elderly crofter. So a visitor would come to our house, genteel to the nth degree, it might be, but with that modish knowledge of the disreputable which gentility must needs have to give it

meaning and purpose. He would apologize for intruding. 'Not at
all,' Father would reply, with equal courtesy. 'I've just been
frigging around.'

After I grew up my visits home often saw me torn between
amusement and embarrassment. When I found the latter emotion
predominating I would sometimes try to remember linguistic
pitfalls I had fallen into myself. Wriggling in my corner I would
seek the comfort of analogy. The message 'You have been here
before and survived' is the greatest gift that memory can convey
to the beleaguered.

Pondering such mishaps I recall now one incident from my
childhood. It relates to the word 'whore'. I had come across this
word once or twice in my reading and knew roughly what it
meant, or at any rate sensed that it was a word to be employed
with discretion. However, I had also heard, playing on the streets
of Govan, the dialect pronunciation 'hoor', without ever con-
necting it with the word of my books. 'Hoor' to me was merely
an all-purpose intensifier, which was the use it was commonly
put to in Glasgow. 'Bloody hoor of a mornin' ' was the sort of
thing one heard on a wet forenoon in the working-class districts.
Naturally, there were professional 'hoors' aplenty in that city,
who would one day direct my attention to the human substan-
tive. But I was not yet of an age to be interested. I added my new
word proudly to my growing stock and came the fateful day
when I dropped it casually into a family conversation.

I was showing Father a model ship I had built and I became
concerned to point out, with a totally false modesty for which the
gods were about to administer condign punishment, some supposed flaw in its construction. 'I made a hoor of a job of the
after-deck' was perhaps what I said.

There followed, instead of the flood of praise and reassurance I
had confidently anticipated, a stunned silence. Then the back of
Mother's hand, which at that stage in my life I sometimes
imagined to be attached to my ear by a length of elastic, leaped
out from her cardigan sleeve and rang on my flesh like a pistol
shot: 'Don't you ever use that word in this house again!'

Father, seeing my bewildered innocence, proffered a dutiful
explanation. 'A "hoor" is an abandoned woman,' he told me,
before changing the subject. So I gained a small piece of knowledge at least and it says volumes about the sort of child I was that I
grasped the meaning of his somewhat pedantic definition im-

mediately, whereas an attempt to enlighten me in streetcorner terms might have left me as ignorant as before.

It was not the blow I minded so much, apart from feeling that on this occasion I hardly deserved it. Between home and school I was quite used to the idea that a physical retribution existed and that it was—generally—fair in its application, an acceptable and readily understood method of keeping the world in orbit. What cut more deeply was the loss of face, the shame of having participated in a public gaucherie. My parents were plainly highly embarrassed by the incident and this rubbed off tenfold on me. No one minds such happenings as all-consumingly as the child minds them; the blush of adults is skin-deep but the child blushes to his very soul.

Gradually one develops a carapace in life, building it up segment by segment in a series of small and painful victories. Yet one remains vulnerable in certain circumstances. Nothing pierces my armour so readily as being compelled to witness the embarrassment of others.

I remember one occasion when the hazards of language and a stranger's blushes coincided remarkably for me. The occurrence was trivial in itself yet in my memory its colours have stayed vivid, its impasto bold, while much that was larger in canvas and more striking has flattened to a dull grey.

It comes from a later period in my life when I was a National Service infantryman. I was stationed in that unhappy but fascinating country, India, and I was, when it took place, engaged in what I nearly always seemed to be engaged in out there—I mean travelling.

The war was over by this time, only just over but military life under the Raj was already settling back, as if nothing had ever disturbed its world or ever could disturb it, into its age-old, infinitely comfortable, infinitely boring routine. For the common soldier this meant the re-imposition, after the tiny amount of relaxation necessarily allowed him under threat of combat, of the disciplines and drills of the peacetime British Army. These were a unique mixture of the sinister and the farcical.

As conscripts intent only on the quickest return possible to civil life National Servicemen were a mulish encumbrance to that Army, grit in that smoothly inefficient machine. We were trundled mercilessly from camp to camp, in a desperate attempt to fit us in where we might spread least corruption. To and fro we went across the vast subcontinent, on journeys often lasting for days. We travelled always by train and outside our carriage windows the flatlands of central India rolled interminably past: paddyfield, plain and jungle; jungle, plain and paddyfield. We sat by ourselves in European splendour, for all that we scarcely merited, in any other sense but geographic, that resonant adjective; indeed, as far as my squad was concerned, we were but mostly rough corner-boys from the back streets of Glasgow. We were equipped with space, if not with cushions, on a scale so hugely in excess of our needs or deserts that even then—half-educated, callow, unused to any sort of moral precept beyond the simple and tacit ones of home—I had begun to find the privilege embarrassing. We lounged for the most part unmoved while in their own section of the train Indian civilians jammed the compartments and at times clung clustered to door and roof like so many brown bees. ('Brown b—s,' my comrades would have said.)

Late one afternoon a train I was on stopped in some small town or another. I never did learn its name. One was forever stopping just as one was forever travelling and save for a glimpsed and generally meaningless nameboard or two the halts were for us as shrouded in mystery as the destinations. Out of nowhere we came and into limbo we departed. The British Army, as far as its lower ranks were concerned, invariably moved in secret; less out of politic awareness of the sharpness of enemy ears, I always felt, than out of total indifference to the curiosity and intelligence of the soldiers who served in it. One would have been transported beyond the galaxy in the same contemptuous silence.

While we were stopped and my mates yarned or played brag for the small copper coins of the country I leaned out of the window. I saw before me a typical Indian railway station: home to hundreds of people; vibrant with heat and stench and seething with humanity in all its shapes and postures and occupations and stages of life, from the womb to—no doubt—the deathbed. In a little clearing in the midst of the swarm, a cool territorial imperative hacked out by a century of conquest, a group of European sahibs stood chatting. And on the edge of this group, close to me and in profile, was an extremely beautiful girl.

She was tall and fair, white-skinned, full-breasted, round-buttocked, long-legged. I did not need to guess at her attributes for, very clearly indeed, she had left off whatever of her garments she legally could in the interests of comfort. Sandals and a gauzy silk frock were absolutely all she wore and the sun of India, rampaging mutinously through a gap in the station buildings, had outlined her to a hair's breadth. Nippled and bushed, in essence naked, she posed for my delight, a lush oasis in my desert of prematurely worn-out and haggard poor Indian women.

I think that such unexpected largesse, coming just then, would have stuck in my mind of its own accord but what happened next riveted the memory to me permanently. Down the platform, dodging in and out among the crowd, came a boy, a little Indian pedlar with a bundle of English newspapers under his arm. He shouted as he came but what he shouted I did not immediately grasp. He passed between me and the girl. As he did so he called out again at the top of his voice: 'Fucking papers! Fucking papers!'

The girl swung round, looked at the boy, caught my eye and flushed deeply. Not merely did her face and neck blush but the rest of her, too. Through the transparent flimsiness that draped her I saw a huge tide of crimson pass over her body. I drew in my head. The train jerked into motion.

Easy enough, of course, to shape a script to that denouement. I picture an earlier soldier, an earlier train window. The soldier hears the unintelligible cry of an approaching vendor and feels, not the springing at the loins that I felt, but a dryness in the throat. Leaning out to hail the charwallah, as he thinks, he settles back disappointed when the little newspaper-seller draws close. 'Fucking papers!' he grumbles.

And the boy continues on his way, autodidactic intruder on our pale realm, overhearing and appropriating this possible key to our incomprehensible language and vast wealth. 'Ah!' he thinks. 'So that is what the sahibs themselves call these mysterious sheets of writing that I sell. "Fucking papers" is it? Oh, very good!'

At least I hope that is how it was, for the alternative scenario involves mischief-making rather than indifference. It involves someone convincing the lad that 'Fucking papers' was the correct English term for what he sold and that in just such a fashion did Churchill sahib's bearer announce his master's *Times* and *Telegraph* each morning.

Probably that is a more likely explanation. One developed a perverted sense of humour fairly rapidly in the British Army and very rapidly indeed if one were serving in India. It was by way of being a defence mechanism.

When I think back now to that station platform I ponder my own role in the affair. Obviously no one had bothered to tell the child that he was making a mistake. Ought I to have done so?

'Listen, son. Those newspapers that you sell are all too often "Fucking papers" indeed. But it doesn't do to admit that when you're trying to palm them off on others. There is no Santa Claus. Arm yourself with cynicism for you stand on the threshold of a cruel hard world and cunning bastards assail you on every side.'

I don't know. It's a big responsibility to take anyone's verbal virginity. Only implant your seed and the personality you have fertilized may swell in a manner you had not bargained for. Nine months, nine years later, see the horror on the midwife's face. Gengis Khan, Caligula, Adolf Hitler, all were little newspaper-sellers once, till some teacher got to them.

My father would have known what to do. Unassertive as he was he yet knew his place in the world and the privileges and obligations pertaining to it. Whatever in life he was unsure about, it was never where duty lay.

I don't recall now whether he 'frigged around' in connection with his 'banger'. Such language would at least have been appropriate to that long-drawn-out story. Certainly when he discussed the matter flashes of bitterness sometimes lit the darkness that normally shrouded his mental processes. To my way of thinking he should have railed cosmically and it was the story of Father and his banger I really wanted to tell.

Men are not generally commemorated by an account of their struggles and adventures while learning to drive. Apart perhaps from those who catalogue the recognized margins of the world, the Arctic or the Gobi Desert or the like, not many chroniclers relate how someone hoped and despaired, schemed and fought, as he tried to keep a form of transport going in a transportless land. Some lands are not usually thought of in that light.

Father, I dare say, would not have chosen to serve as an exception. Yet no aspect of his life was more typical of him or of the sort of existence that fate had condemned him to. The tale is a mixture of farce and tragedy, in pretty equal proportions. I don't know to what extent he saw it that way himself. He liked to refer to his activities behind the wheel as 'motoring' and to an outsider the word must have appeared rife with irony. It all began when my brother, Ian, my younger brother, bought him a second-hand car. Our nearest shop was six miles away—in good weather —and the mobile grocery that had visited us weekly since pony and trap days was already under threat of withdrawal. So a car seemed like an excellent idea and all that remained was to provide it with a qualified and regularly available driver.

Father, the only possible candidate, had turned sixty and had never sat behind the wheel of a car in his life. Indeed he had not often occupied a passenger seat. In his favour one could say that he was as avid of new experience as a crawling baby. He was also a handy sort of person and much interested in the mechanical. Against him had to be noted that he was nervous, unconfident and did not prove to possess the good co-ordination and judgement necessary in driving. Most damning of all, he had a poor teacher.

Ian was a fine driver in his own right but totally lacking in patience and savagely intolerant of the failings of others. The lessons went badly from the start. Father was painfully slow to learn and my brother quickly at the shouting stage. The climax was not long delayed. One day there came a more than usually pronounced display of ineptitude on Father's part. Ian stormed out of the car to the accompaniment of a slammed door and with the added comment that he could more easily have taught the rudiments of driving to our collie, Laddie (who had indeed been an interested passenger throughout and who had displayed some eagerness to get behind the wheel). Father drove home alone and from then on was self-taught.

He was pathetically keen. He bought driving manuals, he bought repair manuals. To the extent of his limited pocket he bought gadgets. He tinkered and polished endlessly. If he did not actually talk to his car as he did to his cows it was only for lack of an obvious hairy ear to funnel his loving voice down.

He obeyed faithfully every rule in the book. Driving between Sanna and Kilchoan in the depths of winter, with the road gale-swept and rain-lashed and the nearest other car probably miles away and garaged at that, he would still give signals. At the Achosnich crossroads some bedraggled ewe on the hillside would be punctiliously informed that Father was about to execute a left turn.

Summer brought a different set of problems to him, including a flood of tourists' cars on our single-track road. In order to complete at least the outward half of a journey to Kilchoan without the need to reverse or squeeze narrowly past, two operations he disliked and was bad at, he took to leaving our house at a ludicrously early hour. As his passenger one would find oneself being bowled unsteadily along in the half-light of pre-dawn, glimpsing only the inhabitants of the Ardnamurchan dark, pedestrians every one but with sense enough, whether substantial or spectral, to keep well out of Father's way.

All this became something of a joke between my brother and me, though at times it was anything but funny. To give his signals (it was an old car) Father had necessarily to abstract his right hand from its navigational task and wind down his window, before waggling the hand about outside. This was very definitely not the sort of action that one would wish to see encouraged in a driver who already appeared to lack an arm or two.

Also, since Father was, *a* deliberate in his movements, *b* one who did everything thoroughly, the signalling sequence tended to occupy a mile or so of highway, during which time the car would be proceeding in a series of convulsive meanders from ditch to ditch. Ardnamurchan ditches, one might add, are in general to be avoided. They are of the type that in medieval times would have been stocked with carp and equipped with drawbridges.

Somewhat later in his career it occurred to Father that he could save bother by leaving his window permanently down. This more or less halved his reaction time, certainly, but I don't suppose it fooled the Driving Test Examiner. Nor, given the exigencies of the Ardnamurchan climate, did it do a great deal for his passengers. It was small consolation to return from an excursion having successfully retained one's head on one's shoulders, only to spend the next few days sneezing it off.

It did not do to tell him that concern for passengers ought to rank at least equally in a driver's mind with concern for other road-users, especially when these were likely to amount to no more than a hedgehog or two. We were never a family who delighted in having anything very much pointed out to us, except maybe scenery and even that we preferred to discover for ourselves. When driving with Father it paid to refrain from criticism. If you did not wish to find yourself decanted in mid-wilderness to continue your journey on foot, you kept your mouth as firmly closed as your eyes, praying inwardly meanwhile for wider roads and quicker hedgehogs.

I think that Father wanted to pass the Driving Test more than he had ever wanted anything in his life. He set his ageing heart on it and to me it seemed a small request to make of his deity after a lifetime's abstinence from more immodest demands. In time he did become half-competent but never really good nor ever an inspirer of much confidence in those who watched him. And he never did pass the Test. On the three or four occasions when he summoned up enough courage to try he did not even come close to success.

When he reached his seventies he began to feel that his age was counting against him. I dare say it was. Unlicensed, he continued to drive. Living where he did and with Mother constantly pressing him about the state of the larder he had small choice. He was never caught, never actually had an accident and no one ever gave him away, though the true state of affairs must have been known throughout the peninsula.

Eventually, I think, he gave up hope, if indeed he had ever possessed it. He wrote to me a year before his death, asking me to send him yet another application form for yet another attempt. As I read his letter I thought of him, an old man on a remote Highland croft, a man with a long hard life behind him and little to show for it, yet a man with a yearning or two left still. I obliged without comment. I found the form, unused, among his papers after his death.

Teacher and pupil, Ian and Father, lie side by side now in Kilchoan Cemetery. The vehicle whose pilotage they quarrelled over, the vehicle that one of them loved, outlived them both. Until a year or two ago you could still see it by the roadside in Sanna, up to its axles in the soft ground and bowing its head slowly to successive winters. Two gallons of petrol remaining in the tank were siphoned out by some nocturnal thief within a week of Father's death.

The old banger, indeed, became an antique at last. One noticed tourists going over to examine it, poking around in its innards without so much as a by your leave. Father would have hated that, being a survivor of an age and an area where the rights of property extended beyond the grave. On clear quiet days, long after he had gone, I used to half-expect that I might yet see him emerge from the house to bear down on the inquisitive, blowing his whistle and fuming and gesticulating.

Eventually my sister called upon the District Council to remove the car. By now it was too much of a temptation, too collectable, and she could not bear the thought of seeing other hands, necessarily philistine in their grasp, resting on the sacred wheel. Workmen came with a vast machine, crunched it up and hoisted it away. I thought that the equivalent of scuttling one's ship rather than seeing it pass to the enemy.

INTRODUCTION II
Ardnamurchan

FOR MOST OF its long life Ardnamurchan has lain as far off the beaten track in history as it does in geography. The great tides that surged to and fro across Scotland, tossing plumes and pennants in their midst and drowning the screams of the dying in their wake, made but a ripple or two here. The Norsemen came and conquered but eventually went. Various feudal chieftains debated the overlordship with one another, when they were not being overwhelmed by the superior rhetoric of the Stuart kings and their mighty vassals, the Campbell Dukes of Argyll. James IV visited Mingary Castle at Kilchoan, in 1493, to pretend that he was receiving the submission of the unruly Hebridean chiefs. Much good it did him, for he was back two years later on the same fruitless errand. After that he turned his attention to the English, who unfortunately were never much interested in pretenders and who were shortly to demonstrate their superior grasp of reality at Flodden. Ardnamurchan slumbered on.

It came to life briefly in 1519 when the Lord of the Isles decided that he might as well add the place to his territories, it being undoubtedly Hebridean and for all practical purposes an isle. The Lord of Ardnamurchan objected and the two met to settle their differences on the flat ground below Craig an Airgid, which is a hill overlooking the present road, halfway between Sanna and Kilchoan. A skirmish only, the engagement rates no mention in the history books, yet it was deadly enough. One wonders in passing how much blood has been spilled up and down the land, unrewarded even by the parrot cries of schoolboys because there were but ninety-nine gallons of it lost at a time, instead of a hundred. On this occasion the Lord of the Isles proved the better butcher. The Lord of Ardnamurchan, however, retained possession of a small part of the field, some six feet by six, being sufficient to cover himself and his two sons. There he lies still, if our new bounty hunters, with their clickety-click machines have not dug him up. Where the ordinary men of Ardnamurchan, who fell in their common heaps around these luminaries, have their burial is not recorded. Perhaps they awaited the attentions of those earlier bounty hunters, the Highland ravens, who also went 'clickety-click' as they whetted their great black bills.

Pretending had another of its periodic Highland efflorescences in the eighteenth century, so beloved of Scottish historians. How satisfying it is to be able to write down merely 'the 15' or 'the 45' and have all men know instantly what you refer to! Here's romance for you, here's fame! Such an internationally-understood shorthand is not often permitted our parchments. It gives one the feeling of being a member of a cosy club, where the password is a mystic number.

Ardnamurchan was hardly a member of this club, for all that Charles Stuart landed nearby. Passing through the area he patted a little girl, who had been brought out from her home to see him, on the head. She was a grandmother of mine, several times great and was ever afterwards known by a Gaelic designation meaning 'the girl who was singled out by the Prince'. There is no record in my family that she became any wiser or richer or more beautiful. The Prince went on to Edinburgh, where the girls were bigger and the patting adjusted to correspond.

Later in the same century Ardnamurchan was to come under the spotlight once more, and finally, when Cruikshank discovered at Strontian a mineral which he named strontianite and from which was later extracted strontium. And much good that did him, or anybody else either.

While all this was going on superficially, as a scum on the surface, no doubt the old compact between man and the land was elsewhere being renewed each spring. One imagines the people of Ardnamurchan, when they could avoid the recruiting sergeant, beginning the slow process of trying to take possession of their birthright. It was a process that was never to reach fruition. Like crofters everywhere we of present-day Ardnamurchan still live on and walk over land that others own, go we north, south, east or west, and still we find that generations of back-breaking toil and starvation have brought no more than a quasi-legal sufferance.

As the nineteenth century approached, then, a pattern of crofting began to emerge in these parts. Slowly the townships took form and filled with men and women crudely sheltered, workers of two or three dyked-off acres, possessors of a cow if they were lucky and a potato patch and perhaps a corn patch; burners of peat; cobblers and weavers of their own rough wear; of a self-sufficiency that was due to the emptiness of their pockets rather than the generosity of nature; essentially tenant farmers in minuscule but without the security of even a quarterly agreement; more accurately, indeed, squatters, though they squatted on land that was theirs if it were anyone's; above all, bitterly, bitterly poor.

The Church, almost the only source of charity, did what it could to alleviate hardship, though it exacted its own peculiar return. The Session Records of those days, still extant for the Parish of Ardnamurchan, make harrowing reading. On 26 November 1789, for instance, the minister and elders, in Session, found themselves to be in possession of six pounds seven shillings in Church funds. They retained one pound for emergencies and distributed the rest among forty-one of their poorest parishioners. John Henderson of Achnaha, aged seventy-seven, received five shillings, for example. Mary MacColl of the same hamlet received two and sixpence and Duncan MacLauchlan (described factually and bluntly as 'a Changeling'; one of several so called) had three shillings. 1790 sees a long list of three- and four-shilling distributions. In 1797 one notes that John Henderson of Achnaha, by now aged eight-one, was allowed eleven shillings 'because his wife, Anne Macdonald, aged eight-three, was equally frail and destitute'.

Sometimes the charity was in kind instead of cash. In 1779 the then owner of Ardnamurchan—and how strange that sounds when one considers it, though as a rule we recognize such strangeness only when we magnify the occasion and talk about, say, the owner of Britain—the then owner, Sir James Miles Riddell, empowered the distribution of twenty bolls of meal among the poor. Archibald MacArthur of Sanna got four stones but Christy Henderson of Swordle only two. One wonders how much deprivation went into qualifying as a four-stone person. One pictures the great day when the Factor's horse and cart arrived to begin the distribution: 'Four-stone people on the left, two-stone on the right.'

The Church paid for funerals, too, when the relatives were unable to do so and regularly among the accounts for this period one sees three shillings for a coffin and one shilling for the accompanying bottle of whisky. The latter item might scandalize some readers. 'How can you claim poverty for these people yet tell us that they splashed liquor around at their funerals?' I have wondered about the whisky myself. Was it perhaps doled out among the grieving relations along the lines of the strong drink that used to be recommended for patients having teeth out? One gulp equals one gap? But, no; one bottle in a crowd of men—a sip apiece—would ensure neither anaesthesia nor licence nor yet serve as the simple stimulant it was later to become. The whisky was surely ritual, and age-old at that; time was when it would have been poured into the ground.

The income of the Church derived from various sources. There were the fines imposed by the Session for moral lapses: non-attendance at divine service or sexual relations outside wedlock. These ranged from one pound to three pounds and in the case of sexual misbehaviour seem to have been imposed jointly; evidently the view taken was that both parties were equally guilty. On 19 July 1837, Duncan Maclachlan, Glendrian and Christy Henderson, Achnaha, for instance, were jointly fined three pounds for illicit sex. She was his late wife's sister.

What nonsense! How better, I should like to know, might one assuage one's grief than in the arms of the next nearest and dearest? For God's sake, what could be more natural or more seemly? And is not three pounds a savage price to pay for a moment's closeness to another human being, bearing in mind that as an object of charity rather than a reluctant benefactor you would be lucky to receive a tenth of that sum?

The Church in Ardnamurchan inherited, too, the interest on a few small legacies and there were also, of course, the usual Sunday collecting boxes. Income from the latter, as might be expected, was pitifully small; a penny-halfpenny was a common total at Kilchoan and a penny at Kilmory.

Fornication was not the only crime that might cost one money then, nor was the Church the only levier of fines outside the civil authority. There was also the Factor to be reckoned with, the right-hand man of the estate owner, serving as his bailiff and his thumbscrews. The Factor, indeed, was essentially the civil law in a place as remote as Ardnamurchan. (It was like being 'West of the Pecos' in early Texas and under the dominion of that brigand and self-styled judge—Roy Bean.) On the 19 July 1837, for example, the Ardnamurchan Factor fined 'a son of James Henderson' and 'a son of John MacGlashan', both of Achnaha, the sum of five shillings for 'spoiling a horse's tail'. (Horse hair had a number of uses, such as providing 'gut' for a fishing line, and if you did not have a horse yourself you might try, as these lads did, to sever a few strands from the tail of one of the estate horses. At five shillings, however—possibly two years' income if you were a charitable case—your fish would be dearly bought.) Again, on 13 January 1838, Alexander MacKenzie of Sanna was fined twelve and sixpence by the Factor for 'cutting saplings in the enclosure at Coirevulin'. (This man, finding himself evicted and shelterless, had returned to his former home to cut roof timbers for a new house. I suppose that few Ardnamurchan cottages were worth twelve and sixpence lock, stock and barrel.)

Estate owners—Proprietors as they were generally called then —came and went and if they ordered their comings and goings entirely without reference to their living chattels it is fair to add that not all of them were ogres by any means. The best of them, however, came up against a problem that all along bedevilled humane and well-meaning landlords in the Highlands (e.g. Lord Lever, the soap manufacturer, who was willing to spend a fortune on his Island tenants). This was the problem of helping a people whose one huge and overriding wish was to be left alone. Ardnamurchan had its own Lord Lever in the shape of a Victorian magnate called Rudd, a former partner of Cecil Rhodes and a very wealthy man in his own right. Across the bay from Sanna lies a hamlet called Portuairk, a classically-marginal West Highland crofting community, huddled on a few poor acres of half-cultivable land between mountains and sea. Rudd once offered to translate the entire village over the hill to better ground where he would provide new houses and new crofts. He was turned down cold and retired baffled to his castle in Glenborrodale.

(It may not be desirable or lovable to be stiff-necked to such a degree but there are worse attitudes to have. Were Rudd to make that offer to some present-day Ardnamurchan crofters he would find not merely his new houses grabbed but would be lucky if his castle were not demanded into the bargain.)

One gets the impression of a people of complex character, pushing independence up to and a little beyond whatever limit was available to them at a particular time, yet utterly lacking that fierce pride to be found in, say, the Plains Amerindians or the Pathan tribesmen. Rather than the latter we see a people gentle and dreamy, biddable—despite their independence—to the point of a fatalistic passivity. The most astonishing thing about the notorious Highland Clearances of the nineteenth century, given their widespread nature, the large numbers of crofters cleared and the frequent callousness and brutality involved, is surely the almost complete absence of resistance. Yet the men who allowed themselves to be thus herded off their land, in the same fashion as the sheep that replaced them were herded on to it, albeit with somewhat less granted them in the way of consideration, were the grandsons, many of them, of the men who charged with hand weapons the English field artillery on Culloden Moor.

Passive suffering is not necessarily an endearing trait. Faced with a man who accepts a savagely unjust burden without complaint, one's reaction is often to add an item or two to his load. At times it seemed that nature itself was becoming irritated with the Highlander. One indication of this came with the devastating epidemics such as smallpox that swept up from the south, creating unimaginable havoc in a folk whose blood cells were as unsophisticated as their minds. There still exists in Sanna, below the present little church, a pond, *Lochan Cuilc* (the Pool of the Reeds), where in 1830 a man called Neil Macdonald, of Portuairk, a man with a freak immunity to the then current epidemic and the only 'old wife' available, used to strip and bathe on his way home after laying out the latest batch of Sanna corpses.

Another such portent came with the mid-nineteenth-century failure of the potato crop, the Great Hunger. Yet none of these plagues became as enshrined in Gaelic legend as did the Clearances, though their effect, even considered severally, was much more severe. No doubt they were somewhat less amenable to the folk-song treatment or sounded less pathetically glamorous when trotted out with the whisky at the evening ceilidh. You would have to be a dull raconteur indeed not to be able to draw a tear or two with the story of how your great-granny was rifle-butted by the soldiers and had her rafters burned above her head. It is harder to make capital out of pustules and diarrhoea.

Of the Clearances themselves, the restocking of the great Highland estates with profitable sheep and deer and the forced resettling on still more marginal land of the unprofitable crofters, too much has already been written. Clearances certainly took place in Ardnamurchan. Sanna, for example, though people had dwelt there at least since neolithic times, was settled in its present form about 1830 by crofters who were evicted from further up the peninsula, from villages like Swordle. But the Ardnamurchan clearances seem to have been more for non-payment of rent than because the Proprietor had discovered a better use for his land. A year's notice was given and there was no burning of houses and no physical force. Perhaps in the long run the evicted crofters were no worse off, in the harsh sense that they went from being dirt poor to being dirt poor. In Sanna, certainly, new houses had to be built and new crofts hacked out of a bog and patiently coaxed into something resembling fertility. At least the incomers had the grim satisfaction of reaching the end of the road: literally, for having been driven to the very tip of the peninsula they could be driven no further; and financially, for having been robbed of all they owned they could not be robbed again. A more positive benefit occurred when the international outcry over the genuinely bloody-minded and occasionally bloody Sutherland clearances at last brought crofters everywhere what security of tenure they now possess.

To blame the Clearances for all the ills of the Highlands or even for most of them is a belief so distorted as to bear no resemblance to reality, though it is a belief that seems to hold a fatal charm for many Highlanders. There is something in the Celtic character continually seeking to draw a perverted nourishment from dwelling on disaster, continually fostering in the dark of the mind a lovely sense of betrayal. Your Highlander is your scab-picker extraordinary. Truly, one might almost say that if the Clearances had not taken place it would have been necessary to institute them. Of course, they provided readily identifiable villains and an easy short-cut to the emotions—of natives and pseudo-natives —and that is a lot simpler than thinking hard about the problem of the Highlands and evolving a complex solution in which you yourself might have to shoulder part of the blame.

Ardnamurchan reached its apotheosis as a crofting area as the twentieth century dawned. People were still very poor but it was not exactly the grinding and deadly grub-in-the-fields-for-roots poverty of the previous two hundred years. Not quite. Paying work was obtainable—mostly elsewhere, it is true, but communications and transport had improved to the point where a man could go off for a year or two to earn some money. Most crofters now owned a brace of cows and a scattering of poultry.

Crofts and the art of working them had reached their final perfected form. Families were large; there were bodies enough and to spare for both private and communal endeavour. Young folk remained in their villages; there was a pool of potential mates and potential child-bearers. Education was freely available and good; in the width and depth of their knowledge and in the extent of their thirst for it crofters of my father's generation could put many school-leavers of today to shame. Tourism, that *ignis fatuus* of the modern Highlands, had not yet begun to lead astray those it purported to be guiding. Bureaucracy had not yet strangled initiative nor initiative become so lacking in taste and so self-centred as to require bureaucratic check. It was a late flowering and while the blossom was still opening the rot was creeping up the stem.

It is difficult to say what happened. Part of the answer is suggested in the body of this book and implied in the above paragraph. Findings might be subsumed under some such heading as 'The Onward March of Time'. Ardnamurchan has suffered a bad attack of history. There was never anything immutable about the old West Highland way of life; like much else of interest and nobility it came, achieved its hour and passed. Crofts and crofters evolved in response to a specific set of circumstances; those circumstances have now altered out of all recognition. If they come round again, as well they may, I shall not see it. But when I reflect that I knew that way of life, even in the yellow leaf, I am filled with pride and love.

I have always looked on the ferry that crosses the Narrows of the Linnhe Loch at Corran as a kind of mobile decompression chamber where various kinds of pollution were drained from the blood and I was fitted to breathe pure air again. On the far side lay Ardgour, with its jetty and its huddle of white houses. Once across one was in the *echt* Highlands. The road turns west at Ardgour, or the best part of it does; if not yet within sight of the Hebrides, the heart of Gaeldom on earth, one is at least within reach of their spell. To go on is to be protected and fed; if one is lucky enough and receptive enough, touched with goodness.

That road winds down through Strontian and Salen and Glenborrodale and Kilchoan and at last trickles to a halt on the *machair* at Sanna. Beyond land, here at land's end, lie only a handful of islands and Labrador. Electricity arrived two years ago. Most of the houses now have piped water and septic tank sewage. There is even a weekly refuse collection. Yet the nearest shop and the nearest post office are six miles off, in Kilchoan, the nearest policeman and doctor thirty, in Strontian, the nearest town and the nearest hospital fifty, at Fort William. If you include book-shops among your necessities, as I do, you have a hundred and twenty miles to go, to Inverness.

In the small hours of one night my father had a heart attack. A nurse had first of all to be summoned (six miles). She inspected him and authorized the rousing of a doctor (thirty miles). The doctor came, made an examination and called out an ambulance (fifty miles). It was decided to take the patient to the better-equipped hospital at Inverness (a hundred and twenty miles). By the time Father was at last stretchered away from Sanna it was well on in the forenoon. The initial thirty miles of his journey were over a single-track road notorious for its roughness. He lasted as far as Salen (twenty-five miles). Still in the ambulance he had a second and massive thrombosis and died.

Respect and admiration for the past do not always balance the difficulties of the present. If, like my crofting ancestors, you have no choice about where you live or the means by which you encompass your living, that is one thing. Choosing such a life of your own free will is another. There is no spiritual value in poverty or in isolation in themselves, or if there is I was too busy being hungry and lonely to find it. I am rendered ill at ease by luxury but I have never seen why one should deliberately elect bone-bare circumstances when one might own a modest degree of comfort, and I am all in favour of combining the best of both worlds in this world, if it can be managed, since I do not count greatly on the world to come. There exists today, among certain of those who forsake the town for the country, a cult of the spartan, a notion that—for instance—where electricity is avail-able and can be paid for it yet should be rejected in favour of oil lamps. I have no sympathy with such thinking. Living in Ardna-murchan offers consolations many and sweet, some of which I hope emerge in my pages, but it is not all scenery and skittles, even for those of us who can afford to stay indoors when the gales blow. Television reception in Sanna is poor and, such as it is, requires special and expensive equipment. Radio reception, even on VHF, is equally bad and the best programmes are the hardest to get. Obtaining the better newspapers varies from difficult to impossible. There are no concert halls, theatres, cinemas or libraries. If by chance you find yourself a little depressed one day and decide that a grilled chop for supper might offer solace —forget it. You will discover neither restaurant nor butcher on the corner. There is no corner. Extract what joy you can from a tin of beans.

And if these things do not matter to you, reader, then you are fortunate; they matter a good deal to me. Of Sanna I may not be the reluctant lover quite, but I reckon myself a clear-eyed and clear-headed one. Above all, I am not in the business of creating glamour where none exists. It is here, perhaps more than most places, a question of deciding how you want to live—and why.

★

I have chosen to extract from the middle of the twenty or so years of my father's journal, selecting in particular two years a decade apart: 1960 and 1970. I have picked the same three days, at the beginning, middle and end of the month, from every month in those two years, this of course that I might not seem to be lighting deliberately on days when a little or a lot was happening. It was the typical I was after, the pattern of the days and the seasons. However, I have, in addition, allowed myself one free day each year.

I have transcribed each entry as I found it, down to the punctuation. But I have altered the names (not always consistently) of local people and for the names of visitors—tourists, I mean—I have substituted successive sets of initials.

If in my comments I speak of my brother, without qualification, I mean my younger brother, Ian. He occasionally, and I much more often, flit in and out of Father's pages; he would be present when he had a holiday from his job and I when factory life in the south became once more intolerable and I inserted myself into the midst of my long-suffering family for another six months or so (mostly to immure myself in my room and write). My elder brother, James, was rarely at home. My parents, of course, and my sister, Janet (Jessie), were permanent residents.

Most of the book, save for preface and epilogue, was written in Sanna, in the years immediately following my parents' death, though little of it in my parents' old house. I was therefore editing my father's journal, for the book, and keeping an—occasionally conflated—account of my daily life while doing so. I was undertaking this task, moreover, not from the house where the journal was actually written, the house where I lived when I featured in its pages, but from another cottage nearby. To add to the complications, the book was later revised while I was once more staying in the family home. I shall not trouble the reader with the reasons behind all this (chiefly they sprang from my efforts to maintain a roof over my head while getting on with my writing); I shall merely say that if these complications cause any confusion of place or season or tense or person I apologize in advance. Dwelling so much on the past, in an area already reeking of it, I sometimes found past and present, summer and winter, old house and new, blending uncontrollably in my mind. No doubt I did not always manage to separate them on paper.

My original intention was to let my father speak entirely for himself, reproducing him without remark. In the event this did not seem wise. Though he had hopes, I think, that his record would outlive him, as a piece of social history, he wrote it chiefly to be a working tool to his own hands. So much of what he said needs explanation or expansion that, apart from anything else, it would be grossly unfair to him to let his bald narrative stand. The result has been much more of the son than the father and the reader would do well to remember the relative values to be attached to concise prophet and prosy commentator. To the extent that I have imposed myself on his pages—for this intolerable deal of sack—forgive me, reader. Forgive me, Father.

FATHER'S JOURNAL

[Alasdair's parents towards the end of their lives]

FATHER'S JOURNAL, 1960

January 1st 1960
Heavy rain and strong southerly wind in early hours. Dry from then on
with continuous sunshine and very good visibility. Wind dropped to
calm in afternoon. Usual daily chores and replaced projection board
which the storm on Wednesday had blown off south end of house gable.
No post this evening. Visit from Mr and Mrs A. at night.

Father's journal shows a continuing and detailed preoccupation
with the weather and its effects. Sometimes, indeed, this constitutes almost the entire entry. There was good reason for this.
Townsmen, it seems to me, are largely ignorant of weather-
related matters. They are aware in a general sort of way if it is
blowing hard, for example, but they could hardly tell you the
direction of the wind, far less the state of the tide or the time of
sunrise or the phase of the moon. Unless they had heard a recent
forecast they could not give you a likely guess as to what the
weather might do over the next few hours. In short, they are
largely separated from their climate, from the source of much of
the rawness and realness of their world, though they might deny
the separation indignantly as they were buffeted at some street
corner.

This insulation makes their lives easier, no doubt—or appears
to—yet in many ways it is an unnatural existence. I would not go
so far as to suggest that all who live an urban life should be
subjected to a daily drenching in a wind tunnel for the good of
their souls. Even in this day of Californian cults, when the bank
balance of the latest guru is often in direct proportion to the
amount of sadism he can inflict on his followers, that would
hardly be popular. Besides, a number of city-dwellers, in Britain
at least, might well claim to be already undergoing such an
ordeal. Yet I do wonder at times whether those who enjoy such
protection from the weather do not suffer some degree of spiritual erosion as a result. Or I do wonder, to put it less specifically
and less startlingly, whether nature is not up to her old game of

outflanking us, of taking with one hand while she yields with the
other. I think it may well be that our increasing mastery over
nature, as we believe, our continuing economic gains and our
gain in comfort, are all being subtly cancelled out under our very
noses.

Of course it is easy to forget about nature when one lives in
town. When I am a denizen of the streets I lose the habit of
periodically raising my eyes to the heavens. The great passion and
drama of the skies rage quite unobserved overhead while the
gutter takes all of my care. I creep about with my head bowed.

To the crofter, on the other hand, clinging by a mixture of
instinct and experience to the remote fringes of these islands, the
weather is a god. It is the difference not merely between a pleasant
and an unpleasant life but between success and failure, until the
advent of the welfare state between—possibly—living and
dying. Until you have gone about your daily business under the
thumb of the weather you can have no conception of the extent to
which it orders your life. You cannot grasp, for instance, how
laborious and time-consuming, how literally exhausting, the
simplest outdoor task may become when performed in a howling
gale.

Winters in Sanna can be, and frequently are, appalling. Gales
often blow for days on end, accompanied for much of the time by
rain. The ground around house and outbuildings, with the
constant to-ing and fro-ing of animals and people, becomes a
churned-up quagmire, a constant drag and hindrance to everything one tries to do. Everywhere is supersaturated earth which
will accept no more moisture yet still hills and heavens pour it
down till there are pools and streams on every hand. The prospect
from the house window, at any time from November to February, may be of such unrelieved bleakness as to strike a chill into
the heart.

Even to enter or leave one's house, if it lacks a back door—and
most of the old cottages did—may be a hazardous operation in a
gale and a door once opened may not be easy to shut again. I have
seen old people in Sanna go from house to steading on hands and
knees, being unable to proceed any other way. For of course the
life of the crofter did not come nicely to a standstill in winter,
though it may have grown a little more leisurely. Animals still
had to be fed and watered and their dung removed. They had to
be allowed out if possible, then rounded up for readmittance.

Milking cows had to be milked. Fuel for the house had to be fetched, and food. The moorings of haystacks and sheds had to be checked and if need be reinforced. All this and more.

Life under such conditions could be a long nightmare, not only for the man of the house but for the woman as well. Consider, for example, the effort involved in keeping the family clothes clean and dry. And doing it, as my mother and her generation did it, with no assistance other than that provided by a wooden tub, a tin scrubbing board and a bar of coarse soap.

Crofters' wives deserve everlasting glory for what they endured. More than once, as I grew up, I came across my gentle mother in some corner of the house, reduced to tears by the cruel exigencies of the life she was trapped in. The acquisition of a stone sink and piped cold water in the 1940s were the only refinements she ever achieved. She began scrubbing for her family, she told me once, as a mere girl, on the death of her own mother. When she herself died in 1973, more than sixty long years after that harsh initiation into the womanhood of the poor, she was still at it.

January 15th
A fine day. Mainly cloudy with light wind from North to East. Did not get to winkles because I had to motor to Kilchoan to meet Gowanbrae Stores van to collect bag of flour and other groceries for ourselves. Also two bags—one bruised oats and one Indian meal—for N. Macaskill. Received a khaki shirt for Alasdair from Cameron's Stores, Inverness. For a while each night I have been copying some of the data from the Kirk Session Book, which the minister lent me last week, the principal aim being to record the names of people who resided in the various townships in Western Ardnamurchan commencing 1775. Frost all away.

The winkles that Father did not get to were the small edible shellfish, *L. littorea*, that grew in profusion round our shores and that were gathered by many crofters for the Billingsgate market. The more common Highland name for them is wilks, a corruption of whelks. The use in our family of the English name, winkles, was originally facetious, the sort of adoption that Father was fond of.

Gathering winkles was—indeed still is—an important addition to the income of many crofters, often the only such addition readily available. You collected a hundredweight in a sack, canful by canful, and shipped them off with a covering note to your chosen merchant, generally several sackfuls at a time. In due course back came a very welcome postal order (though naturally the freight charge was a debit and an increasingly exorbitant one), plus a bundle of clean sacks to start you off again.

Various merchants tended to be in favour at different times as word got round the townships that so-and-so was offering exceptional prices. Some firms in Billingsgate must have been puzzled to find their supplies from a particular area suddenly drying up while a competitor was swamped. No doubt it all came even in the long run.

One of the memories of my childhood is being allowed to browse through an old dresser in our house that was crammed with all sorts of detritus, kept because it might one day come in useful. (Crofters were the original recyclers.) Among this junk were long strings of shiny oval labels made of embossed tin, each bearing the name of a Billingsgate merchant. These, of course, were supplied by the firms, to be sewn onto the sacks, and some of the names on them were almost fabled in the West Highlands, a matter of common household conversation. Some, on the other hand, might well have gone out of business long years before, for aught we knew to the contrary. It was as though you were dealing with distant gods. You despatched your offering, clearly specifying the god whose favour you were seeking, and after a suspenseful period you received your reward, though never so lavishly or with such a degree of certainty that you could afford to become complacent about it. Gods do not operate that way.

The strings themselves were like Brummagem necklaces, the sort of thing the early explorers took to Africa with them. I was fascinated by them. Now they are the coinage of the past, the stuff of the folk museum. You do your own labelling. It is a do-it-yourself age.

The price obtainable for winkles has naturally varied a good deal over the years. When I last collected, in the early sixties, thirty shillings or so was an average return for a bag. A decade later that had risen to seven or eight pounds. Today your bag of winkles will probably fetch you fourteen or fifteen pounds and there are occasional reports of eighteen.

You might, if you were really pushing it and everything were in your favour, gather some six or eight bags in a week. That would realize around eighty or eighty-five pounds, let us conservatively say, at present prices. Eighty pounds a week is a lavish income by Highland standards. So why don't the crofters abandon the unequal and unprofitable struggle with the land and take to the shore in droves?

Well, of course, it isn't as simple as that. Nothing about crofting is as simple as that. I know of no way for a crofter to make money that doesn't carry with it at least one fairly crippling drawback. Gathering winkles has several.

For a start it is, or was, a seasonal occupation, though the old belief that one ought not to eat shellfish during the summer seems to be going by the board. It is also a tidal occupation. Naturally you can only collect when the tide is out and only, really, when it is the time of the spring tides for only then can you get out to the big beds where the sea-fruit lies thickest. (If you have to pick up your winkles one at a time rather than scooping them up collecting becomes that much more laborious and that much less profitable.) Already, therefore, you are cut down to—at best —one week in every two. Then there is the onset of darkness to consider. You can only put your spring tide to full use if low water comes in the middle of the short winter day and tides are not always as obliging as that.

Then there is the weather to think about. I have gathered winkles in wind and rain, hail and snow, and it was no fun. You have your hands in and out of water constantly, for many of the beds lie in rock pools, and after half an hour of that, on a bitter day in winter, you feel as if you had a snowball stuck on the end of each finger. Grasping objects becomes a matter of faith; your eyes tell you that you have picked up something but your sense of touch refuses to confirm it. You cannot wear gloves, either, but blue and brittle must get on with the job as nature made you.

What elderly people endure under such conditions may be imagined. But they do endure it and I have watched them at it, my own parents among them.

The weather, indeed, may utterly inhibit collecting. If, under the lash of an onshore gale, twenty-foot waves are charging up the rocks, jumping on one another's backs to get at you, you will be well advised to stay at home. In the wake of such a storm you will be lucky to salvage any winkles you may have already collected but not yet sent off, even though you will naturally have left these in a crevice and weighed them down with rocks.

(Winkles ought not to be left for more than a day or two without being refreshed by sea water, hence the need to store them where they may receive this benison naturally, or where it may be bestowed on them without too much effort. The reaction of a bag of thirsty winkles to a good splash of Mother Atlantic is delightful. For a few minutes all is creaks and squeaks and bubblings, as though a buzz of winkly conversation had broken out. As for the power of the sea, few townsmen or upland people have any idea of its awesomeness. The length of ocean behind a wave—its 'fetch', as seamen say—bears directly on the height of that wave, and on the west coast of Scotland the Atlantic enjoys a two-thousand-mile run at its victims. A force which can pick up hundred-ton breakwater blocks and carry them off as a tigress carries off kids is a force to be reckoned with.)

Other factors conspire against the winkle-gatherer. Every seventh day that unfolds to him, possibly an excellent collecting day otherwise, is inconveniently a Highland Sabbath, with 'Thou shalt not' tolling out its mournful monosyllables. In Ardnamurchan not all now go to church on Sunday but few, among the natives at least, are prepared to break tabu to the extent of being seen to work then. The Commandments were implanted in childhood, up to and including my generation, and it takes major surgery, of a severity not everyone would countenance or could survive, to deposit them dripping bloodily on the theatre trolley.

I have said enough, no doubt, to indicate that one does not readily become rich by collecting shellfish for market. Compassion might well stop at this point; craftsmanship in writing certainly would. But I owe it to generations of dead crofters not to be overly nice with my readers, nor overly biased in assessing the claims of art as against life. There is more.

Winkles often occur in huge quantities but their numbers are finite and they do not replace themselves overnight when removed. A full-sized winkle may be reckoned to be several years old. If a number of you, then, are gathering on one particular stretch of shore, as happened in poor villages, you will quickly find your quarry becoming scarce. That means going further and further afield, without infringing on another village's territory, and carrying back what you collect on your own bowed back. A sackful of wet winkles, I might add, has the weight and texture and degree of malleability of a sackful of musket balls.

I recall my parents and me, one winter when competition was

fiercer than usual, transferring our collecting ground from Sanna to the neighbouring deserted township of Plocaig and at last ending up on the boulder-strewn shoreline under the Carraig Cliffs. That meant something like a two-mile carry-back, and over the very roughest of rough ground: gullies, streams, bogs, hills, hollows and heather; whatever horrors of landscape weary legs can conjure up that walk includes. My parents were then in their old age. Sometimes, when I think of the system that condemns decent people to a lifetime of such grinding poverty, I feel myself shake with rage.

And yet and yet—the great 'and yet' which in Ardnamurchan so often betrays one out of anger into wonder: our shoreline is never less than beautiful and in places goes as far beyond that as your language and your nerve ends will carry you. When supper is rough and rainy miles away, or when the cold so grips that your marrow plummets in your bones, you have that for a kind of comfort.

I think of Father, conscientiously removing overly-small winkles from his collection, carefully picking out stones and bits of seaweed. Gatherers are not so finicky now. I see them scoop up whatever comes their way and shovel it into their sacks regard-less. 'Why not?' they say when I challenge them. 'We get paid for it just the same.' Yes. And nor do they pay much attention to the winkles once they have bagged them. All too often the sacks lie out under the sun, unwatered, for a week or a fortnight before being dispatched. I should not care to eat their contents.

January 31st
Sunday. Cold and dull with intermittent rain all day. Wind Southerly moderate to fresh. Altogether, not very pleasant. Service in Hall at 3 p.m. by Parish minister. Present. Heavy sleety rain at bedtime.

February 1st
Mild, with moderate Southerly wind. Afternoon mainly sunny. Stella out from about noon. Torrential rain came on at night. Had to lay up in afternoon, stomach very upset.

Stella was one of our cows. She had calved a day or two before this entry and was now, at the first tolerable opportunity, being shoved outside to forage for herself, to pick up what she could in the way of withered herbage. Crofting, among much else, is the art of balancing one's humane instincts towards one's stock against one's dwindling and expensive supply of winter feed.

Father recorded his many ailments faithfully and minutely. Whatever else in the way of an entry might be skimped through tiredness or busyness, whatever illnesses the rest of us might endure unknown to history, that at least would be reported. How genuine these ailments were is a matter for conjecture. He was undoubtedly a hypochondriac and the reader should bear in mind that he reached his middle seventies, having done a hard day's work on the day of his death and with scarcely a serious check till the great check that claimed him. It is true that the stomach upsets which figure prominently in the tale of his ills were given some retrospective colour a year or two before he died by the discovery of a peptic ulcer. However, from his account of that great day in his life, delivered eagerly to his family as he sat at table after the Fort William ambulance had ferried him home, I came to the conclusion that the diagnosis was largely a matter of inspired guesswork on the part of the hospital doctors, or perhaps the awarding of a consolation prize. His intestinal troubles, I felt, were more likely the result of the dreadful patent laxatives with which he purged himself daily. I forbore intruding on his pleasure with comment so dispiriting, however. I let him finish his usual hearty supper in peace.

(Unfair, no doubt, and *pax*, Dad! God knows you had reason enough to be riddled with ulcers, so hard and so long you struggled and against such odds. You believed in your illnesses at any rate. If the foundations you built upon were shaky the terrors you reared were yet solid enough. It is the ulcers of the mind that are deadliest. I, of all people, ought to know what happens when the lining of consciousness punctures and the darkness wells in.)

February 15th
Snow thick on ground this morning, and showers of hail and snow
continued all day. A searing wind swinging from North to Northwest
created blizzard conditions at times. We managed to get the cattle out to
water in afternoon. Molly calved in byre, at about 9.45 a.m.—a bull
calf—Oscar. Took him to hut in evening. No post tonight.

In addition to byre and barn our house was surrounded by a little shantytown of various other outbuildings of wood or corrugated iron. We referred to these by such simple names as 'the shed', 'the annexe', 'the henhouse', 'the sheephouse', 'the hut' and so forth.

My brother and I, on our visits home, often became quite critical of Father's crofting methods. We could afford to, of course, for we shared only some of the work and none of the responsibility. One aspect that we especially seized on—it was, after all, highly visible—was this clutter of structures, which we damned both on aesthetic grounds and because we thought it unnecessary. 'For God's sake,' we used to grumble, 'have one really big building and be done with it.'

But, as I have just remarked in these notes and as I shall certainly have occasion to remark again, it was never that simple. I came gradually to appreciate this. One really big building, with its great expense in constructional man-hours and materials, not to mention its need for a suitable site (not so common), would have seemed to my father, for most of his crofting life, an impossible luxury.

A crofter builds as need arises and as time and materials become available. Materials especially are a problem. Few Highland townships boast a builder's merchant among their amenities and few crofters could afford to patronize one very often were he at hand. Father was a polite and retiring man yet he managed, in his crofting persona, to turn himself into an expert scrounger and picker-up of discarded bits and pieces. Things like old doors and windows and second-hand—or tenth-hand—sheets of corrugated iron were treasure trove to him.

A crofter also bears in mind the simple proposition that it is easier to add to an existing building than to rear a wholly new one. Some of Father's buildings, straggly, concertina-like structures marching inexorably across the land towards the inevitable check of rock or ditch, could almost have been told off year by year like the growth rings on a tree. Adding to what you already have, however, means that you have one side of your new building given and that may make all the difference between the feasible and the non-feasible.

Father did at last erect a totally new and quite large building —meant as a byre mainly—during the last decade of his life. Perhaps the criticism of his sons had a cumulative effect. Perhaps it was no more than the opportune wrecking nearby of a Russian timber-carrying ship and the consequent arrival on our beaches of more new wood than he and his fellows had ever had in their lives. As far as I know the wreck was not of the Cornish kind but it certainly provided a bonanza. To Father it must have seemed like a directive from on high, 'Build!', and he built.

The new byre measured about forty feet by twelve by twelve. It had a concrete floor with drainage, a peaked roof of corrugated iron, was half-lined inside, had two doors and four windows and was covered outside with roofing felt. He built it largely unaided, with a saw, a rule and a hammer and I don't suppose that more than ten per cent of what went into it was actually bought. It stands firm yet and I think will outlast me as it outlasted him.

It took him several years. Even so he left a corner of the flooring unfinished and even so the effort involved almost broke him. He confessed to me a year before his death that this new construction had become a waking nightmare to him, greedily swallowing every spare minute he had and seeming never to be finished. He was then seventy-four.

And even so the need for other buildings remained. Hence the 'hut' to which poor Oscar was taken, to be deprived of his mother's valuable milk almost before he had had a chance to taste it.

February 29th
Dull all day with strong Southeasterly wind. Mild. Drizzle, which started in mid-afternoon, developed into torrential rain which lasted for several hours. Gathering winkles about Traig Bheag and estuary.

March 1st
Strong Southerly wind and driving rain with hill fog in forenoon. Afternoon better with one or two sunny spells. Gathered a bag of winkles in Eilean and estuary. Neill Henderson called at night with clock for overhaul.

March 15th
Cloudy and dull all day, with drizzle at times. Daffodils in bloom. Light Easterly wind. Making bridges in croft. Motored to Kilchoan for stores in evening. Mild.

Some of the ditches in the crofts were so large as to require bridges, generally no more than a plank or two.

Since the shop in Kilchoan kept regular hours I assume that Father, with his evening trip here to collect stores, was going to

meet an itinerant grocer, one or two of whom still found it
profitable to visit the peninsula. These might not reach Kilchoan
till quite late.

March 31st
Wind Southeasterly light to moderate. Dull and cold. Motored to
Achateny, with Alasdair as passenger, to collect 3 bags of oats. Wrote to
James. Received mail from James. Visit from Neill Mackinnon. Spread
some manure. Stopped calves' hay after tonight.

April 1st
Mainly dull, but with a few bright spells. Spreading manure and usual
daily jobs. Left the six bigger calves out at night because I've no hay to
spare for them, unfortunately. This is the worst year yet in respect of
cattle feeding.

Crofting, in its heyday, was a finely evolved system for extract-
ing the maximum amount of nourishment from the minimum
amount of ingredients. It had grown from its feudal roots under
the clan chiefs to become a unique mixture of the individual and
the communal. A crofter was free to run his croft as he wished but
free only within limits set by his peers acting in concert. He might
sow what crop he pleased and by sun or moon; he might reap
when the spirit moved him; he might do much or do little and
certainly whatever profit he made beyond those communal
expenses that had been assessed against him was his to keep or
spend as he saw fit. No matter what he did, however, there was a
point beyond which he must curb his eccentricity or his selfish-
ness.

The criterion was the common good. Our crofter, for example, might cut as many peats as he had time and energy for and
the fireplaces to absorb. He might come at last to despise the
ordinary cubed form and hack out his fuel in the shape of
pyramids or octahedrons. He might consume his handiwork
himself or wrap each block in tartan cellophane for the tourist
trade. What he might not do was to open up new workings
wherever he felt inclined; his peats would be cut only in the place
appointed to him.

Similarly he might delay or advance his hay harvest according
to his private reading of the several factors involved but if he had

not completed it by a time judged reasonable by his fellows that was too bad; his fields would be treated as stubble with the others and thrown open to the township livestock.

It follows that a crofter might not acquire as many cows as he pleased, for his beasts fed on communal land: the Common Grazings of the township. The number he was allowed would be determined by the township Grazing Committee. In Sanna the original figure—the 'souming' as it was called—was two cows for every croft. This, of course, referred to mature female animals. Latterly at any rate, a less strict eye was kept on the number of 'followers' a cow might have, followers meaning calves which, in respect of bullocks (castrated males), might profitably be kept till they were two or three or even, exceptionally, four years old. A cow, therefore, might be accompanied by three or four generations of her descendants and each crofter's little herd amount to anything from four to perhaps eight individual animals.

By the time of these journal entries, however, the traditional Sanna picture had become distorted out of all recognition. My father was by then the only practising crofter and the local Grazing Committee had declined from the great days of its power to a joint operation with the neighbouring township of Achnaha, and at last to one man acting intermittently as clerk. So Father might, in theory, have expanded his stock to take up all the available slack. He might have leaped from two cows to forty, being twenty crofts, the original Sanna number, at two cows apiece. That was the lawful potential of the township and there was by then no one really to say him nay. In reality, of course, other factors limited him severely. Seven mature cows was the highest number he ever attained and even that, I felt, was too much for him.

A crofter normally left his stock permanently outdoors from about the end of April till about the beginning of November, to forage for themselves. During winter they would be pushed out in daylight hours if the weather were at all clement and would have their grazing supplemented by hay and by various—mostly bought—cereals and such manufactured products as oilcake and beef nuts.

Much of the skill in crofting lies in the subtle and profitable management of one's cattle, the most successful operator being he who is best at juggling all the elements involved. One might consider my father here, taking him not as an average, for in relation to a spectrum as wide as crofting yields talk of an average is meaningless, but as a working model (a description that would surely have called forth his rare and sardonic smile). During his lifetime cattle auctions took place twice yearly in Kilchoan, in spring and autumn. Occasionally he might sell a cow: because she was getting old (few crofters could afford sentiment in regard to their beasts and Father's excess of it was often, in material terms, a handicap to him) or because, growing up, she had turned out to be a troublesome, obstreperous creature or a poor milker. More generally, only calves were sold, the best prices being made by hulking bullocks of two or three years old. These would often outsell cows by a considerable margin.

For the sale of such a bullock Father might have expected, during the period of this journal and given a reasonably good day, a hundred pounds or so, or even now and then a hundred and twenty or thirty. When he had several to sell and could come home to toss down five or six hundred pounds on the kitchen table before Mother's astonished and gratified gaze he would be a happy man. He would beam as he seldom beamed. All the hard work and all the heartbreak would for a moment seem worthwhile.

So why, one might reasonably inquire, were the Ardnamurchan hills not thickly clustered with hulking bullocks, given the prospect of such returns? But of course, my reader, already you know the answer—it was never as simple as that.

Here are some of the snags to raising and selling cattle. The list makes no claim to comprehensiveness.

Item. Prices fluctuate a good deal and a hundred pounds plus was not necessarily a norm for this period. Seventy or eighty pounds might have been nearer the average with occasional dips to fifty or sixty.

Item. A crofter would not always have bullocks to sell. Nature is not so obliging. And for less marketable (a euphemism for less butcherable) beasts he might well be offered much lower figures. Father, I recollect, took a fine young cow to Kilchoan Sales with her first—female—calf at heel. He needed the money. For both animals together he was offered a contemptuous eight pounds and this as recently as 1960. He trudged them home again and we tightened our belts.

Item. In trying to take advantage of any theoretical spare capacity in a township's souming a crofter might well overstock himself, as I think Father may perhaps have done, both in relation to his physical abilities and in relation to the actual grass growing on the ground. (Real grass is very different from grass that flourishes on paper: cattle tend to grow bony and dispirited on the latter.) On a large farm, that is to say, with lots of mechanical and human help available when needed, one man may comfortably look after a fair-sized herd of cattle. For the crofter, on the other hand, possibly elderly (crofters do not retire; they die in harness) and possibly single-handed, with only the most primitive of facilities and with a myriad other tasks to perform, it is a very different matter. He may well be overstretched at half a dozen.

And there is this business of grass that you can see and touch as opposed to grass that exists only in a clerical sense. When the founding fathers of Sanna reckoned that the place could support two cows for every croft they were thinking only in terms of cows, for all that they made theoretical provision for other grazing species. But by the time I write of, Sanna cattle had to compete with scores of sheep and hundreds of rabbits, not to mention—as I believe—a slow deterioration in climate and the huge spread of such largely unpalatable herbage as the Common Rush.

(Sheep were not brought into Sanna until post-World War Two. It was a tragically misguided introduction. Rabbits, of course, have plagued us since time immemorial, but in former days every man's hand—and pot—was against them.)

Item. A Sanna croft amounted to about two and a half acres. A crofter with half a dozen cows (plus two or three years' followers, remember) would not get nearly enough hay from that acreage for winter feed. Even if other abandoned crofts were open to him, as they were in theory to Father, he would still have to find time and energy to utilize them. This explains why Father found himself buying four or five tons of hay each year from outwith the district. And by the time of his death bought hay had climbed to over twenty pounds a ton. (It is now about four times that, when you can get it.) Five tons at twenty pounds a ton accounts for the profit from one good bullock. Or actually it accounts for the *price* of one good bullock; most likely it accounts for the *profit* from two or three but Father's bookkeeping was never that precise.

Item. To provide stabling for half a dozen cows would strain the capacity of many crofters. Increase the number and you rule out most.

And so on. Already the picture grows mazy but, in addition to deciding which beasts to sell and when, a Sanna crofter, in Father's day, would face the problem of 'where?'. Our local cattle sales were small-scale affairs, tending to be at the mercy of small-scale dealers, itinerant middlemen buying cheap in the north to sell dear in the south. They knew one another, indeed travelled round together, and dog does not eat dog.

Suppose, however, that a Sanna crofter had decided to oppose the system and sell at Oban, which was then the nearest of the larger markets. This market would attract big buyers from all over; the chances of a dealers' ring forming would be lessened. Oban, however, is a long way from Sanna, awkward to get to and still more awkward to ship an animal to. The crofter might not be able to accompany his beasts (an overnight affair) and consequently would have to rely on an agent to do his selling—at a price, naturally, and without the care or the finely-tuned judgement that he himself would possess in regard to his own stock. Even if present he would no doubt be reluctant to bring an animal back unsold from such a distant market, so facing doubled freight charges and the 'I told you so' comments of less courageous neighbours. He would be the more likely, therefore, to take whatever price he could get and there was, after all, no guarantee of more money in Oban.

Even the weather is important when one is selling livestock. What is the forecast for Sale Day? Animals, like humans, look despondent and bedraggled in a downpour and buyers are uncomfortable and irritable. Prices are unlikely to soar. Sunlight, on the other hand, might so gather on the backs of one's beasts as to dazzle—stranger things have happened—even the flinty eyes of a dealer.

I could go on with the '*Items*' but I won't. Crofting is a complex and chancy business, no occupation for fools. Or perhaps no occupation for wise men.

It is true, certainly, that the sale of your surplus stock provides you, as a crofter, with your one sizeable cash inflow of the year. Much depends on it, not least the continued welfare of yourself and your family. Despite that, I came to wonder if the game was really worth the candle. I suggested as much to Father, without convincing him. A more accurate breakdown of figures, I felt, would have dissipated even the small profits that appeared to accrue. No crofter, I noticed, ever got ahead of the game; at best he survived.

Since those days of doubt I have grown older and more sensible, or if not more sensible at least more tolerant. Money, I now realize, was never really the point of the exercise. My father would have argued, had he ever had the time or felt the need, that the keeping of cattle was his *raison d'être*, the very essence of his occupation. Without that he became as a musician sitting silent and empty-handed. However he fared at selling his stock, whether it showed a profit or no, it was his road through to pride and manhood.

In the entry above Father is paying the penalty for over-reaching, for getting his sums a little bit wrong. By leaving six calves out at night as early as the end of March he is acknowledging that. It was unlikely that they would come to much harm; neither would they benefit. The year's new growth would not yet be under way and they would find little to eat that was both palatable and nutritious. Most probably they would not attempt to forage at all but would simply cluster around the byre all night, 'talking' to their luckier fellows inside. By allowing them the largely theoretical option of grazing Father was really doing no more than providing a sop to his conscience. But why not, I suppose, when that was among his chief of possessions?

April 15th
A fine day, with light variable wind. Mainly sunny. Replaced aerial
and projection board blown off in severe gale two days previously.
Many cars down. Two tents in bent at Traigh Bheag area. Received
application form for sheep subsidy. Fiona Mackenzie crashed their
Austin Gypsy at Grigadale. She escaped with bruises but, apparently,
the vehicle was wrecked.

An eventful day by our quiet standards but Father makes typical-ly terse work of it. 'Projection boards' had better be explained, this being the second time of mention. They were long boards attached to the ends of the roof and following the lines of the gables. Their purpose was to prevent wind from getting under the vulnerable end slates and, it might be, stripping the whole roof. Unfortunately they were themselves vulnerable and ours blew down on several occasions. Father and I eventually replaced them with the more usual concrete abutment type of thing.

'In bent' means among the dunes and refers to the marram grass that covered them, often known locally as 'bent grass' or 'bent'. 'Down', as in the cars that were down, is mere local linguistic convention and the result of living at the tip of a long peninsula. 'Up' would display as much—or as little—logic. You go downtown and I go uptown. We both get there in the end and perhaps it does not matter very much how we describe our journeying, as long as we travel with gratitude in our hearts for the blessed ambiguities of English.

April 30th
Dull at first but sun came through in late forenoon. Miss D. and friends left about 10.15 a.m. Stripping peats at faraway moss and repairing fences. A very cold North to Northeast wind sprung up in the evening.

That bank of ground, sectioned deep into boggy moorland, where a crofter 'cuts' (digs) his peats for fuel, is known in the West Highlands as a 'peat moss' or more simply as a 'moss'. Sanna crofters operated two or three such mosses as a rule, in places apportioned to them or to their ancestors. These would likely be in different areas, deliberately so, and might well produce fuel of widely divergent quality. Dried peat varies in 'burnability' as much as does coal. Some peat is light and brown and spongy; some heavy, compacted, hard and black. The best is almost as good as coal and the point, of course, of spreading mosses around is to produce an equitable distribution of the good stuff. It means that no man has to take all his fuel from an area of poor quality and likewise prevents him from hogging the best.

These mosses would be designated in simple fashion for convenience, hence the faraway moss of this entry, a name that was literal rather than poetic. It was something like two miles off, over our usual rough ground and across a fair-sized stream, the fording of which, in winter spate and when one was laden, was difficult or impossible. It was no small task for an elderly man to fetch back from there some forty or fifty pounds of peat and to do it two or three times a week regardless of weather.

Father, in fact, when he reached his seventies, abandoned the faraway moss and opened a substitute nearer at hand. He would not have been allowed to do so in former days but by then, because of depopulation and the consequent going to pot of township affairs, there was no one to gainsay him nor, for that matter, any need to do so, for he was depriving nobody.

The winning of peats from a bog begins with 'stripping' or 'skinning', that is, removing the top layer of heathery turf to expose the peaty earth below. This is done in a band about a yard wide along the edge of the bank. After this the peats are cut, or dug out, in layers, perhaps three, perhaps four layers deep, depending on how good drainage is at that particular moss and how much water is beginning to collect. The wet peats are cast up on to the bank as they are cut, to dry out. This may involve spreading them around a bit by means of a special three-pronged fork. When they are dry enough to be handled they are 'set up', or propped on end against one another in little three- or four- or five- or six-peat pyramids. When they are thoroughly dry they are ready to be burned and can be taken home by whatever means are available—the human frame with us—to be tumbled into a shed or built into an outdoor stack beside the house. Alternatively—our usual procedure—they can be stacked at the moss and taken home as required. There are advantages and disadvantages in both methods. The purpose, needless to say, of building a stack is to keep the peats dry once they have reached that stage and a well-built stack achieves this despite rain and gales.

Cutting peats—by which I mean now the whole operation—is never less than hard work and, in hot sticky weather, when the midges and stinging horse flies are bothersome, can be a form of purgatory. But it can also be sheer joy, the most delightful part of crofting. You leave home, it may be, early on a spring morning, with the sun shining and a pleasant breeze blowing. You take a picnic lunch with you for you intend to stay all day and neither expect nor want to see anyone till you return at dusk. And you start to work, for your own benefit and pleasure, at a job which has a direct and physical connection with who and what and why you are. Up above you larks are going melodiously mad and all around is the varied life of the bog, butterflies, dragon-flies, half a hundred plants and wild flowers. Behind you grows the story of your day and you can see it and feel your progress in the very depths of your muscles where the unused tissue slumbers. By mid-afternoon a weariness has begun to creep inward from your wrists, from your ankles, and by teatime it centres itself in the small of your back. Cherish it! Work to increase it! One row more. Then another. There is no rebirth without pain.

On such a day one would have to be a clod of clods, deprived of all senses and all hope, not to feel close to the beating heart of the world, not to feel accepted and nourished. I have spent long days out on the bog when I would not have changed places with a king, with an emperor. Even as I think of it and write of it I can feel my bowels turn to water.

May 1st
Sunday. Sunny all day but with a searing North to Northeast wind. Service in Hall at 3 p.m. Free Church. Found one of our best ewes dead, with a partly born lamb, which apparently she was unable to deliver.

May 15th.
Sunday. A fine warm day with light Southeast air and a lot of sunshine. Service in Hall at 3 p.m. Not present. Allan Macdonald, formerly of Grigadale, died at 5 p.m. in Mingary, where he lived with his brother Kenneth and his wife. He took a shock in the morning and never regained complete consciousness again. Allan was unmarried and aged 79.

May 31st. Warm and dull until about 4.30 p.m. when light rain came on. Alasdair and self making a stack at faraway peats in forenoon. Funeral of Duncan Mackenzie from Caim to Kilmory Churchyard, at 7 p.m. Did not attend because of the distance and the lateness of the time. Received Firearms Certificate back from Martin.

Women, by old Highland custom, do not attend the graveside part of funerals, though they may be present during the preceding religious service at the home of the dead person and will normally be responsible for dispensing the subsequent refreshments. Local funerals were, and to some extent still are, pretty faithfully attended by all the available males of the district. (Hence, one supposes, the custom, of giving out something to eat and drink, for a man might have walked miles to be present and would need staying before he set off for home.) The cynical had it that attendance at funerals was due as much to cautious anticipation, an expected quid pro quo, as to piety. One was making a down payment against one's own rites of passage. Of course you gain in prestige by having a good turn-out at your funeral and if you cannot enjoy it yourself, or at any rate are not able to make your enjoyment terrestrially known, at least your family can bask in the glow of your accomplishment. Exceptional turn-outs are remembered for years afterward.

I think that the cynical view of funerals is a little unfair. In country areas at least, good attendance at funerals is surely an indication of tribal solidarity, as well as being a survival from more ceremonial days (ironically enough, perhaps the last such indication and the last such survival). With infinite foolishness we discard our rituals one by one but the rituals which we associate with death will be the last to go, as they were no doubt the first to come. Some little wisdom clings to us still. Not everyone now gets formally christened or wed but all get some remnant of a funeral, however truncated, and those that get most die best in the memories of their loved ones.

A firearms certificate has to be shown or sent to a gunsmith (e.g. Martin's of Glasgow in this entry) before he will sell one ammunition. Keeping down the rabbit population of Sanna was supposed to be a legal obligation owed by my father, as a landholder in an agricultural area, and among the bureaucrats who swarmed in on us was an official with the Ruritanian title of Pest Control Officer, Highlands and Islands (hereinafter known as the PCOHI). His job it was to see that this obligation was met. He descended on us once or twice a year and strolled briefly among the dunes. If by chance he encountered a few rabbits—and one would be hard pushed not to in a village as rabbit-struck as Sanna—he came to us and hauled poor Father over the coals. Perhaps once in all his visits he complimented us on the apparently rabbitless state of grace we had fallen into.

Of course it was all totally unscientific, and the one time we escaped censure was almost certainly due to some freak of circumstance. Someone had no doubt walked through the dune area just ahead of our PCOHI and scared the rabbits back to their burrows. Had he returned a few minutes later he would have found himself tripping over them as usual.

Rabbit control was an onerous duty and an unfair one. It ought by rights to have been visited on all Sanna crofters, present or absent, but in practice Father bore the main bureaucratic onslaught in this as in other matters. That was easier for official-dom than chasing up absentees, who might be represented by mere distant and uninterested relatives of the original family or who might now live on the other side of the globe. Father's habit of timid compliance with all ukases that came his way made it easier still. In his life as a crofter he had several times been leant on very heavily by officials and had once, through no real fault of his own, narrowly escaped prosecution. He had become terrified as a result.

I suppose that no calling in Britain is as infested by petty bureaucrats, trailing their slimy paper trails, as is crofting. It is good to obey the law but it is as detrimental to the law's welfare as to one's own to let it trample one without justification or enmesh one in foolishness. There are times when a resounding 'Bugger off!' is called for.

Our attempts at rabbit control in Sanna were in any event foredoomed. Though I might, in a prolonged fit of rage at being so hounded, dig out our old .22 and kill a score a day for a week, it neither made nor could make the slightest difference. Our rabbit stock, compared to former days, had mushroomed, being firmly dug in on hillside and in hollow, as well as in every corner of the dune area and in all outlying parts of the township. It had reached optimum level, in other words. Such a stock is self-regulating and quite immune to normal human manipulation. It takes a catastrophe such as myxomatosis to produce noticeable effect and even that will be recovered from in time. Any Pest Control Officer worthy of the name would have known all this.

I don't know what happened to our PCOHI. He stopped coming eventually. Perhaps he grew discouraged. Perhaps he was bureaucratized in his turn—little fleas have big fleas—and languishes now in some forgotten office where the Out Trays stalagmite to the ceiling and the tea lady never comes and the inmates sit around like husks, their vital juices long since siphoned off by a voracious computer.

The advent of the PCOHI had one beneficial result at any rate, for it enabled us to prise from the Chief Constable permission to own a rifle. And a rifle has other and better uses on a Highland croft than the ludicrous one of trying to alter rabbit statistics.

> A wand from the wood, taken at will,
> A fish from the stream, a deer from the hill;
> Why grows this gap 'twixt Cot and Hall?
> These three are rights God gave to all.

So runs an old Gaelic proverb.

June 1st
Dull, with fine rain and fog from mid-day onwards. Foghorn
operating. Wind Southerly moderate and mild. In Kilchoan for stores.
Rhu and Plocaig lambs docked and dressed and sheep sprayed. For us 12
male lambs and 8 ewe lambs were the total. After several recounts
Donald and self reckoned that there are 21 grown sheep, including last
year's hoggs. The above tally of lambs includes four pairs of twins, of
which one pair are small. Received 500 rounds HV hollow point .22
ammunition from Martin.

The Sanna area, with its lack of shelter, its bogs and ditches and
precipices, its wind and rain, is killing ground for sheep. Our
stock never rose above the number we started with, each year's
crop of ewe lambs being just enough to cancel our losses.

Lambs have their tails docked, supposedly as a preventive
measure. The theory is that since the tail tends to become clotted
with dung and so attractive to bluebottles the less there is of it the
better. It is true that bluebottles lay eggs on sheep, eggs hatch
maggots and maggots eat their host alive. I have seen ewes so
badly attacked via an invaded flesh wound that their innards were
exposed.

Male lambs were 'dressed', a euphemism for castration. Sheep
owners in these parts traditionally buy rams rather than breeding
their own. Whether this is a wise policy is a moot point. It may
indeed lead to a better gene pool, as it is thought to do, but good
rams are expensive and, as newcomers to a ground, not as alert to
its dangers.

June 15th
Cloudy in forenoon, but afternoon sunny. Wind Southerly to Southeast
fresh at times. Evening became overcast and rain started at 6 p.m. and
gradually became heavy. In Kilchoan for groceries. Alasdair and self
finished the setting up at Lon Bheinn na Curra peats. A caravan came
into Toll nan Conn area at 7 p.m. Wrote to James.

June 30th
A fine sunny day with light West to Northwesterly wind. Found one of
our sheep with maggot and clipped and dressed same. Stacking at Lon
Bheinn na Curra. Cherry out all day. Wrote to James. Visit from Mr
and Mrs E.

Just to be confusing, 'dressed' is used here in the sense of dressing a wound. The wool in the region of the wound would first of all be clipped.

Father refers in this entry to being visited by Mr and Mrs E. Going visiting at night, that is, casually dropping in on a neighbour or two for an evenings's tea and gossip, was an activity developed to a high art in the townships of Western Ardnamurchan. One or two local families grew famous—or notorious —for their skill in visiting. An evening when they remained at home became the stuff of legend, worthy of being marked with a white stone.

Obviously the savings in heating and lighting—let alone tea —that resulted from a thoroughgoing devotion to visiting were considerable. But complications loomed for the incompetent, and sometimes farce as well. For instance, you dared not arrive so early at the house you had decided to visit as to interrupt the family at their proper tea, for the laws of hospitality, iron in character in these parts, would then require them to feed you. And while it was considered all right to stick them for a pot of Brooke Bond and a scone or two, it was thought a bit much to eat at their expense. Besides, when you arrived too early you were then, by crude means, placing yourself in a position to note—and retail—how well they did themselves at table. It was perfectly acceptable to acquire such information by stealth, usually by rooting among the order boxes while the grocery van driver's back was turned, but it was generally acknowledged bad form to obtain it openly.

On the other hand, you had to get away from your own house sharply enough to avoid being visited yourself. It was in the nice timing of one's comings and goings that much of the fun and expertise of visiting resided.

Then there was the hazard of 'crossing', when you arrived at the home of the people you intended visiting only to learn from a surfeit of eagerly informative neighbours that they had gone to visit you. Reports of such contretemps were generally in circulation by the end of the same evening and always occasioned a good deal of glee. (It is true that the Gael is classically a dreamy and melancholy character, but it is also true that he possesses a sardonic and mocking wit and is much given to *schadenfreude*.)

Visiting was naturally an activity that fed on itself to a large extent, and noting the visitors of others was an important adjunct to one's own efforts in that line. It was politic, therefore, to take a night off now and then and spend it perched behind one's lace curtains, ubiquitous Highland binoculars in hand, scanning hill and glen for signs of life, gathering titbits for later distribution. For a visitor who came always empty-handed, absorbing gossip and never yielding any, would soon find his welcome growing thin. After all, the extent to which remote communities are tolerable—viable, some would say—depends on an intimate acquaintance with one's neighbours' affairs.

(Good field-glasses, incidentally, were an important item of furniture in the old-style Highland home and were usually among the first purchases of newly-weds, giving precedence only to the female calf, the dozen point-of-lay pullets and the framed sampler of 'The Lord is my Shepherd'. One regrets their passing for they were cheaper than the television sets that have replaced them and vastly more entertaining.)

Tourists staying in the neighbourhood often took to visiting like ducks to water, especially those whose regular advent had enabled them to scrape a few acquaintances among the natives (e.g. Mr and Mrs E. above). Whether their enthusiasm arose from a determination to be, for the brief space of a holiday, as genuinely Highland as possible, or whether it came merely from a stunned contemplation of the Ardnamurchan alternatives I never managed to establish.

Because my family sold milk and eggs to tourists we were invariably among the first to have our acquaintance scraped. We had decidedly mixed feelings about this. Except perhaps for my sister we were never an enormously sociable lot. A little visiting went a very long way with us and after working hard all day we liked to have our evenings free for such family pursuits as reading and writing and passing round crossword puzzles. We found it a bit much to have visitors—tourist visitors at least—bounding into our midst night after night, full of gusto and bonhomie after having spent their day lounging on the beach.

Father and I grew fairly ruthless about dealing with this. The reader should note Father's scrupulous phrasing in the entry above, 'Visit from Mr and Mrs E.'. He doesn't say 'I was pleased to welcome Mr and Mrs E. and enjoyed a long and interesting conversation with them.' The chances are that he wasn't even there. He and I developed a split-second technique for skipping out the back door whenever voices were heard at the front.

My sister remained behind willingly; my mother stayed not so much out of sociability but because she had a stronger sense of the proprieties and a less pronounced determination to pursue her own affairs. Her awareness of the injustice of this, her knowledge of her own impotence, often made her bitter. 'I can't run away like you and him,' she would complain to me. 'I've got to stay and face them.'

These complaints filled me always with guilt and sympathy but seldom produced much alteration in my behaviour. For an evening or two, it might be, I would endure the tedium, the—to me—genuine agony of sitting in our kitchen making polite conversation with whoever had dropped in, the chalk vainly trying to establish common ground with the cheese. Then another and still more urgent form of guilt would intervene. I would think of time passing and the unwritten masterpieces. Resentment, too, would bear a hand. 'Why should I have to put up with this torture?' I would ask myself fiercely. 'Why the hell should I? What are these people to me or I to them that they should force me to endure such boredom, such feigning?'

Then 'Sorry, Mother,' I would mutter to myself. 'Deeply sorry. But I cannot come to your aid. I simply cannot make myself do it.' And the next evening I would take to the hills or hide in my room as usual.

Our skipping-out technique did not always work with the natives. As a tactic it depended on the willingness of the visitor to stand on ceremony, to knock and wait to be admitted. Not all who came to our door were trained to do that. At one time in the Highlands doors were never locked and no one ever knocked on them. When you visited someone you simply lifted the latch and walked in. Oh, I dare say that if you had sold a calf lately for a record price and had put on a bit of consequence as a result, or if you had merely lived too long in the south, you might shout a greeting from the lobby once you had entered. But that was swanking it a good deal.

A few of the older generation clung to that tradition even as lately as the period covered by Father's journal. You found them pulling up a chair at the fireside before you could do anything about it. It would have been pointless to hide from them anyway. They knew your habits better than you did yourself and were quite capable of rummaging through your outbuildings in search of you. It could be embarrassing to be informed dryly that it was a

fine evening as you emerged sheepishly from behind a column of
baled hay in the barn.

We kept dogs, of course, who normally lay on old sacks in the
hallway and whose duties were supposed to include warning us
that someone was approaching the house. But dogs, we learned,
were never entirely reliable in such matters, sometimes letting
loose a positive frenzy of barks and sometimes, for no apparent
reason, remaining stubbornly mute. A dog's judgement of an
approaching visitor is presumably determined by such factors as
whether he possesses a pleasant-sounding footfall. It has to be
said that the verdicts thus arrived at, while often of great interest,
did not always have a practical application. A visitor might chime
his way into the heart of every dog in creation yet be the biggest
bore unstrangled.

It is all changed now. The houses of Sanna, for the most part,
rest from their labours, like those who lived in them, unvisited
save by bird or fieldmouse, or holidaying owner up from the
south. The ritual of the visit is dying. Radio and television
(latecomers to the Highlands and not available everywhere even
yet) have helped to kill it, no doubt, but the main culprit has been
simple depopulation. Sanna's year-round number of inhabitants
could now be totted up on the fingers of one hand. A self-
sustaining level of visiting is not possible with so few people. You
may go for weeks now without having an aborigine cross your
threshold. Indeed in winter you may go for long enough without
clapping eyes on another human being. Come back, Mr and Mrs
E!

1st July
Some light rain in the morning but a fine day thereafter, with light
Westerly wind. Shearing sheep all day at Achnaha. Jaguar car,
belonging to the people in Morag Mackenzie's went in road drain,
released by council lorry. Mr F. arrived to caravan. I had to lend him
two planks to get across the stream at Glac an Fhaing with his car. Two
caravans came in at 9 p.m. to Toll nan Conn area. Mr G. and party
(two cars) arrived at 10.35 p.m. Suspect Daisy's calf has fractured right
hind leg.

I like the precision of '10.35 p.m.' but such meticulousness in
regard to people's movements is in itself a telling comment on life
in a small community.

The calf had been born with a congenital malformation of the limb, an occurrence which, by the time of the next entry, is to lead to unpleasant consequences (not least for the animal itself).

July 4th
Light rain from early morning till about noon. Afternoon fine and calm with some sunshine. Visit from Dr H. who is camping in Sanna with his family. They were here four years ago. Motored to Kilchoan for stores. The Vet was in Achnaha at Donald's beast so I requested that he come to see Daisy's wee calf. He said, after examining the calf, that the right hind leg was displaced in two places and that nothing could be done to put it right and, also, that even if the calf lived to maturity it would always be a cripple. In view of that, and of the fact that the poor creature was obviously suffering pain, we reluctantly decided to put it out of its misery. Alasdair was good enough to relieve me of that unpleasant duty. We buried it in the 'lawn' below the byre where Susan and the other two calfs we lost are. Jessie called it Bideach Beag.

Bideach Beag, the crippled calf, was shot. Alasdair, so far from being 'good enough' etc., was given no choice in the matter. Father appeared abruptly and uncomfortably in the doorway of my room, where I was writing, with the rifle, loaded, in his hands and the information that the grave was already dug. His request that I shoot the calf for him was my first intimation of his intentions. He might as well have presented the rifle at my head. I could see that the animal had to be killed, either by the vet or, with less fuss and probably more dispatch, by us. I could see, too, that Father would never be able to do it. That only left me.

A crippled calf can be moved around readily, at least when it is small. A crippled cow, that can neither move itself nor, because of its huge bulk and weight, be moved by any means available on a croft, is a living disaster. If this calf had reached maturity the consequences for both us and it would have been horrendous to contemplate. Shooting it was an unpleasant duty for me, too, but unlike Father I could—just—bring myself to do it.

I wheeled the poor beast down to the appointed place in a barrow. At the graveside I decanted it, shot it through the head and heart, and tumbled it in. I shall not dwell on the look of placid trust in its eyes. I remember that two of our neighbours, making a call in the nearby phone box, witnessed the whole operation. I felt hugely resentful that I should have been selected by fate for the role of executioner and more angry still that I should have been provided with an audience. Some remnant of my better nature remained, however, and I filled in the grave as quickly as I could before Father appeared, that he might not be distressed by the sight of the dead animal.

I do not know that I could shoot that calf today, despite the consequences of not doing so. As I grow older I come more and more to feel that all life is sacred. And I become less sure of the dividing line between responsibility and non-interference. I could turn and be a Jain, though I claim no more for my feelings than a sympathy induced by my own growing fragility. Swatting flies is about my limit now and I do that reluctantly.

The whole business of having pets destroyed, or injured or diseased animals, reeks of euphemism and rationalization and plain old-fashioned lying. There ought to be no extermination without representation. Too often when we say that we are putting an animal out of its misery we have no real information on the subject and are prompted merely by our own misery at the sight of it. The deed is selfish rather than humane.

I must take care not to sound superior. On reading over what I have written here I catch myself slipping in the phrase 'poor beast', indicating to the reader my own keen sensibilities without being openly boastful. A little bit of subliminal self-advertising, in fact.

How subtle is language! And how discreetly and daintily, between a comma and a comma, may one wash one's hands.

July 15th
Showery, with fresh Northwest wind. Went by mail bus to Strontian to meet a car bringing Jimmy and Derek. They arrived at 10 a.m. but our bus for the return trip didn't leave Strontian until 1.30 p.m. We spent the interval in Horsley Hall Hotel where we received all hospitality. Sent James a postcard. Many campers away.

Jimmy and Derek were his grandchildren, sons of my elder brother, James.

July 31
Sunday. Forenoon dull and sultry. Wind Southerly moderate. Bright spells in the afternoon. Alasdair took Jimmy and Derek to Carraig

cave. Mr G. and son left at about 1.30 p.m. Caravan arrived at 2 p.m.
Other four caravans arrived in late evening. Service in Hall at 3 p.m.
(Church of Scotland). Not present—chasing cows.

Services in our little 'Hall' or church, actually a corrugated iron hut with a few rows of seats, were held on alternate Sundays by the Church of Scotland (otherwise known as the Parish Church or the Established Church) and by the Free Church, a Calvinistic breakaway group. Church of Scotland members, such as Father, generally attended both services impartially; not so the Free Kirkers, who would have felt that they were risking spiritual contamination in the more easy-going atmosphere of their rival. And Father's cow-chasing (rounding-up) would have engendered horror rather than sympathy among the adherents of an institution which chased its sheep with such grim determination, and which forbade even such simple Sunday pleasures as going for a walk.

August 1st
Dull and calm at first. Afternoon warm and mainly sunny. Heard
several peals of thunder in the distance. Out fishing with K.
MacGillivray and H. Henderson but only caught about twenty saithe,
mackerel, gurnet and lythe, between us. Several more camping outfits
came in. Touch of lumbago.

August 15th
Rain during early hours and until about 9 a.m. Sunny thereafter and
with fresh Westerly wind. Mr I. left for Alloa in early morning. Some
more campers in including a Dormobile. Afternoon sunny but with one
or two light showers. Cut and spread a rig of hay next to the dyke,
beyond first cross drain. Torrential showers at night.

August 31st
Cloudy all day but with particularly good visibility. Cutting in Mary
Anne's croft.

Mary Anne's croft adjoined ours and being unused had been partly taken over by Father in an effort to solve his perennial fodder problems.

September 1st
Sunny and calm from early morning, with a light Northeast breeze,
cloudless skies and a wonderful sunset. Hector arrived with tractor and
started cutting the remainder of our hay at about 12 noon. He had two
breaks for food and finished at 2.45 p.m. His total working time would
only be about 1½ hours. He left a couple of bits uncut, where the
ground wasn't suitable for the tractor to work on. These pieces I hope to
cut with the scythe, and any other pieces that I see elsewhere, worth
cutting. The J. family from Helensburgh, with two cars and caravan,
departed in forenoon. One of their little girls was named Caroline and
the other Victoria. Made one rick and spread some hay. Mail car
arrived at 11.30 p.m. Parcel of damsons from Mary Henderson.

Hector, who came with his tractor, was my cousin once or twice
removed, from a neighbouring village. Two or three of the
slightly more affluent crofters in the district by now owned
tractors and it was sometimes possible for us to have our hay cut
by machinery, at a cost of a fiver or so, plus the driver's meals.
(The latter part of the bargain seems to have been taken full
advantage of on this occasion, but that was no doubt due to
Mother's importuning rather than Hector's greed.)

We did not often get a tractor and there were reasons for this:
we were independent; others were busy; chiefly, our croft was
unsuitable for tractor work, being heavily criss-crossed by ditches, some deep and wide, some half-concealed. Our ground was
softish underfoot, too, even at its driest, and the damage done by
churning tractor wheels could be appalling. Besides, there was
the constant nightmare risk of the vehicle's getting stuck.

Again, though it sounds wonderful to have a machine eliminate two or three weeks of hard labour in the space of an hour,
things—my leitmotiv—were never as simple as that. The cutting
of the hay is only the start of the haymaking process, still leaving a
good deal to be done. But once your hay is cut and on the ground
you have committed yourself and if it is all on the ground at the
same time you are totally committed. You must then press on
with the next stage. If a long spell of wet weather follows—not an
unknown event in the West Highlands—your hay might well rot
where it lies. To lose only a 'rig' (that is, a small strip) in this
fashion might not matter too desperately; to lose your whole
croft could be disastrous.

The modern practice of turning grass into silage instead of

making hay of it, a simple and safe process that does not hinge on the weather, has now spread to quite small farms and ought to be a boon to crofters. In the days of its glory, however, Sanna knew nothing of silage and probably would not have been interested anyway. In the establishment of new practices crofters of Father's day operated at least a generation behind the rest of the country and were quite content to have it that way.

Hay-harvesting old-style, like much else about crofting, is a case of juggling several probably contradictory factors. And when you have done that to the best of your ability you are still jumping head first into the unknown.

September 15th
D.O.A.S. Inspector called at mid-day to inspect the cattle for subsidy. He also punched Dinah's and Oscar's ears for Calf Subsidy. Rain all morning and forenoon. Streams in spate and ground in a deplorable state. Rain, sometimes torrential, continued until 6 p.m. Kept the cows and calves in because the night was raw and cold, and every appearance of more rain to come.

Calves that were to receive a Department of Agriculture subsidy had their ears punched and a numbered metal tag inserted to help prevent fraud.

September 30th
Strong Easterly wind all day. Sunny spells alternating with cloudy periods. Took more hay to stackyard and made three medium-sized ricks. Wrote to Ian. My left arm has been troublesome for some days, being painful and swollen between wrist and elbow. Cold morning and evening.

It was the weather that was cold rather than the author. At least, I think so.

October 1st
E's birthday. Dry, with long sunny spells. A strong Easterly wind prevented us from doing anything at the hay. I gathered a large can-full of brambles off the croft dyke. Ian arrived unexpectedly by car at about 10.45 a.m. Army cadet officers, numbering 70, were conveyed by military vehicles to Salen from the Fort William area and told to find their way to Dunbhan as best they could. One of them knocked on our

*door at 10 p.m. having been to the lighthouse and then to Dunbhan. We
gave him some tea and he returned there to suffer it out till morning and
see if any of his colleagues turned up.*

*Hugh Henderson brought a burden of potatoes, after dark! On above
date I informed Hugh that I had no objection to the main pipeline for
the Lower Sanna water supply being led through my sandcroft,
otherwise known as Dal Dubh.*

Soldiers undergoing the more advanced—that is to say, the more
sadistic—training exercises occasionally surfaced in Sanna. This
man had gone badly astray, having veered off course as far as the
lighthouse (Ardnamurchan Point Lighthouse, a mile and a half
from Sanna as the seagull flies but about six miles by road), before
reaching his target area of Dunbhan (near Sanna). Nevertheless,
he had covered well over thirty miles, across the very roughest of
ground, in something less than twelve hours. This while moving
through a totally unfamiliar landscape.

We heard later that he was, in fact, the only one of the group to
come anywhere near completing the exercise; a worrying statis-
tic, surely, for the generals, for it would appear to indicate that
officers are becoming less fit—or more intelligent.

A 'burden' is a common local word for a bagful, of indeterminate
weight, of almost anything. Hugh Henderson's thanks for a
favour rendered was bestowed after dark for a variety of reasons,
I suspect: he would not wish others to know his business; he
would be afraid of others misconstruing his gift (or perhaps
construing it); he would not want everyone to know that he had
a surplus of potatoes. The absurd lengths to which he was willing to go to keep secret a perfectly reasonable action are all too
typical of the present crofting village. They form a sad contrast
with the more co-operative and necessarily more open older
days.

Hugh, a very decent man, but an impulsively choleric one, did
not always arrive bearing gifts. He came bursting into our house
one day, inarticulate with rage, his arms beating the air with huge
ineffective gestures, like an over-full cormorant trying to take off
from the fishing grounds. When speech returned to him we
learned that he had, but a moment before, come across a dead
sheep, on the banks of the Sanna River, perilously close to the
edge. He feared that the juices of its dissolution would percolate

into his drinking water—drawn, of course, from that same stream—and under the impression that the sheep was one of ours he demanded that Father sally forth with a spade immediately and remove the carcass for decent—and distant—burial.

Father gave his usual soft answer (and was later to discover, on investigating the crime, that the offending sheep in fact belonged to someone else). In my corner I listened to their conversation with that mixture of impatience and wry amusement that village affairs usually drew from me. If Hugh had taken the trouble to trace his precious water supply to its source several miles off in the Glendrian Mountains he would have stumbled on—I would have taken a wager—as many as half a dozen dead sheep on its banks and probably one or two actually in it. And had I not, on many a summer day, watched the local cattle stand for hours, up to the knees in some river pool and pissing and shitting to their hearts' content?

No one ever died from drinking that water (I have swallowed many a gallon of it myself) nor, as far as I know, suffered the slightest indisposition. Mountain streams, in regions as remote as this, purify themselves of all natural 'pollution' within a few yards.

October 15th
Wind Northeasterly light. Forenoon sunny but afternoon mainly dull. Spent some hours gathering brambles along the croft dyke. Did nothing special otherwise. Katie Carmichael and Mary Henderson, Achnaha, went away in the morning. Received letter from Ian. Cattle loose in crofts.

The hay had by now been gathered, the cattle loosed into the croft to crop the stubble and any aftermath there might be. The easing of the work-load is evidenced here; Father permits himself the indulgence of a long bramble-picking session.

Autumn rivals spring in being the most attractive of Highland seasons. In some moods I prefer it. The tourists have mostly gone and one may roam untrammelled, neither intruding nor being intruded on. The October weather is often among the best of the year and the landscape is at its loveliest. After the intensity of summer light, the blaze and crackle of so much positive colour, there are clouded skies once more. One may lave one's eyes with duns and russets and olives and golds and greys.

> Down to the puritan marrow of my bones
> There's something in this richness that I hate;
> I love the look, austere, immaculate,
> Of landscapes drawn in pearly monotones,
> Bare hills, cold silver on a sky of slate . . .

The bustle of harvest is over and winter with its special problems and tensions is not yet. Throughout nature there is a feeling of relief, of letting go; a universal pause. The wild geese fly south, sky-wide sometimes, in huge and heart-stopping skeins, calling to each other, to us, as they go. Everything seems drenched in a gentle melancholy, that unspecific ache that is the heritage of man.

Besides, there are the brambles. To wander at sweet will along the banks and dykes of autumn, with purple hands and mouth, following no inclination more urgent than the slow curve of the earth and one's ebbing sense of duty! Bramble-gathering is a most pleasant and nourishing pastime.

October 31st
Generally a fine day with little or no wind. E. and I motored to Ardgour, parked the car and carried on to Fort William. Had the plaster taken off my arm at the hospital but it doesn't seem any better. We left home just before 7 a.m. and arrived back at 4.20 p.m. Saw Jean Mackenzie in Fort William.

November 1st
Overcast, with intermittent rain and Easterly gale. Morag MacCallum (acting nurse) called in forenoon. Wind moderated in evening and died away at night. The sky cleared giving a fine moonlight night.

November 15th
Moderate to fresh Southerly wind became strong in evening. Drizzle in early forenoon. Dry for an hour or two in the middle of the day. In the afternoon the sleety train became torrential and continued into the night. Did a little more to a new house for Tilly. Gave cattle a little hay. Managed across river at Cnoc Breac peats.

Tilly was a pet sheep, the first of many orphans that we hand-reared. She was a privileged character (I tell her story later) and no ageing butler, slopping the sherry around the salver on his tottering passage between pantry and drawing-room, could have been more conscious of possessing security of tenure or more determined to exploit it. The 'house' that was being built for her was but one indication of her status. Your ordinary sheep shivers it out on the hillside all night, having no roof but the low cloud of winter.

November 30th
Dull and overcast till about 3.30 p.m. when a vicious shower came on.
Showery all evening thereafter. Moderate Southerly gale until
night-time when it became calm. John Cameron cleaning the road
drains near our garage. Repaired puncture and changed the wheels
around. Received mail from James.

'Our garage' doesn't half sound posh. In truth it was but one more of Father's home-made second-hand constructions, of tin and wood. There was hardly room to swing a Baby Austin inside.

December 1st
Overcast with showers of sleety rain and some hail. Wind
Southwesterly moderate. Started small regular feeds for the cattle, with
treacle solution sprinkled on, today. Wrote to James.

Father is talking here about supplementary winter fodder for the cattle. December 1st is late-ish to be starting that but I would guess that, as usual, he would have none too much and would have postponed its introduction as long as possible.

December 15th
Dull all day with strong Southerly wind. Rain started at about 5 p.m.
and soon became torrential, with the strong wind making it a very dirty
night. Usual chores. Tramped to the other side of Benn Dubh in
afternoon but saw no deer nor any evidence of their having been there
recently. Wrote to James. E. feeling somewhat better today.

December 31st
Strong Southeasterly wind at first but veered to South to Southwest. A
prolonged cloudburst in the middle of the day, accompanied by peals of
thunder. Heavy showers of hail, sleet, and rain thereafter into the
night. Mrs Cameron called in evening with a tin of shortbread. Mr K.

arrived just before 1 p.m. Received tin of shortbread from Mrs Maclachlan. Received £4.4/- from Plumb for my 3 bags of winkles. Mr and Mrs Carmichael went to Mull. Duncan Macdonald went to Glasgow.

A quiet ending to the year. One holiday home owner has arrived for a New Year break but three of our sparse stock of indigenous neighbours have got out for the winter while the getting out was good.

Four guineas seems to me a poorish price in 1960 for three bags of winkles but I've no doubt the money was needed and welcome.

Up here tins of shortbread rival caddies of tea as the great and universal present, suitable for all ranks and occasions. They accompany us into the world and are passed around with the platitudes when we leave it. The crunch of biscuit and the slurp of tea have replaced the growl of surf and the splash of stream as the characteristic noises of Ardnamurchan.

Advice to newcomers: when in doubt give both tea and shortbread. Only gold ingots will better ensure you a reputation for good taste and generosity.

FATHER'S JOURNAL, 1970

MEANWHILE TEN YEARS have passed in the journal and for the journalist. One sets down some such phrase and all the intervening entries cry out for justice; a babble of small voices, infinitely piercing.

The material circumstances of my parents have improved in the interval. They receive the old age pension now. It is like saying that the beatings have been stopped and a course of mild indifference substituted. Too little and too late, but to them a godsend. They can be sure of paying the grocery bill now and that is something new in their lives. They are a decade older, however, and indeed by the end of this year's journal will have less than three years to live. The crash and whistle of time against the frail barrier of the flesh is something both are extremely aware of. My father grows obsessive about the need to hand over in the best repair possible to the next generation. My mother dreads becoming useless. 'Oh, Alasdair,' she says to me one day, 'it's terrible to grow old and be a burden on folk.' My cue, of course, to put my arm around her and comfort her. 'You will never be a burden to me, Mother.' That is how I feel but instead of saying so I sit silent and terrified, frozen within my own inarticulateness. The moment passes and my heart shrivels a little.

Crofting, it always seemed to me, was like being deposited by some malignant fate on the middle steps of a down-going escalator, one that was travelling rather fast. Naturally, your instructions were to proceed upwards. You had no chance of reaching the top but if you were young and fit and circumstances not too set against you, you might hope to stay where you were. Father is losing his place now. His old legs pump away still but inexorably he is being forced down. Years of patching, of making do —house and outbuildings, fences and land—have served only to postpone that major reorganization and restoration, the need for which is now massively upon him. It will never be undertaken. It never could have been.

The main characters in the story, the Macleans, are still all present, unshadowed as yet by the devastation soon to be visited on their ranks. Animals have come and gone and their bones lime the bitter earth around our house for yards in all directions, a record of friendship and service. In the village, too, there have been changes, as the coevals of my parents die off and are not replaced. 1970 sees the year-round native-born population of Sanna reduced to four, from a high of approximately a hundred at the turn of the century. (By the end of 1973, the year of my parents' death, it would be down to two, though it has risen slightly since, due to the decision of two elderly couples to spend their retirement in the place of their birth.) The empty houses tumble into ruin or are sold.

Changes in nature are less easy to quantify. Sanna Estate acquired a new owner during this period and campers and caravanners, sensibly if harshly, were banned. Day trippers, unfortunately, have multiplied and the record of their burgeoning is writ into the landscape. Our *machair*, that sandy sea-turf that is so attractive and so delicate a feature of many West Highland coastal villages, became deeply rutted by cars during this ten years, to a depth of two or three feet in places and over most of its long length. Once the thin skin of grass is broken on such a greensward the wind picks away relentlessly at the wound, keeping it open and slowly enlarging it. *Machair*, alas, is ideal for parking on, ideal for saving oneself half the fag of the hundred-yard trek to the beach. So a few careless summers suffice to destroy the patient work of nature over centuries. And once *machair* is gone it is gone for good; like a coral reef you cannot mend it or replace it.

That is bad enough but there was worse. We possessed once in Sanna a landscape feature that we called 'the *Druim*' (that is to say, 'the Ridge' or 'Raised Place'). This was a section of elevated *machair*, seaward of the stretch that now remains. It was a plateau about fifty feet high and a hundred yards or more wide, running virtually from one end of Sanna's long coastal sweep to the other, between village and foreshore. Obviously the remnant of a Raised Beach, a souvenir of the Ice Age, it was a delightful place, a vast and airy island of grass and wild flowers. Sanna's *Druim* was a famous landmark, certainly unique in this area and I dare say unique in a wider context than that. Its destruction has been one of the great topographical crimes of the Highlands.

For destroyed it has been. I have watched the children of

tourists play on it for hours, breaking huge clod after huge clod from the edge and riding them with whoops of laughter down the sandy slope to the bottom. By 1970 that great expanse had shrunk to a poor half-acre. (During the decade to follow it was to vanish altogether, to be replaced by dunes and the all-conquering mar-ram.)

Yet ecology does not offer simple solutions, least of all in crofting villages. Tourism is not the sole agent of destruction at work here; it may not even be the main one. We ourselves, we natives, are greatly to blame. Already in my childhood the *Druim* had split into several parts, with sandy gullies in between them where rain and wind gouged and chiselled; this while Ardnamur-chan was still the great unknown region of the Highlands and tourists creatures to be gawked at, beings from another planet. The crofters' own cattle, that here and there could get up on to the plateau—and were encouraged to do so—helped to destroy it. So, even more, did the later sheep, those vicious nibblers. Ourselves as children, were we not every bit as destructive as the children of visitors? Who bothered to tell us that we were demolishing something precious and irreplaceable? Who knew?

And could the *Druim* have been saved anyway? I doubt it very much. Preserved for a year or two longer, no doubt, but that is all. You cannot put a glass case around landscape. Though on a human scale—that mere millimetre of ours, that infinitesimal fraction—landscape may appear permanent, it is not. *Druims* come and *Druims* go and nature herself is the greatest mistress of destruction there is (though man begins to run her close and may be about to overtake her). As long as it is nature herself that is the agent of change we may rest easy in our beds, telling our dreams next morning over the breakfast table instead of shouting them from the darkened pillow. Nature will fill nature's vacuum and with something equally lovely and equally practical.

This decade, too, saw the virtual disappearance of the Sanna and Plocaig woods, those tracts of hazel and birch and aspen, alder and blackthorn and scrub oak, sallow and rowan and holly. Food and fuel and timber were there and much pleasure besides. Now no seedling dare poke its nose above the ground and the parent bushes and trees, rampaged through by sheep and cattle, are scraped and battered and ring-barked, broken and eaten. They die off year by year.

Of course there were cattle here before, if not sheep, but they were herded during the day and kept in at night. That was the old system of management. Now they roam loose more or less from birth and you may say that all the acres and all the months are theirs to do as they please in. True, the manpower to herd them is lacking; what may be more important is that the will-power is lacking as well.

When I was a little lad and there were still times to be had and getaways to be made there was a 'wood'—actually a kind of half-hanging thicket—of hazel and oak, in extent perhaps seventy or eighty yards by forty or fifty, on the far slopes of Port Plocaig, which is a small creek just beyond the abandoned hamlet of Plocaig. You could scarcely force your way into that thicket, so impenetrable was it, but if you managed to do so you might attain a rocky, mossy islet in the centre, rising above the bushes, a pinnacle on which a boy could be kingly for the whole of a summer's day. How beautiful that little wood was, how dearly I loved it! In my long life as a child I found nowhere else that so generously and fruitfully mingled dreams and plausibilities.

I emerged once from that thicket, after an afternoon's secrecy, emerged onto the flat bottom of the port to find myself forestalled. Tinkers' tents had sprung up mushroom-wise during my absence, tarred sacking bent over withies, black and bedouin. Each tent entrance was guarded by a three-legged pot swinging from a tripod stood over a glowing heap of twigs and crumbs, each heap surmounted by a pyramid of larger peats, so three and three and three in the old way. I was frightened, slipped back into the wood unobserved and went home by another route.

I had no need to fear. These were Highland tinkers of an impeccable and ancient lineage, a harmless, gentle people, true children of the great Egyptian diaspora though they spoke Gaelic and had names like Macdonald.

My thicket was but the seamost extension of a straggle of linked thickets that led inland for half a mile or so on either side of the creek bottom. And these thickets in turn were only a group among groups. It is a shell-shocked landscape now, something out of the Salient after Ypres. The old tinkers have disappeared back into the fairy tales; the new tinkers come in vans, speak Glaswegian and never leave the roadside. Even the very brambles, that once rioted, are hard put to it to survive. You would make a day's hard work of a canful now where once, for serious gathering, buckets were in order.

And so? Well, you cannot force the travelling folk to revert to donkeys. Neither need you foul your own nest for a thin shilling.

In this ten years I saw my last molehill and my last roe deer. I heard my last corncrake. I bade farewell to woodcock, partridge, pheasant and sand martin. There were eagles as close as Plocaig once; not any more. I came across my last peregrine during this period; it was dead.

Sanna is a bare place now, stripped of much of its cover and many of its inhabitants and deprived of many delightful creatures.

★

In reproducing the 1970 entries I deviate slightly from my source, though not, I think, importantly. I omit the somewhat tedious series of figures that by now were introducing each entry, thus: *Glass at 8 a.m. 29.76.* At some point in the decade we have just passed over I bought Father a barometer, an instrument he had long coveted. From then on the morning and evening reading of the glass became part of his life, creating a displacement in the rituals of the day and seismic even in such distant centres as byre and pasture. I should not, beforehand, have wagered tuppence on the likelihood of anything like this ever happening but happen it did. Truly, there is no text so sacred that it may not find itself made over in the service of a new god. How hard was the diorite of Egypt yet Akhnaton's chisels shattered it!

★

January 1st
As I was up long before the other members of the household I carried out the old ritual of going out by the back door, and bringing in a lump of coal by the front door. After that I did my usual daily stint of lighting the fire and making their morning tea for the sleepers! Some showers before daylight. Forenoon damp with intermittent smirr and hill fog. Wind Westerly, light to moderate, at first but veered to Northwesterly in the evening. Showers from mid-day onwards. Afternoon and evening raw and cold. No sunshine. Apart from Eliz's illness, the year just ended was a good one for us in every way. No post tonight.

The old ritual referred to by Father is of course the Scottish New Year custom of the 'first-foot'. According to this custom the luck of one's household is determined irrevocably for the whole of the coming year by the physical type of one's first visitor in that year or, in the synecdoche of the common phrase, by one's first-foot. Women, children and fair-haired men are considered unlucky; the ideal first-foot is a dark, mature male. It is better, too, that he does not come empty-handed and if he carries a piece of coal that is felt to be especially productive of good fortune. There are a number of regional variants to all this but the general principles remain the same.

The propitiation of the powers of darkness by sympathetically-linked dark objects is an interesting pointer to the threat the ritual must have embodied when it was strong and pure, before its own circumvention became a built-in part of it. With what trepidation then would a family have awaited that first visitor! How long might people in remote cottages have had to hang by their fingertips! Weeks might go by before the year's god turned in at the gate. How they would learn to bless or curse that fateful moment, constrained by the rules of the game to be polite to the chance arrival, even when she was a fair-haired woman, like people forced to welcome their own executioner. And how, one wonders, did they fare in the limbo interval before that late arrival, when they were yet stateless persons unrecognized by fate?

Of course the visitor was invited in regardless of sex or pigmentation. That was the whole point of the custom. It was a transaction with the unknown, a gamble in which one was throwing for one's yearly luck and in which one's stake had therefore to be commensurate with the possible prize; in effect one was putting one's life and the lives of one's family on the table.

People in those days did not—dared not—trifle with fate, as we do who are merely superstitious. They were true believers. If, that custom then prevailing, a ladder had been placed in their path, they would have walked trembling beneath it. That is the logic of a belief in the power of ladders. They entrusted themselves wholly to fate. As a result, their lives were given over alternately to terror and joy, shot through with staggering blows and miraculous good fortune, but at least not spiritually crippled by the boringly automatic certainties of today's religions.

We who come after have taken control of our own destinies. We demand that our reward be written into the contract and the resulting ennui is killing us. First-footing, to the extent that it still exists in Scotland, has become a mere excuse, a synonym indeed, for a round of convivial visiting. Or, as with my father, the old menace is appeased so farcically as to render the custom meaningless.

January 15th
Wind Easterly, mainly moderate. Overcast all day. Showers during the early hours. Hill fog in the morning. Byres, feeds and a few odd jobs. Certifying Officer passed and marked our three calves. Showers and drizzle after dark.

'Byres' is shorthand for doing the byres, that is to say, mucking out. 'Feeds' refers to making up the bundles of hay, pails of oilcake and such, that constituted the extra winter rations of the cattle.

January 31
South to Southeasterly gale all day. Overcast, smoky, and frightfully cold. Byres, first thing. Took the banger to the peats after breakfast and brought home a bagful of old sgros—the turf that comes off prior to cutting the peats. These burn well in our grate, so with a few logs and some pieces of coal, we can have an excellent fire to sit at, at night. Feeds after eleven o'clock tea. A number of the usual small jobs in the afternoon. Rain came on around 8 p.m.

Father does not mean that he took the 'banger' right up to the peat moss (that would not have been possible, given the nature of the terrain) but only to the nearest part of the public road. He would still have to carry his bagful of turf to the car and that might be far enough, depending on which peat moss he was using.

Father dearly loved an open fire and a good one at that—a big roaring fire, as we used to call such heapings up—to sit by of an evening (and so do I love a big roaring fire). Especially when visitors were present he took a childish delight in piling the blaze as high as possible. If he could compel them to move their chairs back from the heat that was his evening made. More than once I have seen some half-stripped tourist sweating out his visit in the remotest corner of our living room, with Father smiling quietly to himself. Partly this was pure goodness, partly an unconfident wish to enjoy, through over-emphasis, a reputation for hospitality. And partly too, of course, it was Father's mischievous (and typically Highland) sense of humour.

'A few logs' sounds Dickensian in its extravagance. Father never quite achieved fires of such yuletide proportions. (He never had the means—or the fireplaces.) 'Logs' was merely our word for sawn-up six-inch chunks of driftwood.

February 1st
Sunday. Wind Southerly to Southeasterly strong. Overcast all day.
Raining in the morning and into the forenoon. Dry thereafter until
shortly before 6 p.m. when quite heavy rain came on again. Usual
necessary chores and a walk with Twiggy to the Traigh Bheag. Wind
to gale force at bedtime.

Twiggy was one of our dogs, so named—after the celebrated fashion model—because she was preternaturally thin. She came to us at four or five months old, having been acquired from a shepherd then in the area. We learned later that she had been kept locked in a dark shed for all of her young life and perhaps ill-treated in other ways, too. She lived to a reasonable age but never did put on weight despite being subjected, as all our pets were, to a constant stuffing with titbits. Neither did she quite recover from the psychological battering she had received. Sheepdogs tend to be highly strung and unpredictable at the best of times; Twiggy possessed these characteristics to an unusual degree. The collie's sly habit of circling round behind someone and darting in for a quick nip was a favourite trick of hers. With the family she was all right; with strangers one rather held one's breath.

February 15th
Wind Northerly, light at first but freshened in the afternoon. Severe
frost. Some sunny intervals in the afternoon. A period of heavy snow in
the evening. Byres and feeds. Went to the Rhu after breakfast to look
for Miranda but failed to find her, despite considerable searching.

Miranda was a pet ewe who had reverted to the hills—a recidivist, Father called her. She was one of only two to return to the wild among the scores we nursed. She remained tame enough, however, to come to the hand to be fed dainties, provided it was Father's hand or mine. She was generally catered for in respect of these extras once a week and since by 1970 she had become very old there was always a panic when the would-be feeder failed to locate her. Evidently on this occasion she had simply been keeping her head below weather level in some corner, as well she might with such incentive blowing about her ears; she turned up as usual the following week. She was to die of the maggot in the summer of 1971, after suffering wounds inflicted by a tripper's dog.

February 28th
Wind Southeasterly, light at first but veered to Westerly in the evening.
Hard frost in the morning. Some sunny spells but, also, a lot of cloud.
Mucked the byre and the annexe before breakfast. After breakfast
Twiggy and I made for the Glac Chriche, where I had put out some
pieces of timber some little time back. I carried as much of it home as I
could totter under. Not good for the old physique! Feeds etc. kept me
going till lunchtime, after which I had an hour's sleep, having been up
early to look at some cows which are due to calve. Cindy did calve but
at 3.30 p.m. behind the lower part of the Cnoc Breac. Jessie was on the
spot to do her stuff. Some two hours later we went for them and I put
the calf in a bag and carried it to the stirkhouse. I haven't yet confirmed
it, but I'm told it's female, to be named Fiona. Letter from Ian, posted
Barbados.

My sister, Jessie, commonly acted as midwife to our cows.

The 'timber' put out by Father—'put up' was the more usual local term—was driftwood. Apparently he had found this wood on an earlier walk, had carried it above the high water mark to indicate ownership and to prevent its drifting back out—put it up, in other words—and was now taking it home.

The use made by crofters of the gifts of the sea merits a book in itself: seaweed for fertilizer and if need be for food; seabirds for their flesh and their eggs; driftwood for fuel and for building with; sand for fertilizer, for cement mixing and infilling and to provide a layer of insulation under bedding in byres; and of course fish. There is always the chance, too, of finding something really interesting or valuable. (For instance, there is the semi-mythical ambergris, reputedly worth a king's ransom a lump, which all beachcombers hope for but none ever seems to find. Indeed, one wonders how many would recognize it if they did find it; I doubt if I should!) And there is the beauty, mystery and terror of the great ocean to love and to make a lifetime's study of.

The coast of Ardnamurchan is so finely toothed that it might be a topographical permutation designed to increase one's chances of obtaining these gifts; a hundred miles or so of border, were it straight, becomes a jagged thousand. One of the tinier of these inlets, near Sanna, is still called 'the butter creek' because long ago someone found a case of butter there, just drifting ashore. (Still perfectly usable, of course; the sea would keep the butter cool and fresh without penetrating it, though no doubt the outside of the block would have been pretty salty.) And a famous local anecdote concerns the discovery, on Sanna beach during World War One, of a ship's wooden deckhouse, undamaged in any way, complete with interior furnishings and with the key still in the lock.

Finds like that—and there were a number of them down through the years—were major events in the history of the parish. One would require to have lived through the poverty of Ardnamurchan as it was in former days to appreciate quite what they meant.

When I was a boy in Sanna beachcombing protocol was strict and competition fierce. ('Beachcombing', incidentally, was not then nor is it now a word in local use; we call it 'going round the shore'.) Two or three days of northwest wind to bring the wood in and you would have to rise at peep of day if you wanted to be first on the scene. Often I did just that or even scoured my territory by night if the moon were at the full. I was a fanatic for the beach. I became so good that I aroused jealous resentment in one or two of my most hard-pressed rivals. 'Lucky' they called me, a description that I resented in my turn. Luck was involved, maybe, in a sense, but as in so many other walks of life one made the luck for oneself. If I found a lot on the shore it was because I was there to find it and because I was thorough when I was there. I scrambled in and out of steep-sided creeks and gullies that no one else bothered with or even knew about.

I still adore beachcombing and still it gives me joy to discover —for example—a really fine piece of timber. There is sadness, of course, in carrying one's finds home to an empty house, sadness in realizing that no one now will emerge beaming from the kitchen to admire one's latest acquisition and praise one for making it. Indeed the wood I drag home these days quite often never gets used but lies rotting in a corner of the garden. At best, when I am too poor to buy coal and too busy to cut peats, it gets sawn up for firewood—even sometimes, wantonly, that part of it that deserves a better fate. In securing it I merely observe a ritual. But then that is not so very much of a 'merely'. What better way of honouring the dead? For that matter, what better way of ensuring the future?

As for the rules of the game, in Ardnamurchan of old if you took your beachcombing finds well clear of the highwater mark, so eliminating any possible ambiguity about their status, they were yours till you chose to fetch them or, if you did not choose, till they mouldered where they lay. Generations might pass and no one would touch them. I have seen some handsome pieces of timber disappear into the ground almost, through decay, after having been put up by someone who had died before managing to retrieve them or had gone off to Glasgow and not returned.

This attitude was typical of general standards of honesty, both here and I believe throughout the Highlands. Certainly, in pre-World War Two days in Sanna, you could go away for a year and leave your front door not merely unlocked but wide open. Your house might be invaded by the creatures of the field or the gales rummage among your possessions but no human foot would cross your threshold.

How changed are things now! You scarcely dare leave your shadow unattended for a moment, lest it be ripped from your side, and the locals are as bad as any.

It is sad that progress—for to what we are pleased to call progress one must attribute the decline—should so corrupt those it touches, yet it seems always to do so and the further it is taken the more widespread and deeply rooted the dishonesty it produces. Indeed, what one might call behavioural disaffiliation, of all kinds, keeps level pace with every improvement in technology. Virtually one could lay it down as a law that the more advanced the culture the less civilized the people. It is as if some unregenerate corner of our being were refusing to travel our elected road and were registering its protest in this self-destructive, self-defeating fashion, as a disturbed child might draw attention to its wounded psyche by fouling its surroundings or as a beautiful woman, from the depths of some perverse despair, might go out to sell herself as cheaply as possible and to all comers.

I speak of personal standards, of one's dealings with one's neighbour. Not to enter a man's house and steal his belongings

—that is clear-cut. But goodness is not always so easy of access. Crofters of earlier days had their grey areas, no doubt, and I do not exhibit them as moral supermen necessarily. There are circumstances in which one may be hard put to it to distinguish right from wrong, circumstances in which the question is so deeply hidden it appears not to be posed. It may be that beach-combing illustrates this very well.

In theory, presumably, all flotsam and jetsam is the property of the Receiver of Wrecks, working through his agents the police and the coastguard. In practice it is not so simple. If you found, for example, a washed-in dinghy you would expect to report it. A tragedy might be involved; in any event the boat would be valuable and its owner would wish it returned. Mere firewood, on the other hand, the authorities would not thank you for wasting their time with. It is what lies in between these extremes that can cause problems. Not every beachcomber would rush to notify his discovery of, let us say, a fifty-gallon drum of valuable and useful motor lubricating oil—something I have twice found and, I had better add, reported. In these hard times the temptation for a car owner—which I was not—might prove irresistible.

Coming upon something of value on the beach is not at all like finding money in the street, or one can readily persuade oneself that it isn't. The moral link binding finder to loser is less obvious and more tenuous. Furthermore, the loser is likely to be a corporation of some kind rather than an individual and so less attractive as an object of sympathy, tending as we do to adjust our honesty to suit our estimate of the loser's need. That long-ago crofter, whose patrol of the Sanna tideline ended in his discovery of the famous deckhouse, must have felt himself favoured by Providence. Should he then have rejected the gift? ('Thank you, God, but no thanks. It is plainly my Christian duty to report this find. Some poor shipping company may even now be searching for its property.' And God goes off muttering to himself, 'Right, mate! Not a bloody matchstick do you get from me from now on.')

Morality is never easy to learn and it is the strictly puritanical, not the human compromisers, who are better placed to con it. Should I or shouldn't I? There have been books written on the subject. Nay, whole libraries have been built around it. Meanwhile, on the shores of Ardnamurchan as on the Aegean, the tide rises and falls and the amoral sea delivers itself of its burden.

In Kilmory Churchyard two headstones help number the dead of the Second World War, number but not name for they record the burial of unknown merchant seamen who purchased on that quiet shore a haven from the long Atlantic swells. What crofter beachcombed them out of the water and into the earth, translating them from the bosom of one element to another, I cannot say. Many a man from hereabouts foundered during that great conflict, however, and I have sometimes fancied that these might have been local bodies, drifting their blind way home. Better an unmarked grave in Ardnamurchan than a mausoleum in Eden. Or so people have thought, but I have not thought so.

There are seamen's bodies in Sanna, too, from an earlier war. They lie somewhere beyond the final cove in our string of coves, as one walks along the beach in the direction of Portuairk. No headstones were given them; one imagines there were none to spare. The place where they wait upon us was familiar enough once, I dare say, but the memory of it has been lost. It has disappeared into vagueness, growing from a narrow plot to a wide acre, which is the way of even the best-behaved graveyards.

Of all fates the fate of going into the earth unrecorded is the one to be dreaded most. That is what I think and that was what a poet before me thought.

> Take from me love or the word;
> Let me quickly or slowly die,
> Tremble to pass or be brave;
> Let the hills split for me,
> The lakes go dry,
> So be you mark my grave.

In Sanna once, long ago, there was an old beachcomber who was noted for the amount of ground he covered and the gleaning he subjected it to. 'Waste not, want not' was his motto. A young man played a trick on him, lying down in his path along the tideline, covered over with wrack but with legs projecting. It happened that the young man was wearing a new pair of leather sea-boots. Along came the old beachcomber. 'Ah, poor fellow!' he said when he saw the 'corpse'. 'Still, a good pair of boots.' But when he bent to remove his prize the body came to life. He ran off in great fear, calling on his Maker to save him.

March 1st
Sunday. Neither a lion nor a lamb, just a heavy miserable sleety
drizzle which came on about 8 a.m. Cindy and the calf seem to be doing
well. The calf is black, with a little white. We are not milking Cindy,
just letting the calf help itself. A few blinks of sunshine in the afternoon
and, also heavy sleety showers. Wind Northwest fresh.

March 15th
Sunday. Wind Westerly light to calm. Some hill fog and mist in the
morning. No sunshine but a fine seasonable day otherwise. Byres and
feeds and a walk to the Gorten to feed Miranda. Snowflake calved at
approx. 5 p.m. on the low end of the ridge beyond the Hall. A grey calf
(Debbie). It was a difficult birth, only the head and one foot coming,
although the period of actual labour only lasted about an hour. Jessie
went to the telephone to see if Marian Macdonald, who is a qualified
Vet, was at home, but she wasn't available. During Jessie's absence I
managed, with a piece of coir rope on the foot, to pull the calf out. I
went over again at 7 p.m. and gave Snowflake some cobs and hay. By
that time the calf was up on its feet, so I introduced it to where the
nourishment was! When I left it was helping itself.

Coir (locally pronounced ky-ar) must soon, I suppose, take its
place in that museum of materials discarded by the twentieth
century, discarded, I sometimes think, with more haste than
wisdom. It is a fibre manufactured from coconut husks and
makes up into a cheap rope, reddish, rough and springy, much in
use formerly but now rare. Coir lacked the strength of the dearer
hemp but, in spite of its rough texture, was much kindlier than
hemp and so was especially suitable for use with livestock. Father
treasured his few remaining lengths of coir. Nylon has it all away
now and only such traditionalists as crofters and hangmen cling
to natural fibres.

Young primipara cows sometimes have difficulty in delivering
their calves. Generally no vet was available to the Ardnamurchan
crofters and one simply had to do the best one could. Hillside
births could be wild and bloody affairs. I have known it take three
men, pulling hard on a rope, to drag the calf clear of the birth
canal. That sounds brutal and certainly can't have been any fun
for cow or calf. One imagines that there are better ways of doing
it. Yet I do not recall either mother or offspring failing to survive.

March 31st
Wind North to Northeast strong to gale. A frightfully bitter day. Some
sunshine in the forenoon did nothing to temper the biting wind.
Showers of snow in the afternoon and evening. Also some hail.
Conditions grim at night and snowing at bedtime. Only the necessary
chores and a short while at the job upstairs, where I put up another
piece of hardboard.

April 1st
Wind Northerly fresh to strong at first but moderated in the evening.
Morning bitterly cold, and all hills and low ground covered with snow
which, however, melted away later in the day. Quite a lot of sunshine,
but some hail in the evening. As the morning was so grim, we kept the
cattle in till 11 a.m., giving them an extra feed. Did the usual chores
and very little else. No post tonight.

'No post tonight', a dirge in miniature, tolls a sad end to a
goodish number of Father's journal entries. Our mail came to us
in the evening, when it came at all, and generally well on in the
evening at that; nine or ten o'clock was common enough and later
still not unknown. One did not usually complain. When you live
in a community as remote as ours things tend to reach you, or
happen to you, at the end of a long chain. When a flaw develops in
that chain you will not always find it easy—or at any rate you
may not find it politic—to pinpoint the source of the trouble. The
existence of such a chain, of course, is ideal for buck-passing and
for the dispersal of suspicion. In any event, it is difficult to raise a
shout of protest when you are firmly strapped over a barrel; your
voice tends to get muffled.

    In the more isolated parts of the Highlands you pay for your
beauty and tranquillity in various ways. One way is that you
place yourself under the capriciously broad thumbs of whatever
local Napoleons happen to be in the offing. (One meets that kind
everywhere, granted, but in the city it is easier to circumvent
them.) To complain about your treatment is to be reminded,
often with brutal immediacy, that you can be got at from several
directions. If you jib at the unfairness or incompetence of Mr
Smith in his Number One capacity you may well learn that you
are entirely dependent on him for favours received when he has
his Number Two hat on (or when his son or his grandmother's

third cousin is wearing it for him). And if you seek a replacement for Mr Smith you will probably find that there is none.

If you have money and influence, on the other hand, you need not worry. You will not be troubled. Mr Smith and his friends, you may depend on it, know to a hair's breadth your standing in the world and the amount of leverage you can bring to bear. When Lord Muck comes north for the shooting they detail a small boy with a supply of cellophane bags to follow him around, collecting his farts for later distribution and inhalation. My parents, however, being mere crofters and pensioners, could safely be screwed and frequently were.

When I was younger and it still seemed to be a possibility, I used to long passionately for riches. I wanted them not for the marble stairs and tinkling fountains I could buy my parents but for the independence I could buy them. And their independence would have been my independence, their invulnerability my invulnerability. One can endure personal poverty if need be; it is the poverty of those one loves that puts the balls in a vise. Squeeze! Squeeze! And as the pressure mounts you find your manly tones moving up the scale. *Yes, sir, yes, sir! Immediately, sir! At once, sir! With dispatch, sir! Good sir! Kind sir!*

Money gets you out of livery. It buys you freedom from the cast-down eyes, from the small voice and the pleated hands. Death is your only other patron worthy of the name. The death of your loved ones is as good as a legacy to you. The last time I bowed my head was at my father's grave.

As for the arrival of the postman, when at last he did arrive, it was often the day's big event in Sanna, often indeed the day's only event. During each visit home I was made to realize afresh the importance of mail in a remote village. At times it seemed one's only real guarantee that the outside world still existed. I can even yet hear the disappointment in my mother's voice each time my sister returned empty-handed from the roadside after meeting the mail van. 'Aw, no letters?' Or 'Just the papers?' (Dearly as she loved the papers.) And I would sit there castigating myself. 'More letters! More parcels! You see how much it means to them!' Then I would return to town and the days would slip by and the weeks, and if I lifted my pen at all it would be to write another poem, another item in my interminable and one-sided correspondence with my own past.

Of course, communications other than those maintained by

the postal service were available even in Sanna. We were not altogether stone-age primitives. My parents had a radio. But what of that? It was no more a proof of continuity than the eerie radiance reaching us each night from the prehistoric stars. Somewhere, presumably, there was an announcer but he might have been sitting among rubble for aught we knew to the contrary (if indeed he were flesh and blood at all and not simply a tape-recorded message). One was told of the genocide of yet another Amazonian tribe and one turned in believing disbelief to the day's tasks. With letters from friends, however, the globe grew small and personal once more, true because compassable. Word was received of mishap, of the loss of a job or the illness of a child and one's over-watered conscience, mulched to excess and dying of a surplus, put out a green leaf or two.

April 15th
Wind Southeasterly moderate in the morning but Southerly later and became fresh to strong. Drizzle and hill fog in the afternoon. Spouts of heavier rain in the evening. Cherry and Hector out all day. Usual daily tasks and wheeled a pit prop home for firewood from the shore below the banks at Sanna Bheag. Papers from Alasdair. Colin reported seeing a lamb with Miranda.

April 30th
Wind Southeasterly mainly moderate. Overcast with some smirr and extensive hill fog in the afternoon, but not unduly cold. Wheeling manure. Only Beulah in at night. Beulah for the bull.

May 1st
Wind Southerly to Southeasterly moderate at first but strong in afternoon and evening. Morning and forenoon overcast and very dull. A light drizzle in the forenoon developed into continuous heavy rain in mid-afternoon. That, coupled with the strong wind, made conditions pretty blustery. I spent the time from breakfast to dinner wheeling manure from the stirkhouse midden to Dalmore croft. Rain compelled me to give up then. There are still two or three barrow loads left. Rain continuing into the night with extensive hill fog. All cattle in at night.

May 15th
Wind light and variable. Morning overcast. Heavy thundery rain came on in the late afternoon. The rain was followed by intermittent drizzle

and extensive hill fog. These conditions lasted into the night. All day putting down concrete in the construction (otherwise the new byre) and dog tired when I stopped at 5 p.m. Beulah in.

Why Beulah should have been so favoured as to spend night after night in the comfort of the byre while her companions had to fend for themselves on the hillside I don't know. Certainly the weather seems to have been more like January than May but if that were the reason one imagines that all the cows would have been kept in, as they were on the stormy May 1st.

Perhaps she was ill. Or perhaps the truth is revealed in the entry for April 30th where we come upon the phrase—a splendid pun—'Beulah for the bull'. If she were ready to mate she might have seized the opportunity afforded by darkness, with its lack of human supervision, to wander off in search of easement.

That sounds feeble, however. It would have taken more in the way of supervision than was supplied by my father and my sister's purely nominal shushing and clucking to stop a really determined cow. A cow with the sexual urge strong upon her has the equivalent of an electric prodder up her arse. With no bull at hand she will go careering across the country, bellowing for release at the top of her voice. Miles she may go. Day will be as night to her. High dykes and deep ditches will hardly keep her back, far less herdsmen. I have seen a cow brimful of libido make a dozen nimble men look like standing stones.

Of course, all this can be inconvenient for the stockman, who for various reasons may not choose to have his animal mate at that particular time. Still more, one supposes, may it be inconvenient for the animal. A Sanna cow once, running the gauntlet between her instincts and her stubborn owner, who did not care to see her mate just then, charged in at the front door of a certain house and out at the back, scattering women and children like confetti. It was only due to a merciful providence that both doors were open at the time, else she had taken the house with her. She came back to her home village two days later, with God knows what strange semen fermenting away inside her, yet so demure you half expected her to curtsy as you passed.

There is no modesty in the farmyard. It is all heave and grunt, all bang and stab. The odour of sex is flaunted like a badge. 'Kiss me, sailor' traces its ancestry back through the ages and comes out at the other end as 'Mount me, bull'.

May 31st
Wind Southerly moderate in the morning, with driving rain and fog.
The wind became strong in the late forenoon and veered to Southwest.
Service in Hall at noon by Mr Campbell, Free Church. Jessie
attended. My stomach complaint, and the weather, combined to keep me
at home. The rain ceased in the late afternoon and, in the evening, the
sun shone for a time. Stomach not unduly troublesome today. Walk
with Twiggy to beyond Port na tuinne after teatime.

Later in this entry Father seems to have forgotten that he had
earlier used his stomach complaint as an excuse for not going to
church, for he speaks of it as 'not unduly troublesome'. Or
perhaps it reached a critical point at the time of the Free Church
service and afterwards subsided. There are possibilities in a
stomach as sympathetic as that. Given proper training it could
take its owner places—or not, as the case might be.

June 1st
Wind Southerly to Westerly light to moderate. Heavy rain around 6
a.m. Dry during the day with quite a lot of sunshine. Evening cloudy.
This was an eventful day. As we were completely out of coal Jessie and
I decided to motor to the Ferry Stores for some, after breakfast. We went
to the P.O. for Old Age pensions as well. On the way back, on the
brae above the falls, we noticed steam coming from the bonnet of the
banger. The bottom radiator hose had burst so we had no option but to
abandon the car and walk home over the hill. It was quite warm and, as
we were carrying our stores and two stones of coal, we were pretty tired.
We sat at the top of Bealach Faotidh and ate some biscuits, where Liz
and I had done the same thing half a century ago. Truly, history
repeating itself.

Bealach Faotidh is a pass through the range of hills that separates
the hamlets of Achnaha and Sanna. It makes a fine short-cut
between the two places but only for such natives as have glossy
black wings and a harsh voice.
　Father had no wings. The pinions were never feathered that
could have borne off to kinder climates and easier fates both him
and the heavy weight of his conscience. He was harsh-voiced
only in the mornings, when he left the house with his first
cigarette of the day centrally placed between his lips, sticking

straight out and glowing sporadically, like a little engine pulling him along.

It is true that, on the map, Bealach Faotidh might have seemed a reasonable alternative to a stranger forced into walking at the point where Father was forced into it. The trouble with maps, however, is that they cozen as they charm. Our maps have improved in a kind of spurious precision as they have deteriorated in the amount of worthwhile information they convey. A mist of fine mathematical detail has blotted out the high tops and is creeping down into the valleys. You get the location of your chosen inn with such a wealth of reference you could go straight to the third urinal on the left in the Gents. But never a word about how the beer tastes or the barmaid.

Here be dragons. That was useful knowledge whether you hoped to avoid these creatures or simply wanted to release your home-bred specimens to the wild. No such bulletins come our way in this dragon-ridden age.

As for hills it is small help to look up one on your map and note that its slopes are thickly strewn with contour lines. Obviously it is steep but hills tend to be like that anyway, especially when you reach middle-age. What you really need to know is how many paces your lungs are going to fall behind your legs when you climb it. If the Ordnance Survey were worth the paper it prints on it would be producing a special series of maps for the over-forties, the over-fifties etc. (When you reach a hundred you end up merely with an enlarged plan of your house, with the location of the lavatory clearly marked and a small arrow pointing towards the crematorium.)

In the recording of topography, as in most other things, we need more literature and less science. That is the only way to achieve true accuracy.

It is an old story. Always, as the technology of mapmaking flourishes in any civilization, the engravers leave the walkers and move into superior accommodation.

Having abandoned his car Father could have walked home by the public road. It would have been no longer, I dare say, in terms of actual mileage and much easier in other ways. Over real ground, indeed, he lost by his short cut. He condemned himself to a two-mile slog across rough moorland, tussock-littered and bog-beset, where hillocks rear themselves in the path of the unwary and streams lie coiled in wait. All that plus a steep climb to the *bealach*—the pass—and a goodish hike on the other side of the ridge.

He knew that in advance, of course. Who better? His true reason for leaving the road, I am sure, was to avoid walking through Achnaha on his return journey, with the looks and questions inevitably attendant on his having but lately passed that way in a car.

In his place I might well have done the same. Fifty years previously, had either of us been passengers in a horse-drawn cart that had suffered mishap, it would not have occurred to us to feel embarrassed about our predicament or to anticipate curiosity or teasing. Self-consciousness still lay at the far end of the motorway and that was not even a gleam in a bureaucrat's eye.

Walking as an honourable—a preferable—means of furthering one's distant business is not yet an unknown activity on the roads of Ardnamurchan. Not quite. But we approach that stage. Going about my affairs on the stretch of highway between Sanna and Kilchoan, on foot, I have not met another native similarly engaged and similarly lacking mechanical encumbrance for well over a decade. I have had ghosts for company and most of them barefoot at that.

Not long before I returned to Sanna to edit my father's journal I found myself being roughly interrogated by two policemen in Kirkcaldy, where I live. My offence was to stroll quietly along a public pavement—at three o'clock in the morning, granted, but that was not what really mattered. The policemen, needless to say, were not on foot; they leaped from a car that screeched to a halt beside me, very literally beside me for it was driven up over the kerb so that its wing brushed my clothing. I could hardly have been suspected of very much. I was obviously sober, properly clad and carried nothing. Nor was it the time of day, as such, that counted against me. I was the fox among the chickens because I chose to be a pedestrian. I might have driven past the scene with a bootful of blood-drenched feathers and been waved on my way. Angry and frightened, I must needs scrabble frantically to prove my innocence who in happier times would have been given a civil 'Good night, sir'.

Kirkcaldy is not so far from Ardnamurchan, not as the auto-bahn unrolls, and the man behind the wheel is your only natural man. You may hate and fear the implications of that even more than I do, it is no matter; the body makes its own accommodations with the world however much the spirit may recoil in horror. Did I read or only dream that pregnant women in California now demonstrate an increase in foetal movement and heartbeat while listening to a recording of an accelerating engine? The tiny fists clench and unclench as they negotiate curves not yet blueprinted.

June 15th
Wind Northeast light. Sunny and warm until evening, when the wind got quite nippy. Working in the new byre all day. First of all I sawed an iron pipe into a suitable length for the drain outlet and placed it in position. Then I levelled off the drain with stones and gravel. After that I got it all cemented except for a bit at the near end. If it hadn't been for the various people who bothered me I would have had it all done. Nice card for my birthday from Alasdair, posted Kirkcaldy.

June 30th
Wind Southeast in the morning but veered to Westerly in the evening, fresh to strong. Overcast all day. Drizzle, which came on at about 10.30 a.m. gradually developed into heavy rain, with extensive hill fog. The rain went off in the early evening, which was raw and cold. Went for peats before breakfast. After breakfast I wheeled three loads of gravel up to the new byre, and that was all the work I managed to do. Heavy rain at bedtime.

July 1st
A violent day with gale force Southwesterly to Westerly wind and heavy showers. Glass falling quickly. Liz and Alasdair left home at 6.45 a.m. in Donald Cameron's car on the first stage of the long journey to Edinburgh. Owing to weather conditions it is possible that they may have had to travel onwards from Kilchoan by mail bus to Ardgour, as the Sound of Mull may have been too stormy for the launch to come. Outdoor work out of the question.

Having become a university student in 1966, at the age of forty, I had now, in 1970, completed my course. The journey that Mother and I took to Edinburgh was for my graduation.

Sometime that summer I had reluctantly telephoned the English Department at my university to learn the results of my Finals. I was informed that I had passed and had been awarded a Second

Class degree. I had very mixed feelings about this. On the one hand, I knew that I could have taken a good First had I exerted myself. Late in life I had been given the opportunity of doing something and I had fluffed it; the chance would not come my way again. And though I was not unduly hungry for academic honours, though indeed I had enrolled at university chiefly that I might live for four years at public expense while I got on with what I saw as my main task in life, the turning of myself into a writer, nevertheless it would have been rather pleasant to have overcome the challenge and taken a good degree. It would have been rather pleasant to have proved to myself and others that I could do it. I was not, I thought, a vain person, but little distinction had come my way. I had recently begun to get the occasional poem, the occasional piece, published but without, as yet, any indication of even the very modest fame to come. I could readily imagine myself letting the information emerge— casually, dismissively and, naturally, only after close questioning —that I had obtained a First. But on the surface at least, I maintained to myself and my friends the partial fiction that I did not care. The regret I felt at my Second surprised and a little chagrined me by its keenness.

On the other hand, thinking back on my university career, most of which I had spent either in the Common Room, drinking coffee and gossiping, or in my own room writing; and thinking, too, of my Finals, of my shame-making attempts to fudge answers to questions I had not at all prepared for, I realized that the award of a Second almost certainly represented generous treatment.

Overriding my disappointment, then, was a still keener feeling of relief. It was true that I had no great plans for using my degree, of whatever rank it were; true, in fact, that I intended never again to work—for an employer—if I could help it. But I should not have liked to have been ploughed. I doubted that my fortitude was yet strong enough for that (though several years of writing failure had brought me on wonderfully) and, besides, there was the effect on my parents to consider. Especially there was the effect on my mother.

Our family was clever but I had been the brainy one, the one whose emergence into adulthood, clad in a neat blue suit with a collar and tie and a solid professional career stretching ahead, Mother had most looked forward to. My belated decision to go to university after half a lifetime of drifting uncertainly from one dead-end labouring job to another seemed at last to bring her within reach of her goal: a son she could be properly proud of, a son she could gently boast of to the neighbours, a son, above all, who had taken a First Class Honours degree at Edinburgh University. Perhaps, even yet, it was not too late? 'See and work hard, son,' had been her unvarying admonition to me each time I left home to begin a new term. I might have been a schoolboy. In her eyes I dare say I was. And I think she allowed herself to hope.

So I telephoned for my results and I came back to the house from the kiosk. Mother was alone, rolling out scones at the kitchen table. 'I've managed to get a Second,' I said lightly. 'Whew! What a relief!'

She looked up from her work, not turning towards me but staring unseeingly out of the window. I think she looked into a boastless, dreamless future, a future that was for her now too savagely curtailed to permit of another such half a chance. Her lips trembled a little, then tightened. 'It's no' as good as a First, is it?' was all she said.

I turned on my heel without reply and went to my room. Of course I was hurt; more so, no doubt, because of the guilt I felt. I had looked for kindness. I had wanted, perhaps, to lay my head on that old bosom for the first time since childhood, to console and be consoled, to weep a little together, it might have been, at the unfairness, the intractability of life.

Mother's bluntness, her tactlessness that was really truthfulness, a refusal to fudge issues, often hurt me. I think that her decision to go to Edinburgh and see me capped, after an initial disinclination for the long hard trip, sprang from a realization of my feelings, from an unwillingness to wound me further. I should not otherwise have bothered to attend the ceremony. It meant nothing to me except insofar as it meant something to her.

The impossibility of communicating my true thoughts to my parents often saddened me as they aged. How could I tell my mother, a simple working woman, what it had really been like at university? How could I describe the pressures, the distractions, the emotional entanglements, how explain the discouraging uncoiling of the system, the polite inflexibility, the way one ended up by taking not the courses one wished to take, the courses one had long dreamed of taking, but the courses that one's superiors felt it meet for one to take? How could I, with almost no proof of vocation to offer, lay bare my secret soul and uncover my overwhelming wish and need to become a writer, a poet—as unsolid and unprofessional an occupation as could be imagined? I would look into Mother's old eyes and it was like looking into the eyes of our pet collie—love and a gap.

Whether she got anything out of her Edinburgh trip I don't know. I hope she did. For me it was a mistaken journey. I saw her then, translated to these new and sharper surroundings, as she really was, a small old figure at my side, leaning and creeping, scarcely lifting her head to regard the castled splendours of Princes Street that once she would have revelled in. I knew that she would soon be dead.

July 15th
Wind Northwest to North moderate. Mainly cloudy, but one or two brief intervals of hazy sunshine. Not feeling too good so didn't do very much in the way of work. Alasdair took up some sand and finished the remaining piece of the drain in the new byre. That is the floor now complete. We have, however, to do some building up in two of the stalls, which don't have enough outward slope to them. There is no particular hurry for this.

July 31st
Wind light and variable, from Northeast to Westerly. Fine and sunny until evening, when the sky became cloudy. When Jessie was going to collect the cattle at about 8 a.m. she found our big wether, Julius, dead in the drain at the entrance to Cameron's croft. He was still warm and, apparently, not long dead. This was a blow, coming so soon after his mother, Belinda, died. He was her last surviving descendant 6 years old. I took him home right away and buried him in front of our garden, where so many other fine animals have been put.

August 1st
Wind Southeasterly fresh. Overcast and dull all day. Went for peats before breakfast. Jessie went later. Owing to the ominous weather forecast, and the appearance of the sky, we went to the croft after breakfast and gathered the piece of older hay and put up a fifth rick. Rain appeared to be imminent, so we didn't do any spreading, or turning, with the newer stuff. We could have turned, and probably gathered part of it. Did various other odd jobs, including cleaning out the stirkhouse, where four pet lambs are housed at present. Last but not

least, with Jessie's assistance, I sheared Tilly and that was the hardest job of the week! Letter from Ian.

Sheep are never grateful for being sheared, though one would think that the relief to them, in high summer, would be considerable. Tilly, being a pet and unafraid of people, and being an obstreperous, bossy creature in any event, was always a handful when it came her turn to be lightened. Poor beast, this was, however, the last such struggle that she was to put up, as the entry for August 17th, my chosen free-day entry, indicates.

August 15th
Wind Southwesterly to Westerly mainly moderate. Continuous rain, torrential at times. As no outside work was possible Ian and his family crossed over to Mull with the 10.30 a.m. launch. They were delayed for about an hour on the return trip owing to it being Tobermory regatta and sports day. The weather spoiled what could have been a nice outing for them. Colonel and Mrs M. went away in the evening.

My younger brother and his family had come to Sanna for a brief holiday. Colonel M. was our landlord at the time of this entry. Needless to say, he had his main home elsewhere.

August 17th
The wind was strong Northwesterly all day. Heavy showers in early hours. Dry during the day, apart from a little scattered rain in the forenoon. Also, a lot of sunshine. I went for peats before breakfast. After breakfast I turned some of the older hay, to keep it from rotting. Later, Jessie turned some more. I also had the melancholy task of burying poor Tilly. Jessie found her dead in the sheephouse, and quite stiff, when she went to feed the lambs. She probably died late last night or very early today. Although we were expecting this, there was always the faint hope that she might pull through this time yet. The place won't be the same without Tilly. She was with us since the spring of 19 [The rest of the date is blank in the entry; Father obviously intended to look it up and forgot] *when Jessie took her home from the Dail Dubh as a very puny lamb. We had her in a teabox at the fireside and she was six weeks old before she could walk properly. She survived all of her numerous offspring. Her first lambing, twins, took place in the month of September! Eight months later she had a single lamb. Mrs Maccoll visited in the afternoon with a piece of*

*venison and a headsquare for Eliz. Ian, Alasdair and the rest fishing on
the rocks but the sea was too rough.*

It is time I told a few tales about animals, with so many of whom
our crofting lives became intertwined over the years. Indeed, 'It is
more than time' I hear my father calling from the shades.

One could say, I suppose, that there are no truly wild creatures
left in the world. At least, if there were we should not be able to
see them, for they would vanish as we approached. The more
delicately the prey was stalked the surer one would be of finding it
gone when one arrived. The price paid for language was an
altering vision which changes irrevocably the thing it looks at. It
is not possible to watch a condor gliding high above the Andes
without in some sense putting a cage around it, even if the bars be
tenuously metaphysical only. And man has taken the subtle
corruption of his presence to the top of Everest and to the bottom
of the Mariana Trench.

Nevertheless, there are degrees of domesticity. My preference
has always been for creatures moving of their own free will in as
unencumbered a fashion as may be through as natural an environment as may be. There is an unexamined magic in the phrase
'wild animal' that ought to turn our hearts over. A herd of red
deer streaming across a hillside—that is a marvel.

The best of zoos are the worst of abominations. It is an excuse
that they help preserve endangered species—if they do—but it
is not very much of an excuse. If one were translated into fable
and led before the throne of the King of the Beasts to be judged
for the crimes of man against animal, one would tremble to offer
that as a defence for fear of arousing more wrath than already
existed.

As crofters my family were dependent upon animals to a
certain extent, though as I have tried to show it is arguable how
far that dependence reached. Rigorous analysis, I always felt,
would have indicated a less pronounced indebtedness than one
might have imagined. And insofar as an indebtedness did exist it
seemed to me rather more psychological than financial.

Yet crofting is a way of life, not a business, and rigorous
analysis has little or no place in it. All the members of my family
got pleasure from animals, though for some of us the pleasure
may have been more intermittent than for others. In contrast to
that, one would have to note the number of times that animals

brought trouble of some kind in their innocent wake. Indeed, as far as family friction is concerned, our livestock and our pets caused more dissension among us than any other factor.

Much of this strife centred around my mother's garden, or at least could be typified by it. This pathetic plot extended for a few feet around our house, cowering for its life behind an ungainly straggle of fencing: odd lengths of rusty wire, spliced and res-pliced in an effort to span whatever gap nature or old age presented, and unmatched and second-hand—or tenth-hand—driftwood posts, haphazardly driven in wherever the necessary depth of soil had accumulated—and sometimes where it hadn't, to the further detriment of their sobriety. Within this absurdly insecure haven there struggled to survive, amid a jungle of hydra-headed weeds, a clump or two of daffodils and narcissi, some tansy, some monbretia, some monkshood, a lupin or so and, in the one sheltered corner, a much-prized rosebush. For years, aided only by my occasional assistance, Mother had fought to keep this patch of civilization alive, in the teeth of furious opposition from the elements (the damage a salt-laden gale can do to a garden in a matter of hours has to be seen to be believed), despite almost daily incursions by hens, sheep, cows and alien growth and despite, too, the indifference or, as it seemed to me at times, the obstruction of my father and my sister. Pathetic the garden may have been but it was dear to Mother's heart, dear in a way that only I—or so I felt—appeared to realize. And from this feeling of mine much conflict sprang.

Father simply did not understand. Wrapped up in his own accumulating problems, little given to the lighter side of life and apparently little in need of it, guiltless of any sort of aesthetic sense, any awareness of ordered beauty, barred from comprehension of any need that could not be supplied by rough nature, he stood about as far from the notion of the cultivated yet materially unproductive enclosure as it was possible to get. To him, no doubt, wholeheartedly committed to the croft and the livestock, forced to wrestle daily with the well-nigh intolerable burdens they heaped on him, the garden was a kind of moral extrava-gance. At least, that, I think, would have been how he would have regarded it had he considered the matter at all. He would not lift a finger to help with it and displayed a complete and chilling lack of interest in its welfare. This attitude, as I indicate, came about not through wickedness but merely because he did not view the thing as being of the slightest importance or, more precisely, it did not enter his head. He would, I am sure, have swept the garden into oblivion had it been entirely up to him and had he felt that the needs of his beloved animals required it. At best he saw it as a convenient pen for orphan lambs and indeed frequently used it for that purpose, with no very helpful results as far as the plants were concerned. 'The animals are what we all live on,' would doubtless have been his reply to any criticism. 'If it were not for them we could not survive.'

My sister, though fond enough of flowers, stood with the animals; my brother never became involved in this particular squabble; I, when I was at home, was entirely on Mother's side. I thought her generally outnumbered and too often taken for granted. I knew that, self-sacrificing and self-effacing as she was, concerned as she was to keep the peace among the wayward and wilful Macleans, she would not push her own rights. She needed a champion badly and I was the only available candidate. I hated argument, rows left me sick and shaken, but for her sake I was prepared to raise my voice. Since she was of necessity largely housebound (being house*keeper*, that ironically ambiguous title), deprived, too, through her situation, of novels, magazines, shops, cinemas, all the things she enjoyed, what was there for her left but the garden? And an innocent enough pleasure, I thought fiercely, and little enough for her to be granted. *Why could not the other two see it like that? Why must they stand idly by while this cow smashed down the fence or that sheep thrust itself through?*

Into this tangle of emotions and loyalties, of conflicting loves and needs, individual animals came and went, creating each its own little displacement. I have chosen four, out of the many that passed through our hands and hearts, to represent their kind: Danny and Tilly, two of our pet sheep and among the most characterful of these characterful animals and Laddie and Maid, two of our long line of dogs, companions for most of their lives and hardly separable in my mind when I look back on our crofting days.

Somewhere in the loft of our old home in Sanna there stands mouldering in the omnipresent Ardnamurchan damp a box of family snapshots and somewhere among those snaps one in particular shows my sister seated in our garden, feeding bottle in hand, surrounded—it is a carefully chosen word—by seven orphan lambs. The last time I looked at that photograph, though it was some years after the event depicted, I could scarcely repress a shudder. Seven lambs! My God! Bad enough our usual, our invariable, two or three, but seven! That must have been a year to try men's souls.

Pet lambs are far from being the meek little innocents of sentimental legend. On the contrary, they are noisy, greedy, thrusting and demanding. What's more, they tend to grow into pet sheep and their imperiousness increases as the years go by. It becomes virtually impossible for them to believe that humans do not exist for the sole purpose of feeding them and that any person approaching them, any person seen nearby, must of a certainty intend just that. At times it was difficult to leave our house without paying tribute, in the form of slices of bread or oilcake cobs, to at least half a dozen of these monsters. They would hang about the neighbourhood, nominally grazing but actually more concerned to keep a sharp eye on our door. Anyone emerging they would zero in on immediately, milling, shoving and butting. You had to dole out your bribes and escape while they were quarrelling over the spoils.

My tolerance for all this was limited, quite apart from the issue of the garden. Sometimes—for instance—in the light nights of our northern summer, when the internal clocks of animals and people go a little awry, I would find myself awakened from an uneasy and hard-won slumber. *Bang, bang, bang.* The cause of my disturbance would be one of our pet sheep—Tilly more often than not—hammering with her head on the garden gate (just outside my window), baaing at the top of her well-trained voice, demanding a hand-out. I would lie there cursing, thinking how long it might take me to get back to sleep and thinking, too, of the ramshackle gate that I would probably have to repair yet again. *Bang, bang, bang.* And I would leap out of bed in a fury, dash naked from the house and harry the offender for a hundred yards or more.

Or I would be hunched over my desk, engaged in the intolerable wrestle with words and having my concentration suddenly shattered by the still more intolerable bleat of the year's crop of orphan lambs, in hungry chorus a yard or two away. Again I would be galvanized into action and again I would return upset and angry after dispersing my tormentors, an impossible state of mind in which to practise the art of writing.

Then there would be a row, if not about what I had just done, about some related matter. (Reasoned debate was unknown among the Macleans.) I would defend myself by trying to turn the tables. 'Was it not the height of folly,' I would cry, 'to encourage a score of fat, lazy parasites who did nothing all day but beg?' And I would point to our window from which, at almost any time, one might see half a dozen sheep circling the garden, probing relentlessly at the fence, while a dozen of their comrades lounged on a handy knoll, awaiting the next distribution of manna.

Why, I demanded to know, did it have to be this way always? Why could we not keep ordinary animals like ordinary crofters? Why must we pervert every creature that came into our possession?

Naturally I would receive equally heated, equally biased answers. If things became especially hectic I might even be reminded that the animals were none of my business, that I resided in that house merely on sufferance, contributing little enough to the family economy in terms of either work or money, and that it might perhaps be better for all concerned if I took myself off and looked for a job—a real job, that is, unlike the one that I claimed to be performing. My poor mother would crouch in her chair, wringing her hands as the angry words surged about her.

Unhappy the writer condemned to live in the midst of his family! Unhappy, no doubt, the family. One feels that the Arts Council, with its system of bursaries, is merely nibbling at the edges of the problem. There is a better case to be made for marooning writers on remote islands, sustained in their fantasy lives by occasional air-drops of food and paper and specially-composed adulatory reviews.

Most Ardnamurchan crofters castrated their male lambs, then sold them as soon as they became old enough for the butcher. We generally kept ours. (A castrated mature male sheep is known, in shepherd's jargon, as a wether.) It was true that such beasts, since of course they neither produced lambs nor sired them, added nothing to one's income save from the yearly sale of their fleeces. But what money was there in sheep-raising anyway? At the level at which we operated precious little, as far as we could see. Indeed, since wether fleeces were usually thick and fine and so fetched a higher price, a long-lived wether would almost certainly yield more profit in the end than a sold lamb.

The only real friendship I ever formed with a sheep, if friendship be an amalgam of respect and affection, was with a wether called Danny. Danny was a hand-reared orphan, like the other 'house' sheep but unlike the others he refused—politely —to be turned into a pet. Once weaned he distanced himself. Other lambs, subject to that fate, were readily coaxed by my father and my sister to accept titbits instead and indeed to become addicted to them, changing in the process from ordinary sheep into pests. But not Danny. Never a morsel of bread or oilcake did anyone persuade him to take. He would eat nothing but the green grass of Sanna. Certainly he stayed in the vicinity of the house for the rest of his life, as did most of the pets, but he did not keep as close as they did nor did he mingle with them. He remained perfectly approachable but did not lay himself out to be complimented or cosseted. Danny was a cat among sheep.

(I wonder sometimes about the psychology of taming the untame, though I suppose that taming is what I do myself when I put out crumbs for the birds. One can understand a need for companionship, God knows, and better the unsatisfactory companionship of an animal than none at all. But is that, or compassion for the creature's hunger, really all that is at stake here? What are you doing when you train a wild creature to come to the hand, a creature that—under normal conditions at least—does not require your food or your friendship and might be better off without either? *Here, sheep! Here, robin! Come and be fed!* And you step into the garden with your platter of dainties. How kind you are! Yes, and how powerful.)

The rest of my family took little interest in Danny. They were spoiled for him by the easy returns in demonstrable affection obtainable from the other sheep. With them you put in a half-slice of bread and out came instant—nay, cloying—love. I sought him out, however—now and then. I scratched his back and he seemed to like that. A simple transaction and the extent of our commerce.

What happened to him finally I don't know. Like a number of our sheep he simply disappeared. I missed him and searched for his body but never found it. Presumably he was swallowed up in a ditch or a bog or, feeling death draw near (he had lived to a reasonable age), he withdrew into a corner the better to entertain his visitor.

*　　　*　　　*

I suspect that few people not compelled by some exigency or another to make a study of animals realize how much individuality they possess. The ordinary motorist, driving past a field in which sheep are kept—I had almost said 'parked'—sees them, I am sure, as clones, mental and physical duplicates of some boring old proto-sheep whose genes are entubed in a heavenly Department of Agriculture. He sees them as that if he sees them as animate at all and not simply a newer and duller form of landscaping. In truth, of course, those sheep will display all the variety of character that a group of motorists would, (more perhaps), being good-natured or cantankerous or forward or retiring or timid or brave. Were it not so life would be intolerably ennui-ridden for shepherds and very likely for sheep as well.

Nonetheless, however individual they might be, sheep are largely expendable among the Ardnamurchan crofters. If they live they live and if they die they die. Either way little trouble will be taken over them; they will be left on the hills to increase or decrease, as fate ordains it. If they decrease, as usually happens at last in these harsh conditions, some more will be bought, ferried to the hill and tipped out to get on with it. It would not do, today's crofter thinks, to devote much time and expense to sheep, for this would cancel out what small profit they yield. The only reason for keeping sheep in these parts, it seems, is that they do make some money and make it virtually without effort on the crofter's part. They are out there working for you and save for an occasional round-up for the purposes of dipping or culling you need not stir yourself greatly on their behalf.

After my sister took Tilly home, new-born, a tiny and weak orphan, we contacted her owner and were told to do as we wished with her. He would not accept the bother and responsibility of trying to rear her himself. It was not worth his while. She spent the first month or so of her life in a teabox by our fireside, as Father's journal relates, and was called Tilly, after the old comic-strip heroine, Tilly the Toiler, because she tried so hard to stay alive.

Stay alive she did, against all the odds. Her successful fostering became one of Mother's favourite small boasts. She took her first faltering steps in our kitchen, mincing stiff-legged across the unyielding and slippery lino, walking ballerina-fashion on the tips of her tiny hooves. It was the only sign of faltering she ever gave till the day of her death. She put on self-assurance with every pound, and there were many pounds to come.

Tilly was three years old when she lambed for the first time, quite unexpectedly and out of season, producing twins one forenoon on the hillside behind our house. We had long since assumed that she was barren. If she had allowed little to hold her in before motherhood she allowed nothing after. She almost burst with pride and her conduct towards sheep and humans became more ruthless than ever.

She was eventually to stand at the head of a small family tree. An evil fate dogged all her descendants, however. Neither 'child' nor 'grandchild' survived her. One by one all succumbed to illness or mishap. The last to go, at some six years old, was one of the original twins, a ewe dubbed 'The Goat' because of her peculiarly-shaped horns. By that time Tilly herself was rising ten and no longer became pregnant. I felt as if some noble line had died out.

Until she began having lambs Tilly often accompanied members of the family on working journeys or walks, apparently untroubled by what must at times have seemed a considerable distance to a Blackface sheep, a breed generally very firmly rooted within quite a small area. It was common for her to go with us to the 'faraway' peat moss, perhaps a mile and a half or two miles from our house. This involved carrying her across a ford on the way. She was the only pet sheep we had or heard of who would do this.

Tilly's habit of accompanying the family once brought me an object lesson in humility. I had gone for a walk in the direction of the beach and she had followed me. It was spring and the first really fine day of the year, indeed one of the loveliest spring days I can remember, a day to wrap around yourself and keep for old age. Importuned on every hand by daisies and larks you could not walk through such a day without feeling exultant. Together, man and sheep, we strolled across the *machair*, a sunlit stretch of greensward. Tilly was then in her fourth year and ought, in sheep terms, to have been a sober matron, or so, proscriptively, one might have felt. Suddenly she left my side to make half a dozen little surging runs ahead of me, at the conclusion of each run attempting a stiff-legged jump in the manner of a lamb. Of course she never got more than an inch off the ground, if that, but the whole of her joyful heart went into the effort.

If sheep, why not man, I thought and I launched into a gambolling run myself—alas with many a cautious glance around to see who watched me make a fool of myself.

I suppose, if I had ever thought about it, I should not have expected a mature sheep to pay much attention to the onset of spring, beyond perhaps a dim awareness that the weather had improved of late. Yet there was Tilly and if she was not that day transported with delight I do not know what the phrase means. I was moved. I berated myself for having appropriated to human-kind the whole of a feeling in which we had by rights only a share.

Tilly was, I think, in her fourteenth year when she died, a truly venerable age for a sheep. In that summer of 1970 she began to ail. She took to resting for much of the day, eating little. It grew obvious that she was for the road, though we pressed her to stay with possets and potions. When we judged that her time was near we carried her to an empty shed and made her comfortable with straw, that she might depart in peace without being troubled by the vulgar, among sheep or among people. Early next morning I looked in, privately, to see how she was getting on with her death. She lay stretched out on her side. I had brought a crust with me, waybread for the journey. She took it into her mouth and held it there, correctly making no attempt to eat it. I stroked her for a moment or two, running my hand over the flank that had been sheared with such a commotion only days before. After Father's none-too-expert work with the clippers her fleece ran jaggedly in long diagonal ridges, like prentice work in a hayfield. I left her then to finish what she had so well begun. When my sister looked in later she was dead.

Maid was a local dog, a pure bred collie, small, neat, handsomely black and white. Laddie came from a farm in Ayrshire, through an old Clyde Trust colleague of my father's. No one seemed at all sure of his genetics but we took him to be a mixture of labrador and collie. If that is so I can advocate the blend. Laddie was the best all-purpose dog I ever came across. He was good with sheep and cattle, or would have been had he been given proper training and discipline. He was also an excellent hunting dog, big, strong, rangy, fast, a dog who could easily catch rabbits in the open or point a pheasant in as classical a pose as any well-bred gundog. He, too, was a handsome animal, blackish mainly but with patches of brown and white. He had a collie's feathery tail but a labrador's flat, broad head and floppy, silky ears. Both dogs were good company, entirely amiable with humans if not always with their own species. Laddie as a rule attacked other males on sight but melted in the company of bitches; Maid hardly distinguished in terms of sex but simply bored in with flashing teeth.

They differed markedly from one another in respect of personality. Maid was all high courage and nervous energy; Laddie, except when it came to fighting other dogs, was extremely careful of his own skin, a great husbander of adrenalin. One day in winter these two and I encountered an otter on Sanna beach. It had come ashore to eat a fish, as otters do, and Laddie, racing ahead of us, had cut it off from its watery base. Laddie and the otter sparred for a moment or two, the otter standing up sturdily on its hind legs, its forepaws flicking in and out like a boxer's gloves, its teeth at the ready, Laddie circling his opponent, barking furiously but keeping a respectful foot or so away. When Maid and I came running up to join the fun the otter turned its back contemptuously on Laddie and slipped into the sea. Maid had to be restrained from going in after it.

Maid would not tolerate a strange dog of either sex around our house. A neighbour of ours, a summer visitor, once entered our garden, on his way to the door to buy milk. His dog, an inoffensive spaniel called Lucky, came trotting in at his heels. Unlucky for Lucky. There was a flurry and a snarling and the next thing anyone knew Maid was on top of the other dog, had grabbed a mouthful of long ear and was in a fair way to transforming it into spaghetti. Lucky's owner hopped around the mêlée on one foot, using the other to stamp ineffectually—and somewhat incautiously, I felt, watching the scene and knowing the mettle of my own beast—on the struggling animals. I had a brief vision of Maid's spaghetti becoming flavoured with cavalry twill and brown suede. Eventually I persuaded her to disgorge. Lucky was wheeled off for repairs and we crossed another customer from our list.

Bitches in heat drove Laddie wild. He could scent them across the width of a parish and off he would go, throwing home and duty to the winds. If he could not get to mount the bitch immediately he would take up vigil outside the home of her owner, prepared for an indefinite stay till his opportunity arose.

So engaged he cared naught for food or shelter and was deaf to all commands. Of course, these urges sometimes came at inconvenient moments for his nominal owners. If you were trying to eject a lamb from the croft, cursing and sweating as you thrashed about unavailingly in the growing hay, it was small consolation to know that the one whose job you were doing, who could have done it effortlessly, was off somewhere increasing the canine population of the world.

Father, in urgent need once of a working dog, spent an hour trying to coax Laddie away from a neighbouring house that he was encamped outside. (Needless to say, the house contained a bitch in heat.) He ordered, he cajoled, he promised dire retribution. Laddie listened to it all with every appearance of regret but refused to stir. Retribution duly followed. When Laddie eventually slunk home some hours later he was well beaten for his pains. One could only hope it had been worthwhile.

The beating made no difference. Laddie was following an instinct stronger by far than any poor training he had been given, any training he could have been given. Nature's obedience classes are much more effective than man's.

Father, despite his great love of animals, his great need of them, often lacked patience with them. He could not brook to be thwarted. I ought to add, however, that only very rarely did he resort to physical chastisement and it was never really severe; shouting was his usual reaction. The inconsistency of attitude that resulted from this goes a long way towards explaining why our dogs were never more than half-disciplined and half-obedient at best. A dog that is indulged to the point of spoiling one minute and roared into a quivering heap the next is well on the way to being useless.

Apart from sex, the great joy of Laddie's life was chasing deer. He would catch a scent when you were out walking with him in the hills and off he would bound. You could call him till you were black in the face and he would pay you no heed. Hours later perhaps, long after you had returned home, he would show up, his tongue hanging out. Of course he never caught any and would not have known what to do with them if he had. It was all sport to him and how purely he loved it.

Both dogs made bad ends, bringing out once more the opposing attitudes to animals and to the death of animals that existed within our family. When Maid was about five or six she developed epilepsy, an ailment that intensively-bred sheepdogs are sometimes prone to. The fits came on her entirely without warning, or at least offering no warning that she could convey to any of us. They were often savage in their effect and horrifying to watch. She would fall over on her side, her body snapping backwards and forwards uncontrollably and with frightening rapidity. Sometimes she would end up yards from where she had begun, jack-knifing across the floor or through the grass as though possessed of demoniacal energy, coiling and uncoiling like a tautened spring that had escaped the watchmaker's fingers and on the benchtop taken on a life of its own. While all this was going on she would foam at the mouth and become so drenched in sweat as to soak the ground around her. When the fit was over she would lie for an hour or more where her last movement had taken her, without stir or blink, in an exhaustion that resembled death and must have been close to it in more than just looks.

Father consulted the Vet, who informed him that the illness was both incurable and unappeasable. 'Have her destroyed,' said my brother. 'You may think you're doing her a favour by letting her live. You're not.'

I was uneasily neutral. Was the putting down of a sick animal an acceptance of responsibility or an evasion of it? How could one tell? Pets, I felt, were often put down too readily, even where something of a reason existed and the owner had not simply become fed up or had come to grudge the expense. Was not the euphemistic phrase 'put down' itself a give-away, a pointer to the shuffling-off of a problem? And yet, such suffering as Maid was patently enduring—here, if anywhere, was sufficient excuse for interfering.

In the event, nothing was done. Maid lived on and was to live on for another three or four years. Towards the end she became a wasted wreck of a beast, virtually blind, concerned to drink water till one could hear it wallop about inside her.

I looked on in wonder and anguish, quite unable to decide. What price a cold death in the Vet's kennels, a puzzled death even if a sudden one? Was the creature not now among friends and in familiar surroundings? Were there not still long fitless days, weeks, when the sun shone and, perhaps, she was aware that it did shine? Should I not judge for her as I would wish to be judged and had not life at all costs always been my great rallying-cry?—I who had some small right to that cry, having endured, it might be, more than my share of mental and physical illness.

When, a few years later, Laddie died, at the great age of sixteen, the old arguments were trotted out, with whatever embellishment experience had suggested and we were beginning to accumulate quite a lot of that.

Relatively speaking, in graspably human terms, Laddie had survived more than eleven decades. Had he been an old man he would have been awe-inspring, a loving link with the past, someone whose youth had been spent when—say—Abe Lincoln had occupied the White House. He showed his age. How he showed it! He grew stiff and blind, turning up milky eyes to the light. He shrank visibly. His body became thin and began to curve like a bow. His nails, through lack of wear and tear, lengthened grotesquely till they curled back underneath his paws, like Turkish slippers in reverse. He would allow no one to cut them and there was, at least, nothing wrong with his teeth or his jaws. When, now and then, he dragged himself to his feet and went for a mooch around the kitchen, he would perhaps collide with a chair that someone's thoughtlessness had moved to an unfamiliar position or, being unable to get any sort of traction on the bare sections of lino, would slither about helplessly.

I had become a little less neutral or, maybe, a little more bitter. Only in my family, I thought, would matters be permitted to get so hugely out of hand. Indeed—or so I sometimes resentfully felt—only with us did such absurd situations ever develop. And what on earth was going on with us anyway? Were we displaying love, of however harsh a variety, or merely indulging in a feckless non-interference, a procrastinating hope that tomorrow the problem might magically resolve itself?

Of course I do not mean to suggest that Father looked on unmoved while all this was happening, sternly and Calvinistically counting off the minutes till some fore-ordained sequence of events duly worked itself out. No doubt he bled, no doubt he doubted. But essentially he did nothing. 'Every creature has a right to live,' he said. 'I am not God that I should wield the shears.'

'But you are God,' said I. 'That is precisely the point. To Laddie you are God. The only one he will ever know. At least dope him somehow and cut his bloody nails.'

I was away from home when at last Laddie died and only learned the manner of his end later. It seemed that on the day of his death he began to whimper, so much so that no one could stand it. My sister carried him over to the untenanted byre and there, some time later, found him dead.

I was sad for his going and sick about the fashion of it. My family, having accepted responsibility for his living—and ultimately I felt I agreed with that decision—had rejected responsibility for his death. At the last they had failed to come up to the mark. They had allowed him to die alone, a tamed and domesticated creature who had never been alone, who had been 'family' like us virtually from the day of his birth. That was a betrayal of trust. If I was sure of nothing else in the whole sorry and complicated mess I was sure of that at least.

August 31st
Wind strong to gale all day. Southwesterly in the morning but more Westerly in the afternoon and evening. Heavy showers throughout the early hours and during the day. One particularly vicious shower of sleet in the forenoon. Some blinks of sunshine in the afternoon. Went for peats before breakfast. Jessie went later. I then went round our fourteen ricks adjusting the stones on them. The forenoon was passed packing fleeces, the total of which gets less each year. We still have several unshorn sheep around the premises but have so far been unable to catch them. Also one up the hill. Violent sleety showers in the late evening and into the night.

The stones on the hayricks that Father went round adjusting had of course been hung on them to prevent their being blown away. The weight of these stones naturally tended to flatten the ricks, eventually causing the stones to be grounded. They had then to be re-hung higher up. But for a full account of harvesting see Sept 30.

It is some indication of the uselessness of our dogs, in matters of work, that we should have had to catch our sheep ourselves. I have vivid recollections of sheep-stalking, the bated-breath approach, belly possibly to the ground, the final frantic plunge that was often disappointed. Sheep are a good deal warier than one might imagine—and a good deal more nimble. It was all fine sport and great exercise but God alone knows what our neighbours thought of it.

September 1st
Wind Westerly, strong at first but moderated to fresh in the evening.
Showers in the early hours and in the morning. Some sunny intervals.
As far as work was concerned this was a profitless day. Apart from
cleaning out the annexe and the new byre the only other job worth
noting was to shear Oscar, which Alasdair had caught yesterday. The
reason for such a strenuous cleaning of the annexe was so that hay can
be stored in it, as it won't be required for animals—we hope! Evening
quite cold.

Oscar, a huge brute of a wether, evidently represented one of my
successful stalks. I must have been in good form that day.

September 15th
Wind variable light. Some rain in early hours but fine and sunny
during the day. After breakfast I spent some time re-stowing hay in the
barn and the annexe. Jessie and I later carried another rick from
Seaview croft, some to the barn and some to the Annexe. In the
afternoon we respread the hay that had been lying in Dalmore croft for
weeks, and lifted a lot of it on to higher ground. Small bottle of
Penicillin from Vet by post. Lulu, the cripple lamb, in the croft with
the others, but not eating at all. I'm afraid she won't be better.

Among the trades in his Jack-of-all-trades list a crofter had to be a
fair-to-middling veterinary surgeon. Our regular Vet practised
out of Fort William, some sixty miles off. We did not care to
summon him except for something quite serious.
    Lulu was an abandoned lamb, almost totally crippled, that I
had carried home some weeks previously from Dunbhan. The
entry for September 16th records her death.

September 30th
Wind Westerly strong to gale. Frequent heavy showers and a few sunny
spells. Spent most of the day cementing in the new byre and, we hope,
finished there for the present. Hung extra stones on our hayricks.
Perhaps we can save some of them from rotting or being blown over.

Haymaking is the chief preoccupation and business of the crofting year and its greatest glory. It is a long, complex and hazardous
process, beginning in these parts about the middle of July—give
or take a week or two, depending on how good the season's

growth is—and continuing usually into October or even November. Indeed I have known us to conclude our harvesting in December, more than once I have known that, and I have known it not to be concluded at all.

Haymaking begins with the cutting of the hay, insofar as anything so cyclical can be said to have a beginning, and I suppose that Father's old croft, when I cut it for my sister in the autumn of the year he died, may well have been the last in Ardnamurchan to be hand-cut and I myself the last of the scythemen. Yet though I passed for a reasonable hand at the game by the easy standards of today I knew myself to be a bungler and an incompetent compared to the men who cut the Sanna crofts in the past. I have watched my grandfather and his coevals at work, among them men locally famed for their skill. These were the scythemasters, who measured their day's production not in puny rigs or strips as I did but in acres.

The scythe we used was not the small straight-snedded one, often seen further south. That we looked on as a garden implement, a toy. Ours was the tall scythe with the big blade and the curved sned. (Strictly speaking, the handle or handles of a scythe are the small projections that you grasp when you are using it; what the layman might call the handle is more properly, in the north at any rate, referred to as the sned.) A man might spend the best part of a day adjusting a new scythe to suit him; hammering, wedging, heating; altering the rotation of the blade around its axis or its angle to the sned; altering the position of the handles or their vertical or horizontal angle. There were ancient guidelines to help in this. For example, if you stuck your left leg straight out along the ground, as in a goosestep, the correctly-positioned blade, in its sweep, ought to pass just beyond your toe. (It paid to get your adjustments approximately right before you actually tried this experiment.) A man might also spend a week or more in the field getting the shop edge off the blade, the edge that had passed for sharp when it left the factory, and fitting a real cutting edge to it. Much of a good scytheman's artistry, indeed, lay in his skill with the sharpening stone, the specially-shaped piece of sandstone that he kept forever by him as he worked. You might, after all, swing your scythe as prettily as any man in Ardnamurchan; that was of no avail if you had to stop every minute to hone it.

My grandfather was supreme with the stone. A few swift

passes along the blade and he was good for thirty swathes or more, depending on the width of rig. When he stopped at last for a sharpening I always felt that he was acting in the privileged tradition of the labourer, taking the hallowed momentary breather, rather than doing something he really needed to do. My father could take out perhaps twenty odd swathes on one sharpening. I thought myself doing well if I managed a dozen.

You cannot be taught how to sharpen a scythe any more than you can be taught how to swing one. You can watch someone else doing it, of course, and get a rough idea of what is happening. You can, perhaps, have one or two pitfalls pointed out to you. But in the end, as with making love, you are on your own. You will build up your own effective but no doubt slightly different technique through practice. Or you will not.

A badly-honed scythe butchers the hay instead of cutting it, making the work twice as hard and half as proper. Naturally, too, you lose time if you have to stop at the end of almost every row to do some sharpening and you break your rhythm and concentration. Also, too much use of the stone is hard on the blade, eating it away at a great rate.

A well-sharpened, well-balanced scythe is a joy to handle, a good man using it a delight to watch. See how he swings from the waist above sturdily-planted feet, backwards and forwards, never pushing or pulling, letting momentum carry him round, letting the weight of the scythe do the work. He takes the same size of 'bite' at the hay each time, so that his rows will be straight, and his blade clears the ground by the same inch, so that he is neither shaving the turf nor leaving too wasteful a stubble. You can tell by the sound and style of his cutting, by the resistless crunch as the blade passes through the standing grass and by the clean fall of the hay, that his scythe is sharp. And on he goes and on, never hurrying, always sweet and easy, and the hayfield disappears like the chalked letters on a blackboard as a duster is drawn across them.

A hayfield is cut always in the same direction year after year, going with the grain, as it were, going with the prevailing wind and the slant of the stalks. You cannot cut a hayfield 'backwards'. I have tried it, unbelievingly, and it simply does not work.

A hayfield is cut always at right angles to the long length of the strip. You begin at one side, you reach in something like three feet or so, depending on the length of your arm and the height of your ambition, and you take out a swathe of that width all the way across the rig. Then you walk back to the side you started at and you repeat the process.

Scything is hard work if you are unfit or if you are a beginner. If you are both, as I was for most of my career, it is murder. I have seen myself in a sorry state after a mere half-dozen rows: the sweat pouring from me and that from my forehead stinging my eyes like fury; my breath coming in gasps; my aching muscles, unable to sustain a rhythm, having to push hard to force the blade through the grass; the skin on the palms of my hands already broken and bleeding. (The labourer who spits on his hands is not indulging in a meaningless ritual, a piece of working-class affectation. Saliva is a lubricant; it helps.) Nothing I know of unlards the waistline as quickly as cutting hay.

Scything, of course, is two-handed work, for if you try to swing one-handed you may shortly find yourself one-footed. It pays to remember that you are shuttling a heavy steel blade back and forth in an arc about your legs, a blade of razor sharpness. This need for having both hands on the job while scything is well known to the insect life of the Highlands. Horseflies, ordinary flies, midges, all will home in on a man with a scythe from miles away.

Anyone who has never experienced Highland midges in action has never experienced the ultimate limits of physical torture. I have had them round me in a cloud, a tall dark pillar, all biting and tinily whining, in my hair, in my eyes, in my ears. I have dropped my scythe at last and run home howling.

Once I heard someone from South America boasting about the voraciousness of piranha fish. Out there, he said, it was a common experiment, an entertainment for hotel guests or the like, to dangle a live pig into a piranha-infested river. Ten minutes later you pulled your pig out, its flesh stripped to the bone. I would back a Highland midge against a piranha any day of the week. I think that if you kept on cutting hay on a really midgy evening in Ardnamurchan you would soon resemble the figure of Death in a medieval woodcut—a skeleton with a scythe.

The stage after cutting is spreading. A rig of hay, if the crop has been very thick and heavy, may with profit be left for a day or two in rows, just as it has fallen from the scythe. It will shrink a little and dry a little and be somewhat easier to handle. But

normally, in these parts, where thick heavy crops are the exception, cut hay will be spread as soon as may be. It will be gathered
up in forkfuls, that is, and shaken out thinly over the available
space. Spreading hay has its own modicum of skill and if you see a
spread field filled with patches of clear ground and half-shaken-
out lumps of hay you will know that a poor workman has been
abroad.

Spread hay may be left for three or four days or three or four
weeks or forever, depending on how lucky you are with the
weather. When at last it is in good part dry it will be gathered into
rows again by means of wooden rakes. These rows will be left for
a further day or two to complete the drying process, being
meanwhile rolled over once or twice with the rake. We call this
'turning' the hay and it is the easiest and pleasantest of the
haymaking jobs. You turn with the wind, of course, and if there
is a decent breeze the rows of hay, now light and fluffy (with luck)
will almost turn themselves. I have turned a field in half a gale and
had my rows of hay threaten to take charge and go bowling off
like tumbleweed.

You are on the last lap now, though it may turn out to be the
hardest and longest. You will gather up your dried hay into
stacks, or ricks as they are sometimes called, siting them merely
where they are handiest to the area of field you are working on.
You will not, of course, stick them on top of windy knolls or in
hollows where water collects and you will cover them with
sacking or nets, weighted down with stones.

These are what one might call working ricks, a convenient
stage in the haymaking process and a help in the further curing
and compacting of the hay. They are not meant for over-
wintering. They will stand up to a good stiff breeze and perhaps a
gust or two more but the steady gales of winter would topple
them. They will take a shower or two but not weeks of downpour, not without becoming soaked and turning mouldy. Besides which, the cattle would eat them when at last admitted to
the stubble field. So you will eventually transfer as many of these
ricks to your barn as the place will hold, carrying them bundle by
bundle on your back and your wife's back and your children's
backs, till you have crammed the building to the ridgepole. Then
you will tramp it all down and cram in some more.

If turning hay is the most pleasant part of harvesting, tramping
is the least. It is hot and stuffy and uncomfortable. The hay gets

into your hair and down your neck and into your boots. The dust
chokes you. Never does the sky seem so blue, the air so sweet and
fresh, as when at last you finish and can close the barn door
behind you.

The bulk of your hay will still be outside, however, unless you
have an exceptionally large barn (not common in the Highlands
for many reasons) or have had an exceptionally light crop. This
leftover hay you will make into your big winter stack, which you
will build in your stackyard, a small fenced-off square adjacent to
your croft. The building of the winter haystack is probably the
most important single operation of the crofting year, certainly
the most critical and the most fraught. Consider what is involved:
the remaining working stacks will first have to be carried to your
stackyard, which means that for several hours they will be lying
about the ground in broken heaps. The bulk of your hay crop,
therefore, will be totally exposed to whatever weather comes
along. For a crofter that is to be vulnerable indeed. And once you
have started the operation you have committed yourself and there
is no going back.

Remember, too, that your winter stack will very likely be built
late in the autumn, perhaps into November even, when good
days have become scarcer. So you will seize on the first reasonably promising morning to come by, for you might wait long
enough for a better one. For a whole anxious day your heart will
be in your mouth and every five minutes your gaze will turn to
the sky, your attention to the weather. Are those clouds getting
darker? Is the wind rising a little or is it just your imagination? But
when at last you complete your stack, when you see it loom
above you in the gathering dusk, its rounded ends, its orienta-
tion, appeasing the prevailing wind, its bulk well-thatched with
reeds and well-weighted with stones, you can pat yourself on the
back and think with satisfaction of the lighted windows of your
home and the pleasures of the supper table. Your harvest is over
for another year.

I have simplified a bit for convenience. If, for example, your
croft is 'dirty' you may have to go in for 'picking' as well. This is a
back-breaking job which involves going along the drying rows
of hay one by one and picking out the noxious and the inedible,
plants such as knapweed and reeds. But fundamentally the process is as I describe it; a mere page or two, ironically, suffices to
illustrate the operation at the very heart of crofting, an operation

that must have evolved over generations and that at its best worked economically and well.

Yet one ought not to scant or ignore the fact that it did evolve, that the passing centuries must have seen many changes in techniques, in materials, in social circumstances, in climate even. Finite evolution is a logical impossibility, a contradiction in terms. For as little long as crofting lasts there is no reason to suppose its changes at an end.

The crofters of my father's youth, I think, tended to do just that. Crofting, in Ardnamurchan at any rate, had ossified by then. Its former fluid adaptability had become something written down on tablets of stone: *this is how it always was, this is how it always will be.* And of course that is not true. The modern availability of large polythene sheets, to take just one example, has made possible small-scale silage operations, croft-sized operations, and the potential by-passing of the entire risky hay-making process. This was undreamt-of a decade or two ago.

It is foolish, I am sure, not to respect our forefathers. In almost everything that matters they were before us. Here and there we begin to find it necessary to reoccupy positions they once held, strong places we ought never to have abandoned. Such recourse to old knowledge will, I think, increase in the years ahead. But it is equally foolish to suppose that we cannot occasionally refine that knowledge to our advantage or that we dare not attempt to purify a corrupt tradition. I have seen both attitudes illustrated in Ardnamurchan in my own lifetime.

When I was a child here hay was left in the fields to dry for as long as possible. The old crofters dreaded the thought of a stalk or two of greenish hay getting in among the cured stuff. It was as though they were dealing with a contagion that might spread and wreak havoc. And as a preventive measure they baked their hay under as much sun as nature cared to send. The end product was creakly, brown and bone dry; drained of all juice and, one imagines, deprived of much of its nourishment.

By the time of Father's death we had cut the drying period to days rather than weeks and though the change was, in origin, largely forced on us by circumstances, it worked very well. Dry greenish hay became our aim. We produced something that was sweet and juicy and scented. The cattle loved it.

That was to the good. Other outmoded or wrong practices, however, were rigidly adhered to and to suggest alteration was to risk the charge of heresy. Then, too, not all changes were advantageous or appealing. I can remember Father, in the days when we had a tiny corn patch, deliberately abandon the age-old custom of securing the first cut sheaf to be plaited into the 'Maiden' and hung above the fireplace till the next harvest, when it would be ceremoniously burnt. He had become the last local crofter to keep up this practice and had grown self-conscious about it.

That was not at all to the good. The crofter of today is already too much isolated, this being the paradoxical effect on him of the impingement of the outside world. As he becomes more and more concerned with the materialistic and the mundane so he separates himself from tradition and ritual and from the genuine communion with his fellows that these bring in their wake. He meets the other crofters of his parish only in pub or in market place and knows of them only what they wish him to know, knows them at best only on a superficial level. He does not see them under fire, as it were; naked and trembling in the presence of the god. His old attachment to nature disappears, for he does not think himself beholden to her. He loses the instinct underlying his Christianity, the instinct that filled his landscape with joy and fear, with awareness of the unknown. All the religion he recognizes is cleansed and tidied and packaged, trapped feebly within the walls of a church or squeezed half to death between the pages of a book. Of course it does not satisfy him; his soul knows that if his mind doesn't.

My father, to the end of his days, was reluctant to linger in certain corners of the neighbourhood, where he felt too strongly the influence of the spirit of place. I did not laugh at him for his tenets; indeed in some part I share them, though my sophistication will hardly allow me to talk openly about spirits, though it leaves me in that modern intellectual limbo of belief without true acknowledgement, without ceremony, without even terminology. And no matter how I choose to describe my feelings it pleases me when, in my walks about these hills, I catch a glimpse of something that is not my own reflection, something that was here before me and my kind and will survive our departure, something that merely watches and waits. I have blundered sadly and often but I have at least been wise enough to know that in the inexplicable lies whatever meaning there is in life.

For all that, I do not honestly think I could get back to the

'Maiden'. But if I were still an Ardnamurchan crofter I should at least go through the motions. We must look to the future to reanimate our dead forms, hoping that it does not do so out of too bloody a necessity. Meanwhile let us not wantonly discard.

I have wandered from my subject but I have, I trust, been turning in a circle. Haymaking remains haymaking. Work is always work and it is often both brutal and heartbreaking. If I were heavily engaged in it I should not be writing these words; I would not have the time or the energy. I am not going to construct great paeans of praise to the dignity of labour and the therapeutic value of sweat. Nevertheless, physical work can be intensely satisfying. I believe firmly that the man who works only with his mind works only with half of himself. Whether he knows it or not discontent breeds in his heart like the worm in the bud. If I have done nothing else in my life that will count when the time for counting comes I have at least sat on a hillside in Ardnamurchan and looked down on a croft that I had harvested unaided and against considerable odds. I have watched the shadows creep out from the dotted ricks and the stubble take the evening light in the impress of the vanished swathes. And if I felt sad at being the last in a long line I also felt for the first time, truly and confidently, that to be last in a line is still to be part of that line.

October 1st

Another birthday for Eliz. Wind Westerly, fresh to strong at first but increased to gale force in the late afternoon. Heavy showers in the morning and forenoon were followed by continuous rain, which continued into the night. Altogether, a cold and wild day. No work could be done outside. I pushed the old banger out under the elements and left one half of the garage door open, to see if these poor cattle, Cindy, Mungo, Bridget, and Fiona, would shelter there at night. I feel sorry for them but until the cement in the byre has set properly I can't let them in there. Mrs Donaldina Macgillivray (widow of Hector) arrived to Mrs K. in the forenoon. Apparently she had been stormbound at Tobermory since Monday last. [Father wrote these words on a Thursday.] *She certainly would not have got across in the afternoon. My plan of putting the young beasts in the garage didn't work. They ignored it and carried on to mill, and mess, at the byre door as usual.*

Getting around the Highlands by public transport has always been a complicated and chancy affair, with the traveller too often finding himself victimized by the utter indifference or even the active hostility of those charged with his welfare. Such comments, of course, would fit most transport systems in Britain today but they inherit a peculiar aptness when applied to the north of Scotland. The Ardnamurchan journey, in particular, could become a protracted nightmare of discomfort and there were times, indeed, when life and limb were at no little risk.

Modern technology has not lessened our local difficulties. Neither did the emergence, in the sixties, of another way of getting here, made possible by the appearance in the peninsula of a passenger-carrying mail bus. Granted one may be less at bodily hazard now but not less exposed to wearisome and unnecessary delays, ill-planned or unplanned linkages and a degree of the uncaring or the insolent among operators and authorities that would rouse to fury anyone but your well-cowed West Highlander.

For all that it scarcely offers an improvement most travellers today elect this newer route, coming up from Glasgow to Fort William by train or bus (if they are northbound), switching to another bus to get to Corran Ferry, crossing the ferry as a foot passenger and joining the Ardgour-Kilchoan mail bus on the other side of the Linnhe Loch. The journey depends on fine timing and if a connection is missed anywhere along the line the lack cannot easily be remedied; one is stranded then for twenty-four hours (forty-eight if one were travelling on a Saturday and I have omitted discussion of possible problems in getting to Glasgow or in proceeding onwards from Kilchoan).

Thus from the sixties on, if one so chose. For most of the period I deal with, however, anyone bound for Ardnamurchan came via Oban rather than Fort William, boarding at Oban a steamer which took him through the Sound of Mull to Tobermory. Disembarking at Tobermory he took a ferry back across to the mainland—if mainland be the right word for Ardnamurchan —stepping ashore this time at Mingary Pier, Kilchoan.

The main potential trouble spot in this itinerary was the Tobermory–Kilchoan ferry, which was actually a small launch. If the Sound of Mull were at all stormy—and the Sound here is more or less at an end and has widened into open Atlantic—the launch crew generally refused to make the run. It did not matter if the crossing, though rough, was yet possible; if they did not feel like it they did not stir and there was nothing one could do about it. Though supposedly tied in with the national transport network they had in actual practice a good deal of autonomy. Naturally, too, the launch skipper had—or adopted—a sea captain's authority in regard to his vessel and claimed to be the sole arbiter in all decisions affecting her daily running and risk.

Once in a great while, on the other hand—I think when complaints became too loud and too prevalent even for those conveniently deaf to ignore—that same crew would display all the seafaring enterprise that one could wish, and perhaps a little bit more to boot. I have made that crossing on days when all was noise and welter, when the launch went from crest to trough like a bobsleigh and from trough to crest like a badly-overloaded lift, when I had to wedge myself between bulkheads to avoid being hurled about the cabin and had to leap for my life when the vessel at last made a flying pass at Mingary Pier.

But derring-do of that order was very much the exception rather than the rule. Normally, arriving from the south on a blowy sort of day, one would discover H—, the launch skipper, in his usual spot outside the freight shed on Tobermory Pier, huddled under the shelter of the overhanging roof, waiting patiently for the bar of the Mishnish Hotel to open.

'Any chance of getting over, H—?'

'Aw, man, no chance at all! Couldn't possibly risk her! Man, there's gale warnings out all over the place!'

And there one would be, marooned for perhaps two or three days (like Mrs Macgillivray in Father's journal entry), while across the strait the white cottages of Kilchoan, one's destination, gleamed fitfully and irritatingly.

The launch was operated by MacBrayne's Ltd and that, to anyone who knows the region, explains a good deal. For longer than I can remember this company has had a stranglehold on West Highland transport, in all its ramifications, and has been notorious from the beginning for its utter indifference to the welfare and comfort of its passengers. How clearly I recall from my childhood, how often, boarding the old *Lochearn* at Kilchoan, to return south with my parents after a holiday, and finding its scanty and spartan steerage accommodation already full of the Outer Islands poor, picked up at the start of the voyage. They would be sprawled out across every available foot of space, sick, white-faced and miserable after the long trip down from the Islands and the crossing of the dreaded Minch. There would be shawl-wrapped women with babies, men with shiny blue serge suits and soft hats, on their way to the Labour Exchanges of Glasgow, to the tenements, with their pathetic luggage, their possessions, piled around them.

It was scarcely an advance on the emigrant ships of the nineteenth-century Clearances. Indeed Macbrayne's were all too often in the same line of business and operating at about the same level of concern. Yet the *Lochearn* was a blue riband liner compared to earlier MacBrayne vessels. It is enlightening, if harrowing, to persuade old people in the Highlands to talk about such rust-buckets as the *Plover* and the *Cygnet* where, frequently, one shared accommodation—if that is the word for what was on offer; it was, at any rate, MacBrayne's word—with a herd of often-terrified cattle, plunging, bellowing and skittering.

It should be noted that the doubtful privilege, granted post-war to Ardnamurchan passengers, of using Mingary Pier, was itself a revision of the earlier barbarous practice of embarking and disembarking in the open roads off Kilchoan. During my childhood the custom was for the steamer to anchor there (if the captain felt he had time for such minor diversions). One was ferried out and back from a small jetty in the village, in a tiny undecked boat that was invariably piled high with goods and luggage. The hazards of this operation in stormy weather may be imagined, especially if one were elderly or disabled.

Here, from the mid-1920s, is M. E. M. Donaldson on Mac-Brayne's. (She was an English travel writer, belletrist and novelist, who lived for some time in Sanna and who, in fact, built the present 'Big House'. In her day she was a well-known authority on West Highland topics. The book I quote from, two brief extracts from a long passage on this subject, including reports of parliamentary questions and answers, is called *Further Wanderings Mainly in Argyll*.)

On the last occasion I had the misfortune to travel on this floating slum [she is talking about the *Cygnet*] I took a seat under the bridge, which is all the meagre shelter the upper deck affords . . . Very shortly afterwards, however, we were all roughly ordered off—because we were steerage passengers. Whilst the poor woman [a fellow traveller] went away below with her husband to seek what shelter was available amongst the cattle and the cargo in the unsavoury hold . . . I elected to remain on the upper deck and sit out in the rain, as at least the cleaner alternative.

And a little later in the same passage:

MacBrayne exercise what amounts practically to a despotic monarchy in the Western Highlands, and treat the public as they please, without let or hindrance. They charge 1s. carriage for a single joint of beef on the half-hour's crossing from Tobermory to Kilchoan. Compare, too, the freight of 30s. per ton charged from Bombay to Glasgow, a thirty days' voyage, with the average of £4 per ton exacted by MacBrayne for a two days' sailing from Glasgow to Kilchoan.

Plus ça change . . . Iniquitous freight charges still cripple all commercial enterprise in the West Highlands and add pounds to the cost of the family shopping basket. And the 'despotic monarchy' still exists, its attendant arrogance no whit lessened by the fact that MacBrayne's is now largely State-controlled. In the Highlands they have a rhyme which mothers teach their children:

> The earth unto the Lord belongs,
> With all that it contains,
> Except, of course, for the Western Highlands
> And that's owned by MacBrayne's.

October 15th
Wind Southeasterly, fresh to strong at first, but fell away to light in the evening. A thick pall of smoky haze all day prevented the sun from getting through. I did various odd jobs including fitting a shaft to the head of a square spade which someone had dumped in the hollow. This task took some time but, at any rate, we now have a serviceable spare spade.

'In the hollow'—in Sanna, in the days before rubbish removal became the duty (the perquisite, I am tempted to say, being myself an assiduous scavenger of dumps) of the local Council, the unwanted material of the domestic economy was disposed of in convenient hidden spots. The houses in the upper part of the village used for this purpose the then bush-covered 'hollows' or gullies that ran from the lower slopes back into the hills. Needless to say, little was thrown out for the inhabitants were necessarily expert at re-using and repairing. Nevertheless the middens did swell over the years, eventually becoming small gold-mines of delectable and well-made early artefacts. Collectors from outside, unfortunately, have grown wise to the existence of these middens and one's chances of finding anything both handsome and useful, even in such a remote place as Sanna, are now slim.

October 31st
Wind Southerly to Southeasterly strong to gale. Overcast with driving rain all day. After morning tea I set off to go for peats, but turned back when I saw the Plocaig and Rhu sheep being gathered. Knowing that dipping was due, I had breakfast and then walked up to the fank. After waiting there for some time, and no signs of sheep arriving, I crossed over to Achnaha, chilled to the bone. At Achnaha Hugh told me they'd decided, owing to weather conditions, not to dip but to dose instead at Plocaig. After coffee from Eilidh I went on to Plocaig with Hugh. Coming home later I found the river risen so much that, to chill me more, I got my Wellingtons filled with water, crossing the stepping stones. I only counted five sheep for us and three lambs. If we have more I didn't see them. Mrs R. and daughter arrived to Braeside at 6.30 p.m. Wind increasing at bedtime.

Sheep dipping resembles initiation into the illuminated Baptists in that total immersion is required of the candidate; (it differs, of course, in the addition of disinfectant to the water). Those whose job it is to plunge the candidates end up half-dipped themselves (or half-baptized, as the case might be). Presumably dipping was abandoned for the day, in Father's entry here, because the prospect of becoming even more cold and wet, in such dreadful weather, was not to be borne: (I should not have thought myself, judging by Father's description of conditions, that there was much in it either way.)

'Fank' is an Englishing of a Gaelic word meaning pen—in our area generally a dry-stone or wooden fence enclosure. The sheep are driven into the enclosure with the aid of dogs and held there temporarily while they are undergoing the various sheep-keeping procedures. 'Dosing' (against liver fluke and the like) involves the forcible injection of a capsule down the sheep's gullet.

Sheep, encountered close up in the confines of a small pen, are bigger and stronger and a whole lot livelier than the layman might imagine who sees them peacefully grazing in a roadside field. They do not care for being dipped or dosed (or anything else) and given half a chance will buck and twist and heave like broncos in some ultimate rodeo. A day spent wrestling with them tells on the muscles even of the young and fit.

November 1st
Southwesterly gale raging since late last night. In the early hours of this morning it was blowing very strongly indeed. It was a relief, when daylight arrived, to see that the new byre, henhouse etc. were still intact and standing. As the day went in the wind gradually eased and, by evening, it had fallen to moderate and backed slightly. Cloudy all day with one or two rain showers. Usual necessary chores. No service.
Went to look for Miranda but there were no sheep over the usual area because Angus Mackenzie was prowling about Rhu and Dunbhan with two dogs.

A backing wind changes direction in an anti-clockwise fashion; a veering wind, of course, moves in the opposite way. Whether the wind backs or veers matters a good deal in the type of weather to follow.

No doubt it is unnecessary to tell the reader that this was a Sunday, hence 'No service'. God knows, no other kind of service could have been expected.

November 15th
Wind calm at first but light Southerly in the evening. Touch of frost in the morning. Sunny and cold during the day. Necessary chores and gave Miranda her snack. No service. Jessie visiting in Maclachlan's at night.

November 30th
Wind Easterly light to calm. Forenoon sunny. Afternoon cloudy. Feeds, peats and odd jobs. Raining at night.

December 1st
Wind Westerly fresh. A few sunny intervals, and wintry showers. Usual necessary chores and a few small odd jobs. Papers and magazines from Alasdair.

December 15th
Wind Southwesterly moderate. Overcast and mild, with hill fog and
showers, some very heavy. Usual chores. Papers from Alasdair. Hector
called in the afternoon with the cattle subsidy money—£118.15/-, most
welcome.

Hector would receive the cattle subsidy payment in his capacity
as township clerk. I had forgotten to mention this payment when
I spoke of cattle raising. I do not feel, however, that a hundred-
odd pounds a year for raising seven cows on a boggy West
Highland croft constitutes much of an addition to life's pleasures
nor that my omitting to note the sum involved a very dreadful
crime.

December 31
Wind Easterly light at first becoming variable in the afternoon.
Freezing all day. Mainly sunny. Dusting of snow on hills roundabout.
Mail van at 10.30 p.m. with James Macpherson driving!
    The year just ended was a good one in every way for ourselves. We
enjoyed good health and many other blessings.

THE END OF AN ERA, 1973

IN MARCH 1973 my mother died, stopped in her tracks late one evening by a massive cerebral thrombosis; an event I had long dreaded was hard upon me. Summoned by telegram from our various jobs and geographies we three Maclean brothers straggled home one by one. I arrived in my turn to find Father in an alarming state of grief and shock. Scarcely could he get speech out for the continuous sobbing that racked him. His great concern, it seemed, was to smooth over old wounds, to keep the family together as much as possible. We were to present a united front to loss, as though by doing so we could defy it or could forestall a Diaspora that had long since taken place.

'You and I have had our difficulties in the past,' were his first coherent words to me. 'I think we won't have any more of that.'

'Oh, all right,' I assured him, politely embarrassed, as always, by an emotional challenge.

A little later he said, 'You don't react as we do. You don't show anything. But I think maybe you feel it more than any of us.' He looked at me doubtfully through his tears, with a look I knew too well already, a look that was a strange mixture: part sadness, part pleading, part incomprehension; all this with, it might be, a trace of resentment thrown in; all. For a moment it was like old times.

Later still he told me, 'You were always her favourite, you know. Maybe I shouldn't say that but you were.' My siblings were present. 'Oh, well—,' I said.

'You'll want to see her,' he remarked next. It was a statement. I had not, in fact, intended to view Mother's corpse and prepared a defence: 'Not for me. I prefer to remember her as she was.' Yet perhaps that was a cliché after all, born of a desire to be different or born of a feeling that that would be the more modern, the more sophisticated reaction. Tradition, I now thought, might be the truer guide here—if this impression of being towed along irresistibly by events were indeed tradition, as I took it to be. Following it, at any rate, would produce the only course likely to be understood or likely to avoid hurt. I accompanied Father dutifully into the bedroom.

He folded back the cover. I kissed Mother's brow, aware that a gesture of some kind was expected of me, aware that I owed such a gesture to myself even, if I were not to be set down as utterly inhuman. I felt nothing. I noticed only—and hated myself for noticing—the absurd accoutrements of death: the frilled white mob cap that was evidently part of her shroud and from underneath which straying wisps of hair attempted even yet to furnish some semblance of real life; the cotton wool that plugged the nostrils; the ludicrously huge family bible bulking out the sheeted body, making it look for all the world as if we were to bury her with a box on her breast.

Father nuzzled Mother's cheek with the back of his hand, rubbing the knuckles up and down. 'Eh—eh—eh,' he sobbed. I could think of nothing to say that would not be offensive to him or to myself. When I judged that a sufficiently decent time had elapsed I edged towards the door.

With two days still to go to the funeral Father's grief began to give us cause for serious concern. At last my sister quietened him by reminding him of a long-ago tragedy in the old hamlet of Plocaig, where a mother's sorrow for her dead daughter, a sorrow that had similarly threatened to break bounds, was reproved by a neighbour. The burden of the reproof had been that such a degree of emotion would disturb the spirit of the dead child, chaining it to the immediate vicinity rather than allowing it to depart in peace.

I was not present when my sister drew this possible parallel nor did she tell me about it. It was Father himself who relayed her remarks to me. 'I had to stop crying then,' he said. 'That put the wind up me.'

From that point on his outward demeanour became calm. Of course he did not really stop crying nor was he ever to stop, I believe, till Death came along and hushed all his noise. It was merely that his sobs turned inwards and those were exactly the sort, I felt, to echo the more loudly in Mother's ears, if so be she had any hearing left for our kind of sounds.

After the ritual at the graveside groups of people began to drift away. I left the cemetery and walked up the slope to the roadside where the mourners' cars were parked. Father stopped halfway to accept someone or other's condolences. I watched from beside our car as the person, whoever it was, said his little piece and moved off. Father stood there alone, where the conversation had left him, for a moment so utterly bewildered and disorientated that I thought I should have to go and retrieve him. Overnight, it seemed, he had shrivelled. I saw, with a sudden piercing clarity, a small, bent figure, huddling frailly into his coat against the March wind or against whatever wind assailed him. 'We shall soon be back here,' I told myself. 'All of us, as we are, save that one will play a different part.' I had yielded up a father to grief and received an old man in exchange. My long childhood was over; I was the father now.

There was a distribution of keepsakes. James, my elder brother, asked for and was given Mother's walking stick. 'But that's mine!' I shouted silently. 'I made it especially for her from the woods in Plocaig. She loved that stick. She used it all the time at last. It joins us. I want no other remembrance.'

What Jessie and Ian received I do not know, nor indeed if they asked for anything or wanted aught. Father, however, approached me later with Mother's trinket box in his hands. We were alone at the time. He opened the lid. A gauze-skirted ballerina unfolded herself, rising surrealistically from a pivot on the balls of her feet and pirouetting uncertainly to the tinkling strains of 'The bluebells of Scotland'. Inside the box were clippings from local newspapers relating to my maternal grandparents: the award of a prize for Highland dancing; marriage; retirement from work; death. There were also a few scraps of cheap jewellery.

'And there was your grandfather's gold watch and chain,' said Father. 'She always meant you to have that. You were named after him, of course.' He poured the chain into the palm of my hand. I could remember its outstretched length from childhood, the little heart of polished amber that dangled from it and that had, I now saw with the keenness of the occasion, a tiny chip out of one side. 'I've got the watch upstairs,' Father added. 'It doesn't go. But if you leave it with me I'll have a look at it by and by.'

'No rush,' I said.

I came across the watch long afterwards, in the middle of a small box of screws and wheels that were slowly coalescing around it in the damp Sanna air. I broke it out like a kernel. Father hadn't looked at it. At least, you could hear nothing when you held it to your ear. Perhaps it was ticking once a century, slowly releasing its poison into the atmosphere. I stuck it in my pocket anyway. I was a poet, I reminded myself; I was the possessor of a non-transferable immunity.

There had been one more item, it seemed, among Mother's treasures, an item which Father now told me about. Some years previously he had had to go into hospital for an operation. The matter turned out not to be very serious but while still a patient and either feeling that his illness was worse than he knew about or simply covering himself against all eventualities he had written Mother a letter. In it he had expressed his appreciation of their life together. This letter—surprised to find it still in existence, deeply moved that it had been kept—he recovered from Mother's effects after her death.

Told the story of that letter at an earlier stage in my life I might well have reacted cynically or irritatedly. 'Little enough to show,' I might have grumbled, 'for those long years of devotion and drudgery. One bloody letter.'

I thought it possible—just possible—that I was a little wiser now. Love takes people in different ways, some with a desperate and daily muteness, and the most expensive of its gifts are often the least tangible. A lifetime of marriage, of struggle and poverty and child-bearing and child-rearing, is not a matter to be dismissed out of hand nor subjected overmuch to analysis and comment by outsiders. Still there is mystery. Who was I to say what storms of passion had not rocked that bed, what murmurs of love had not been transferred from tongue to ear and round the back of the brain and home again, murmurs swelling there, growing in power and confidence where none might question their lack of orotundity? Love and death are great teachers both and as for which is the better master we shall have to wait and see. Meanwhile there was the letter; a chalked blackboard had been set up in front of me if I cared to read the message.

Summoned once more in August I reached home to find my elder brother before me. He met me at the garden gate, hand outstretched in greeting. 'Well, Alasdair,' he said. 'It's the end of an era.'

Yes, I thought, it's that all right. It was indeed the end of an era, as it had not been when, say, my grandfather died and my father took over. I wondered who among us, who in Ardnamurchan, realized the full significance of the death that had just taken place. I wondered if I realized it myself.

We buried Father from the church, rather than from the house as Mother had been buried, and we decided on an ecumenical service. It seemed a proper enough notion when mooted. Though Church of Scotland ourselves we had always gone indifferently—those of us who were churchgoers—to Free Church services when these were held in Sanna on alternate Sundays in the old days. Kilchoan Parish Church was full. As family we sat at the front with the coffin on trestles before us. Father gleamed in polished oak, a better piece of wood than he had ever had to work with in his life. His brass plate, I noticed, bespoke him as 'John' rather than the Gaelic 'Ian'. That, too, was in keeping with the occasion.

Mr X, the Free Church minister, rose to speak. And speak. And speak. He droned on and on, dwelling lengthily and lovingly on the gloomier prophets, delighting especially in Jeremiah. It was scarcely worthwhile coming into his world, to endure but a short moment in sin and misery and to creep off at last to one's eternal brimstone bath under a burden of guilt and shame as high as Everest.

I tuned out after a moment or two, returning only briefly from my contemplation of the waiting and fatherless croft to take in some more than usually inept illustration. Mr Y, our own minister, sat beside the speaker, drumming his fingers and growing—it was obvious—more impatient and more annoyed by the minute. After half an hour he could stand it no longer. 'I think, Mr X,' he interrupted, rising to his feet, 'we've had quite enough.'

Mr X, chopped off thus brutally in the middle of a sentence and black in the face with fury, strode off down the aisle, his gown billowing out behind him like a dark cloud. His departing footsteps echoed throughout the building till the slam of the heavy oak door stilled them. Mr Y continued the service, somewhat more positively. The congregation, half scandalized and half delighted, settled down again on their benches to compose their stories for the benefit of those unlucky enough to be absent.

'What a lot of tosh it all is,' said my younger brother to me afterwards. 'Save for parents or the like who would go through with it?' Or save for oneself, he might have added.

I was sorry for Father's sake, of course. The interruption to his service would have shocked him profoundly. Contretemps aside, however, funerals seemed to me no bad thing; an ordeal perhaps but an ordeal that one was the stronger for later. Burials had evolved, I surmised, less to dispose of the dead in a hygienic and orderly fashion than to comfort the living. Observance of the ritual mattered more than the feelings of the participants. You carried out Routine A and, almost automatically, you achieved Result B. That is what rituals are for.

We returned home and had tea. The house already had a transit camp feel to it. My brother read the will. It was short and to the point, with no surprises; a touching effort to see that everyone got at least something. Father had distributed his few goods as equitably as he could, according to need where the croft and the little bit of money were concerned, according to taste in respect of what was left. I inherited his shelf-full of books, his well-thumbed library that he had been so proud of.

In the afternoon I went for a walk alone, taking the path by the side of the croft, directing my steps towards the river and the original croft boundary. I passed the lines of rotting posts, never worth pulling out and re-using, that marked successive retrenchments where Father had pulled back his fences year after year till cultivation had shrunk to a square in front of the house. 'It's the sheep to blame,' he had always said. 'They're getting in down there where they can't be seen from our windows. I can't keep them out. Better a small croft adequately protected than a bigger one half-eaten.'

But it was old age that troubled him more than the sheep. It was an obeisance in the muscles, a half-turning to meet the better reaper who was advancing towards him over the fields.

I carried on across the brook, across those same stepping stones that had been insufficient to keep Father dry on 31 October 1970, as he recorded in the journal entry I was later to edit. There before me was the old hamlet of Plocaig, one of the many ghost townships of Ardnamurchan, the ruined houses procryptic now, subsumed by their background. This had been a favourite walk of Father's. How eerie it was, how wonderful, to think that never again would he come this way, or come to be seen and touched, whatever other senses he might appeal to. I could not master the strangeness of it.

My brothers packed their bags to return to their new lives and their new loves. I was to stay on for a while, being a free agent. I was to harvest the croft for my sister.

'Don't grieve for me,' Father had said when he was carried from the house on a stretcher, after his first coronary and before his last one. 'I'll be with your mother.'

My younger brother had been greatly struck by this anecdote almost in spite of himself. 'Do you think there's an after-life?' he asked me now.

I gave the question the serious consideration it deserved. 'Who knows?' I said eventually.

'I don't believe it,' my brother continued. 'Never have done. It's a fairy-story. Yet I like to picture them meeting again. Up there, you know. They've earned that if anybody ever earned it. I like to think of flower-strewn meadows, all that stuff. Father a young man once more, running across the grass. Mother waiting for him. What do you think they would say? How would they greet one another?'

I thought of Mother, her exclamation 'My!' when anything impressed her and how much had impressed her despite her unimpressive surroundings. I could not at first get words past the sob in my throat. 'O that's easy,' I replied when at last I could contort my voice into something resembling normality. 'He wouldn't say anything at all. She'd just say, "My! Ian! You weren't long!"'

> Fear no more the heat o' th' sun,
> Nor the furious winter's rages;
> Thou thy worldly task hast done,
> Home art gone and ta'en thy wages.

ALASDAIR'S JOURNAL

[General view of Sanna]

ALASDAIR'S JOURNAL, 1979–1980

Moreover, I, on my side, require of every writer, first or last, a
simple and sincere account of his own life, and not merely what he
has heard of other men's lives; some such account as he would
send to his kindred from a distant land; for if he has lived sincerely,
it must have been in a distant land to me.

Thoreau: *Walden*

September 20th

A cold bright morning, followed by a fine winter's day—good
walking weather. The wind was northwest but with rather more
of the north than the west in it. I pictured it crossing long miles of
the high Atlantic, thick with drifting ice, sucking up coldness as it
came. I felt its bite both indoors and out.

I woke at eight, listened to the news headlines and after the
essential cup of tea headed for the shore and my constitutional. I
walked from one end of our beach to the other. That would be
about a mile, I suppose, in a straight line, though I suffered so
many fits and starts and undertook such a number of lurches and
lounges and detours that I believe I covered three or four times
that distance. There was so much of interest to see, that was the
trouble. It is hard work being a walker of beaches.

I did not lack for company on my travels. Boot, my sister's
collie, spotted me leaving the house and came with me. He had
been playing in her garden, fifty yards down the hillside from my
own. I had decidedly mixed feelings about my unlooked-for
escort. The truth is that I regard a dog as an encumbrance when I
go for a walk, a responsibility tugging at the edge of my mind,
pulling my attention towards it when I had rather devote all of
my faculties to my own concerns.

It does not help that Boot, though entirely amiable towards all
creatures except field mice and rabbits, is also entirely untrained
and not particularly obedient. In a crofting township, even a

decayed one such as this, you cannot have anarchic spirits like Boot hurtling about the countryside unsupervised. There are still sheep and cattle here and they are easily panicked, with possible dire consequences. Sheep, especially, tend to flee instinctively at the mere approach of a dog, regardless of its intentions, and our Sanna sheep have been so harassed by trippers' dogs that they would rush off at a glimpse of a chihuahua. So an eye has to be kept on Boot, an eye that cannot really be spared by someone with the grand parades of nature and his own mind to watch (with wildlife, you might say, clamouring for notice both before and within).

After which aggrandizement it is suitably chastening to report that I saw little exceptional or recordable on my walk; little, I mean, outwith the ordinarily miraculous sights of a northern beach. Nor do I remember thinking any great thoughts. A handful of small waders flushed up once from some distance ahead, this during one of Boot's mad dashes. They wheeled away in a wide arc over the sea, then landed again behind me. So unified were they in their movements that they resembled a single organism.

I think they were ringed plover. I think my other sighting, the solitary waterfowl that steamed off seaward as I approached the estuary, was a mallard drake.

But 'think' is not quite good enough. You cannot inflict 'think' on your readership too often, not even in a journal with as few scientific pretensions as this one. You may pass off one or two 'thinks' per half a dozen entries as a nice hesitancy, appropriately modest in the face of nature's huge storm of options. More than that and you are in trouble. Your reader says to himself, 'Here is a wilderness, yet this man who would hire out as my guide conceals his ignorance behind a hedge of qualifications.'

A reminder, therefore, to myself: I must carry my binoculars at all times, even if I only go to the stream for water. It is always when one is unprepared that ornithological or botanical history takes a giant stride forward. Descending some hill in a daydream one trips over an unforeseen object. One regains consciousness in hospital with a tragically distinct impression that one owes one's enforced leisure to the roots of a Great Peruvian Pitcher Plant, recorded only once before, by von Schlepp's expedition to the Andes in 1708.

Or driving along a riverbank road, with an importunate and

massive lorry on one's tail, one catches a glimpse of a swimming bird that might just possibly have been a Buff-breasted Chinese Water Pigeon, never previously encountered in these islands.

Too bad on Boot, then. But since he and careful observation do not mix and since I am too soft-hearted to send him home once he has joined me (I don't suppose he'd go anyway) I must learn to sneak off without him. That will be good stalking practice.

I spent the rest of the day writing; chiefly I began my main work of editing Father's journals, of making a representative selection from them for publication. Now I bring my own journal up to date before going to bed. I intend this to be my daily routine.

I am unused to writing at such length, however. I can see that it is going to be a question of whether I can complete the day's stint prior to dislocating my jaw by yawning. This kind of work represents a whole new world to me. When you write poetry you can afford to be prodigal with your day's supply of creative energy. Or your week's supply or your month's supply. It does not matter as long as you produce some verse. Indeed, you would achieve nothing by trickling out your quota; only lavish bursts, only a pouring forth of all you have, produce a high enough voltage for the transformation to take place, for the water to be turned into wine. A worthwhile quatrain, a phrase or two even, and you can be reasonably satisfied. One bright flash and the day's work may well be over.

When you write extended prose, on the other hand, you have to husband your resources. It is the difference, I suppose, between a sprint and a marathon.

Little else happened today of even trivial note. Only once, when I raised my head from the window table where I sat, with its ocean view, I saw a ship going past, a small coaster heading south. So heavily laden was she that she could scarcely have had a foot of freeboard. When she dipped in the troughs her low-lying main deck disappeared altogether from my sight, leaving her fore and aft superstructures to stand up like two islands in the waves.

I wonder where she was making for? It is midnight now as I write these words. Eight bells. If she is still at sea the watch will be changing. The helmsman will be passing the course to be steered to his opposite number, his relief; the crossing officers will be exchanging navigational snippets. The lucky pair will head below, to mugs of tea and warm bunks; the newcomers will remain, one straining to read a dimly-lit compass, one peering anxiously into the rushing dark for lights.

Small centres of human activity moving through the night while I sit here writing! In my mind a sense of wonder mingles with a strange sadness when I think of it. I imagine myself out there, as I once was. To be alone on a ship's bridge at night, forging through blackness, is to experience almost at knifepoint the mysteriousness and overwhelmingness of the universe.

I came back here yesterday, to this hamlet of Sanna in Ardnamurchan, to write a book about the place. I pass for someone who comes from here, though I do not quite in the strict sense of birthplace (as I have been reminded once or twice in the past when I have taken it upon myself to make a few pertinent remarks). I am high-yaller trying to pass as white, trying indeed to pass as a member of the kind of organization of Mayflower-lineage that one gets in the United States—the Daughters of the American Revolution perhaps. Such is the degree of exclusiveness attached here to local birth. It is the Return of the Near-Native.

I have been lent this cottage for the winter. It is late September now and I have scraped together enough of funds to see me through to March or April, with careful husbanding. My house is situated on the hillside above our old family home, now inherited and occupied by my sister. I could stay with her, of course, but I prefer not to. Writers and families, even such reduced families as mine, do not mix, and I speak as one of the world's leading authorities on the subject.

Besides that, the isolation and—with luck—the objectivity of my present residence should better suit my task as writer. And perhaps the irony will, too, this house being a former croft cottage now owned as a holiday home by someone with even less claim to be a native than I have.

September 23rd

I saw a wren today as I walked the shoreline. Or rather I did not quite see it but glimpsed it, creeping among the rocks. What a skulking slithering side-on creature this bird is! I was strongly tempted to make the old sign of avoidance. The wren is the true bird of ill-omen and not your obvious childish raven. One can readily understand why they held wren hunts in the experienced

Middle Ages, why whole villages abandoned themselves to sticks and cries and madness. You may find a wren in your tame garden but that is only because it was there first. Wrens have undomestic souls.

I can hardly remember seeing the front of a wren. All one ever glimpses, as a rule, is that broken-off tail, upturned at a sharp right angle—a signature gone awry as the writer clutched at his heart.

October 1st
Blue-violet is the coldest hue. So says the artist's colour wheel. In practice it depends on the context and perhaps on the viewer's mood as well. So I thought this morning when I sat for a while on a seaside rock to study the Atlantic. It was composed of a range of greens of almost infinite extension but with no member of the series looking more than a degree above freezing. How unfriendly it seemed! I shivered as I gazed. Yet here were no huge combers, forged in some mid-ocean armoury and hurled with implacable fury at the land. Indeed a stiff offshore breeze was blowing and the surface of the water appeared merely wrinkly. This was a closed-off sullenness, inner hostility rather than open rage, and the more convincing for it.

I marvelled that such a source should pour out so much nourishment. Yet it does, even on its margins and even for those not of its kind. Every day since my arrival in Sanna I have encountered a small flock of starlings on the beach, picking their way along the tideline, surviving the winter in their own admirable fashion. They were there again today, hard at work. Hoping not to disturb them and the tide being out I passed below but they rose in a body as I came opposite and flung out to sea on the wind, tearing over my head like a shower of big black raindrops.

There is something unnatural about wind and water working against one another as they did on our beach today. You sense a different situation, a tension in the air, as soon as your foot hits the sand. You feel it instinctively before you realize what is causing it. Then you notice the sea, with the incoming waves being chopped off at the base and blown backwards, the whole bay stretched out stiffly and angrily before you, like a great cat being stroked the wrong way.

Consonance is all, no doubt. Or perhaps it is only that we see

nature through a film of art and when we say that something is
unnatural we mean no more than that it is inartistic.

October 8th
It is two o'clock in the morning and I feel very tired. But a point of
terminology nags at me and I may not rest till I have said
something about it.

I have been describing this record of mine, I notice, as a journal,
not a diary. What is the difference?

I think that a diary functions at a lower level. It represents—or
is thought to represent—a lesser species of literature. It is more
gossipy and slapdash, more concerned with jottings, more practical, less obviously intended for other eyes. So we speak of
Pepys' Diaries but of Dorothy Wordsworth's Journals and mean,
I believe, to denigrate Pepys a little when we make the distinction. Yet who would exchange the former for the latter? Not I, at
any rate, though I am fond of both.

I suspect that nowadays at least, there is an element of snob-
bishness involved in the journal–diary antithesis. Schoolgirls,
archetypally, keep diaries; poets, therefore, must write journals.
(It is true that Yeats wrote a *diary* but true also that he took the
precaution of dignifying it with a fairly resounding title:
'Estrangment'.)

My father, old seaman, was unbothered by such nuances and
called his daily notes a 'log'. I shall stick to journal.

October 9th
As dusk fell today and for a purpose that is neither here nor there,
I climbed the hillside to the east of my house, walking upwards
along the rim of the accompanying hollow. In the deepest,
steepest part of this depression a poor sheep was trapped among
brambles, fettered as with brass by half a dozen stout stems.

It was easy to see how it came to be caught. It had been tempted
into danger through desire of the very bush that held it. Sheep are
fond of bramble leaves, seeming not all incommoded by the
prickles. A few such leaves lingered here from summer, somehow keeping their colour and, I suppose, their food value; bright
spots of energy in a sterile wilderness.

I ventured gingerly down on a rescue mission, edging out,
when I reached the bottom, on to a heaving platform of peat,
mixed in with tins, bottles, crockery, old bedsteads, God knows

what all; the hollow having been in long-ago times a rubbish dump for the nearby houses. It was in the middle of this debris that the brambles grew.

The sheep panicked as I approached, plunging desperately against its bonds. All that happened was that its momentum, unable to achieve a forward release, swung it to the side, entangling it more elaborately still. The brambles, I soon discovered, were truly vicious. They had become embedded in the deepest layer of fleece, in where, close to the body, the wool is almost felted. On one side, several stems had been so braided by the struggle as to form a rope as thick as a man's wrist. A cage would have been no more secure.

Unforgivably, I did not have my pocket knife. Between my ill-preparedness and the creature's frantic bounds I had a job to free it. When at last I succeeded it was at the cost of a pound or two of wool to the prisoner and ten thousand scratches to me.

The sheep turned out to be one of the spring lambs, not yet fully grown and never, I think, intended to be. A runt and in poor condition at that. It will do well to survive the winter, yet if it does is likely to be culled next spring for its pains.

Sufficient unto the day—. When I released it, it trotted up the opposite bank, not much afraid now, and began to eat furiously. I was very pleased.

That sheep was doubly lucky, lucky that I came along (the hollow being a place that I visit only at irregular—and extended—intervals) and lucky to have escaped the attentions of the crows and the blackbacks. These birds quarter our countryside indefatigably and are ever vigilant. Nor are they always so nice as to wait for death to blunt the edge of their butchery. A trapped sheep, its eyes ripe for the plucking, is treasure trove to them, with two easy titbits for consolation while they wait for the struggles to subside.

Foolish, no doubt, to regret this. Gulls and crows must eat as well as sheep and have the same hard winter to get through. Come spring I should miss the crow's purposeful straight lines across the sky and the gull's free wheel, were they no longer available to me. I should miss those distinctive voices.

Yet one does regret it. Against the crows and gulls of the world we operate a hierarchy of sentiment. Mammals in general go to the top; snakes and sharks are at the bottom with the winged scavengers not far above them. In part this is obviously an evolutionary ladder. The more primitive the creature the more it is likely to evoke disgust, incomprehension and fear. It is not totally biased against predators, however, not even predators on man. We have taken the tiger, for instance, into our hearts and homes through the likes of Tigger and Tiger Tim. Yet when these characters were first making their appearance and achieving great heights of popularity, man-eating tigers were causing untold misery in the Kumaon.

So the matter, I think, is more complex than simple evolution. We tend to sentimentalize those creatures that we have added to our families by adoption, such as horses and dogs, or those we habitually anthropomorphize because they are cute and cuddly, such as certain bears (koalas and pandas) and certain birds (robins). When we do accept a genuinely savage animal into our totem we are likely to emasculate it in the process. So Eeyore is a reasonable approximation of a donkey but Tigger bears little resemblance to a real tiger.

Any creature that we feel to be touched by the infernal, any that survives in our despite, these we hate and fear.

And the fear that we have of certain animals, is it conditioned or innate? Would we thrill with terror when a Great White shark came along if we had not heard so many tales and seen so many films? I think we would. There is the awesome power and menace of its appearance for one thing. But more than that, I suspect that there is a something in our fear of sharks harking back to the deeps of time, perhaps all the way back to the sea itself.

I saw a memorable shark one day as I fished from a rock in Plocaig. I had not noticed its approach and first became aware of it as a massive presence, a great dark shadow in the water just below me. My bowels recognized it before I did. The shock to some primitive nerve was piercing.

October 12th
For the good of soul and lungs I did some hillwalking today. I climbed the ridge that cuts off Sanna from the larger world and went as far beyond the crest as would give me a view of the other side.

Of the climb I have little to report. I saw nothing that lived except, high up, a handful of sodden sheep, sticking patiently to their appointed task.

It was wet and windy on the ridge, with a cold persistent drizzle slanting in off the Atlantic at my back. Going a few yards downhill on the Achnaha side, however, I found tolerable lee in front of an outcrop and there I perched for an hour, gazing across the land.

There was nothing to see. Or, rather, there was infinity but not such a version of it as I felt I could subdue on that particular occasion. Over the wide waste of our peninsula, as far as my eyes could carry me, no beast walked or bird flew. If there were people left in Achnaha, under my feet, they kept to their firesides.

I had become cramped and chilled and was on the point of retracing my steps when I became aware of movement. Far below and to my right two cars were coming into view, creeping along the ribbon of road, heading towards Sanna.

Nothing unusual in that, of course. The place attracts a tripper or two, even on an inclement day in mid-winter. But I was struck by the travelling procedure adopted by the drivers. Though they were not, as I later ascertained, together, yet for all of their journey that I could see, and for a good deal more of it than that I would have wagered, they kept within a car length of one another.

This is a phenomenon I have often noticed and puzzled over. Indeed it is very puzzling to me whose instinct, whether at the wheel or afoot, is entirely the opposite. What prompts such a strange affinity? Why should two drivers who were in charge of, quite possibly, the only vehicles that day on the road in the whole long length of Ardnamurchan, permit—insist on—such nose-to-tail behaviour?

I have studied this problem a little. It is one of several important fields in which I am, as far as I know—I take a melancholy pride in it—the sole investigator. For a long time I favoured a solution involving magnetism—the cars were, quite simply, attracted to each other. (In a purely metallic way, I hasten to add. It is true that cars are becoming more and more intelligent but we have as yet—God preserve us!—no reason to suspect any other kind of attraction.) The attraction was cancelled out only at very close range by some remnant of self-protection on the part of the drivers.

This was an interesting theory in that it helped to explain one or two lesser puzzles—for example, motorway madness. The excitement that motorways engender in their devotees removes the remnant of caution. And before they all know where they are—or where they are going to—as many as a hundred cars are firmly welded together in a long unwavering line.

(It might, indeed, be simpler to build them that way in the first place. Then with the addition of a few amenities such as corridors, restaurants, lavatories—plus tracks to engage the wheels of the vehicles and keep apart opposing directions of travel—one would have a very pleasant and civilized mode of transport.)

My magnetism theory, unfortunately, left me ultimately dissatisfied. It seemed to premise that the cars were largely in control of the drivers rather than vice versa and no driver I spoke to agreed with this.

I went on to fancy, briefly, that the affinity was a reaction to wilderness on the part of the cars. I imagined two of them closing ranks against the forces of nature. In my mind I heard a tinny voice saying, 'We machines must stick together, old boy,'—a sentiment that was occasionally interpreted a shade too literally.

This idea, however, ignored the fact that the affinity operated in town as well as country. Currently I am considering the notion that the attraction is after all between drivers—quite simply, blood calls to blood.

I came down from my mountain cold and wet, made a pot of tea and sat by the fire in good heart to drink it. The high sheep were still grazing when I passed them for the second time and I saw one butt another quite fiercely away from its own little patch of ground. Long live the territorial imperative!

October 13th
I wrote here a week or two ago of the effect of being on watch on a ship's bridge at night, of the extreme sense of isolation produced. Something told me once by a neighbour in Sanna bears on that entry. I shall call the neighbour concerned 'Norman' and he is, like me, a former seaman.

It seems that in the days of the windjammers crew members sometimes played a game called 'Jack all alone'—only 'game', as we shall see, is something of a misnomer. One player, only, took part at a time. He went forward into the bows of the ship, at night, climbed out on to the bowsprit and lay there at full length, on his back, looking upwards. He secured himself against falling as best he might, for danger was not the point of the game, or at least not danger in the immediate and direct sense. What the player waited for was for the great rush of wind and water, the tearing sky overhead, to have their inevitable effect on him, to crush him into an unendurable awareness of his own smallness and loneliness. The 'winner', of course, was he who hung on longest.

Norman played once, though in a modern steamship, which naturally lacked a bowsprit and was not wind-driven. He had to content himself with lying down on the deck, as far forward as he could get. The effect would be much less potent, obviously, but it was still potent enough to disturb him considerably. He withdrew from play after a few minutes.

I think that in the days of sail, when the silence of the sea was not broken by the alien throb of engines but was underlined, rather, by the creak of timber and cordage and the onward hiss of the forefoot, such a game might have been quite terrifying. It would have been so, at any rate, to an imaginative man, and what seaman lacked that quality at a time when ships were not mere floating machines but personifications, as individual as the girls who waited on the quaysides and as much loved or hated?

I have not played 'Jack all alone', though I should like to try. One would get a little of the same sensation, I fancy, from walking solitary through the corridors of a large hospital late at night. A job I had once entailed just that. The seeming miles of utter emptiness that were yet well-lit, warm and humming gently with unseen machinery, produced a powerful effect on me. It was as though one had stepped aboard some huge abandoned spaceship, some Mary Celeste of the galaxies.

October 28th

The possession of creative talent, the history of art reminds us, is no sure barrier against the inroads of vanity. Nevertheless, there seems to me to be a chance at least that the trained and seriously-intentioned artist, with the whole weight of tradition in his particular discipline behind him, will be rendered aware of his lack of originality, even if his public and his critics have failed to grasp this. There is a chance that when even merited praise comes his way he will temper his thought and his utterance accordingly. Should conceit ever take hold of him he may yet be recalled to a more modest hope in regard to his eventual stature when he remembers other artists who were unshakeably convinced of their own greatness but who failed utterly to produce any de-monstration of it that posterity would accept.

If conviction does not force a becoming reticence on him, that is to say, fear may bring him to heel. And better a politic modesty than none at all.

Popular entertainers lack even this degree of protection. The history of football is no part of the training of a professional footballer and if the Beatles were at all aware of Schubert as they played and sang it was only because a treasonable clerk or two had insisted on the comparison. Such people are likely to mistake a moment in history for the totality of human endeavour. They go to work unhumbled and therefore vulnerable. Tell them that they are giants and they will believe you, for they have not been to the museum where the bones are kept.

(It is a pity, I often think, that mass entertainment is so hugely trivial. One is led to feel guilty about studying it, and that is really too bad when its sociology is so unfailingly rich in interest.)

The other day, on television, I watched a certain well-known athlete win a ten-thousand-metre race by a matter of a yard or two. For as long as the cameras lingered on him afterwards, which was a long two or three minutes, he urged the spectators first of all to applaud him and finally to put more effort into it.

Perhaps he went on conducting this hymn to himself after the lens had departed. I feel that he may have done so. I was embarrassed. As so often when I watch television, as one used to see children do in old-style infra-red photographs taken in cine-mas, I found myself putting my hand over my eyes to blot out something painful. The following morning my athlete was re-ported in the newspapers as having said after the race—his first success for some time—'The King is back!'

About the same time, again on television, I watched a player score in a football match. His immediate reaction, a reaction that becomes increasingly common, was to seek the adulation of his team's supporters. The congratulations of his fellows, effusive though these were, were not enough for him. Indeed he shook off their intended hugs with some roughness. He was after a headier wine. He ran straight to that part of the field where he might best focus the enthusiasm of the fans. With raised arms he stood before them and on the packed terraces they mirrored in their thousands his solitary gesture. The camera pulled back beautifully and one witnessed the scene in all its fullness and richness: the tiny god central among his serried worshippers.

Of course adulation encourages response. It does so among men, let alone among present-day gods (after all, a later and lesser order of creation). If you offer a god that sort of fare he will naturally welcome it and in time, even, come petulantly to expect it. He cannot do otherwise for his continued life as a god depends on it, just as his place in the pantheon depends on the amount of it and the quality of it. Worship is both the source of his strength and the only proof that he is a god.

We have trained our gods to be like that. Christianity swept away the old order of gods who really were superior, who in their wildness and remoteness found their own deeds sufficient. These were gods whom one could imagine pre-dating the period of their worship and continuing to exist when it had ceased. They might even be indifferent to it. What came in their stead was the domesticated deity who had been forced into a dangerous amount of reciprocity with his followers. Unconditional worship was replaced by conditional. *We would have a sign!* 'If you produce miracles to order', a god is told now, 'we will adore you as no other god has been adored. But if you fail us you shall be thrown down with a suddenness and a brutality that will destroy you.'

We have reached the era of the god-human who, of course, cannot respond in a truly god-like fashion, or can do so only occasionally and luckily. And we have done with surrogates for those gods who have gone fallow, surrogates who could be sacrificed in their place. If we set up a false god now, one who will not serve us truly, we make a real sacrifice of him. But after all, why not, I suppose, when gods have become so plentiful and so easily manufactured?

November 8th
Today is a Fast Day in the Parish. That does not mean a day devoted to fasting, as an outsider might innocently imagine. A Fast Day is a sort of buckshee Sunday, a day with all the rules and regulations pertaining to Sunday save that it lacks a church service. To thoroughgoing believers, deprived of the chance to congregate for a good gossip or a great sucking of peppermints or a counting of heads and a labelling of them or a flaunting of new

bonnets, the Sunday atmosphere without the churchgoing must be like the work without the wages.

Fast Days are sprinkled lightly among our seasons, at a rate of perhaps two or three a year, but upon what principle they are established I have never been able to determine, nor can I ascertain how one knows them to be what they are.

One can always speculate, of course. It may be that a specially-endowed parishioner awakes on a given morning with a Fast Day feeling about him. He sees his room whiten into certainty and murmurs to himself, 'Yes, this is a Fast Day all right.' And he rises and goes out to spread the word.

Mind you, anyone can tell what day of the week it is in the normal run of things. That is something you feel in your bones. There are days, for instance, when you know as soon as you open your eyes that it is a Saturday, whatever the calendar may say to the contrary, and you govern your actions accordingly. At least, you do if you are wise enough and reverent enough. I often feel a Saturday about me, especially on a Monday. But I have never felt it to be a Fast Day. That must take an extra degree of sensitivity.

Or it may be that the person who nominates the day as a Fast Day achieves his knowledge in a more direct fashion. It may be that he regains consciousness of a morning to find God perched on the end of his bed, tail switching impatiently, red eyes boring into him, long dirty nails pinching his toes awake. 'I've decided that today is to be a Fast Day in Ardnamurchan,' says God hoarsely. 'Tell the rest.' And vanishes backwards through the bedroom wall, leaving only an acrid hairy stench that clings to the blankets for weeks afterwards and a white drift of plaster on the carpet, like a hard residue of fact.

When my parents were alive it was easy. 'It's a Fast Day today,' my mother would announce at breakfast. 'How do you know?' I would ask. And I would consult the calendar. *Ferry Stores, Kilchoan*, it would say. *Telephone 201. Cash Terms Only. Goods Delivered As Required.* Above this legend would be a coloured photograph of two puppies sticking out of a pair of wellington boots or a kitten playing with a ball of wool. And it would be a Tuesday or a Friday or a Bank Holiday in Ballybunnion but devil a bit of a Fast Day that I could see.

'You won't be able to do anything outside,' Mother would add. Meaning that I would have to Sunday it from dawn to dusk and not be able to hammer nails or saw wood or whistle or scuff my feet or any of the other things forbidden out of doors on a Highland Sabbath, where one's neighbours might see and hear.

Mother was always right. It was always a Fast Day when she said it was. But how she knew I never learned. She died and took that item of knowledge with her, among items of more moment.

I blunder now among Fast Days as it were among mines. They explode under my feet. At least, some of them do, though I am sure that others must slip by unnoticed but for that faint disturbance at the back of the skull that we all suffer from occasionally, that vague, unattributable malaise that makes us look down to see if we have different-coloured socks on.

Today was one that did not slip by. I was sitting on the foreshore in the quiet of the morning, next to the old track that leads down from Achosnich, when I was pounced upon by Friend Jonathan, one of our local lay preachers, come down from that hamlet for the day to round up his little flock in Sanna for a prayer meeting in someone's house.

There will be bruised knees and stiff joints in the township tonight. It is all in the kneeling with these people. God is summoned to attend by a series of creaks and groans that must be worth a penny a share to the embrocation makers.

Friend Jonathan is a Fundamentalist but none of your common seekers after texts, your village chapter and verse men, eking out the dregs of Gaelic culture in the pews and pulpits of the militant west, searching the Hebrews for pertinence like an ape searching for fleas. He has been given instruction in the colleges of the persuasion in the American South, where they worship not God but the bible. So he is doubly armoured, clad all in shining. Argument bounces off him like ping pong balls off a rhinoceros. Blows themselves would have no effect on him. I could take him and trip him and work his head up and down on the grass till there were post-holes all around us. It would be no great matter. He would rise and shake the dirt off and be as impregnably a dolt as if nor reason nor force had been invented, nor Greek nor Goth bestrode the earth.

We met on the sandy turf; good footing there for a struggle. He was the hammer, I the tongs and the flash and fire of our encounter was visible across the bay in Portairk, where they took it to be autumn lightning and unplugged the television sets. I was sitting on a rock with a scrap of paper in one hand, a lump of charcoal in the other and the surly, curly bay before me. I was graving an image when he came up behind me.

'Good morning to you, Friend Alasdair,' said he. 'You're back.'

'And forward,' said I.

'Today is ordained a Fast Day within this Parish,' said he.

'Fast or slow,' said I, 'it will catch up with us all about midnight. And you can run as you will, Friend Jonathan.'

'God is not mocked,' said he. 'He sitteth in a high place, a quiverful of judgements ever at His side, all primed and smoking like thunderbolts.'

'Poets are exempt,' said I. 'We being in the same line of business as Himself. Poets and children and the disturbed of mind or heart.'

'Then I must leave it to yourself,' said he, 'under how many counts you qualify.'

'I come under the one count only,' said I. 'The Count of Monte Cristo.'

'I say to you a second time, God is not mocked,' said he. 'Have I not seen them in a vision, the poor fools of the Apocalypse, men and women and babes in arms, dragged to the lip of the furnace, their sins puddling about their feet? What! You do not know the smell of brimstone, Friend Alasdair. I tell you even at five hundred paces from the pit the lining of the nostrils peels and blanches. There is a sal volatile to wake the dead!'

'It is not the dead who need awakening,' said I. 'They rouse all too easily. He would be a benefactor who could put them in their place. And I remember the smell of brimstone very well. They dosed us with it in the madhouse to keep us from the female patients. A lively odour, certainly. But as to whether they fed it to the females also, that I could not say.'

Friend Jonathan is under the impression that during my time away from here I was taken to a place of confinement, of the type of high-walled haven where they burn the mischief and the melancholy out of one with dials and wires and the sort of plugged-in catechism that leaves the nerve ends leaping and pulsing like a gaffed fish in the bottom of a boat.

Perhaps he is right. It is hard to tell.

'I pity you, Friend Alasdair,' said he now, 'that you should spend your days in idle vanity, putting a line to a line in quest of ornament. As well make daisy chains. Learnt you naught useful in the Asylum?'

'Only to jerk my knee when the Herr Professor came tapping with his little hammer,' said I. 'A conservative occupation.'

'I say to you a third time, God is not mocked,' said he. 'Nor does He let His servants be made asses of. When He grips you by the waist then will you squeak. Yea, in no tongue known to men will you utter, yet all who hear you will interpret freely. O my friend Alasdair, then will your eyeballs grow to testify the wonder of His strength until they hang upon your cheeks like pumpkins.'

'As for pumpkins,' said I, 'they held candles in my childhood. A soft light. A heavenly glow.'

'But we live in hard times now,' said he.

'No matter for that,' said I, 'so be we have the preachers to match the times. But in my house we keep to the old ways.'

'You say "we",' said he. 'But you live alone.'

'A woman comes to me at certain times,' said I. 'She wears a daisy chain. Naked else.'

I rose from my seat. 'How do you go?' asked I.

'Why, on the track,' said he. 'You know that. Ever on the track.'

'My way lies through the dunes,' said I. And we parted.

November 15th

An appalling start to the day with long curtains of rain sweeping across the hillside. One by one they passed before my window and vanished from sight. The procession continued for hours, or seemed to. Perhaps it was only, I thought at last, that the curtains were circling the hill and coming round again. At any rate, they revealed nothing when parted but glimpses of bleakness.

I did not work but sat with my nose pressed against the pane, hypnotically watching the downpour, as one does when a child. I came to feel presently like a spectator at a dada play, where the same bare set is continually revealed and covered, never advanced by so much as an ashtray at any unveiling, so that eventually pointlessness becomes point—as it always must, the human mind being so constituted; hence the impossibility of truly pointless art—and one loses not merely all sense of beginning or end but all wish for either. This is how it always was, one thinks;

this is how it ought to be. Away with actors, scenery, everything; the stage is the thing.

By mid-afternoon, however, the rain had faltered to a stop. The cloud base began to lift, the sky to brighten. What was left of the day was fine.

Since I had not been out of doors at all I went to the garden gate as the first few thistledowns of darkness began to seed the air. I went to lean and to ponder and I leaned long and pondered hard. I think I added a little to my store of riches though I should be in difficulties were I asked to state exactly where the profit lay. At least I watched night take the islands, blue becoming indigo becoming velvet black, these poor terms standing for a thousand delicacies of colour, till all labelling was lost in the general anonymity of night.

And it seemed to me as I watched that a point occurs during the coming of the dark when the spectator stands with a foot in both worlds—or in none—and is creature of neither night nor day. Briefly the spirit is freed from the bonds of convention. For a moment—a century, a nothing—we step outside time and its tyranny. All things become thinkable.

The period of release is tiny, alas; too small to utilize (though with training maybe?). I continued to lean and so became thrall to the night.

A southerly wind had got up while I dreamed and was soon whistling dolefully about my ears. I was struck afresh by the thought of how very frail our civilization is. In the middle of a great ocean we strain to navigate a chip of bark while all around the sea rages in turmoil. Huge billows rear and plunge and towering liners crash past in the darkness, their names as unknown as their crews and their destinations.

Sanna shrugs off restraint as readily as if it had been bound with paper chains. Give it half a chance—a dark night, a rising wind—and away go firesides and bookshelves and all your comforts, whirled off into limbo, while an old and easy menace comes dropping familiarly into place, welding itself to your shoulders like a hump.

November 16th
The fancies of childhood are persistent, staining upwards through the layers of the years, tenacious of essence and purpose if not always of form. Many of the creatures that I encounter

today, as I wander across the tundras and moraines of my imagination, I recognize as the offspring, several times removed it may be, of earlier creatures who rushed out at me when I was three or four. Generally—and is it 'thank God!' or 'alas!'?—they are monsters no longer. One would not know them to be in the old way of business save that a family trait carries through, a curl of the lip or a tilt of the head, and can wreak a little havoc still in a dim light or at a distance.

A few there have been, of course, whose descendants have prospered exceedingly. Their shadows crash across my path like the racing chasms of an earthquake. They hardly need to work for a living any more. It is enough that they stand between me and the sun.

When I visited the dead hamlet of Plocaig as a boy, appearing suddenly between the ruined walls and stepping on to the old drying green, I imagined that the spirits of the place froze at my approach. I could never arrive quickly enough—or slowly enough—to surprise them and I could not see them as long as they did not move for then they blended, chameleon-like, into their surroundings.

This camouflage, I reasoned, could be no more permanent than anything else under the sun. Years later, though it would be beyond my time, these spirits would become visible when their present background vanished. Nature, grieving always for her lost acres, would at last overwhelm the familiar scenes that had tethered them and sheltered them. 'What!' she would say. 'Carve a croft out of Ardnamurchan? Furrow the bedrock? Absurd! Down with these feeble walls! Efface these scratches from my fields! Long live the wilderness!'

Displaced then, the spirits would coarsen into sensation. They would fall easy prey to the hooked beaks of the ghost-hunters and like everyday vulgar white ladies and headless knights would no doubt come to enjoy the limelight.

Meanwhile, they being local still and fine, one had to startle them into visibility and I never quite could. Oh, once or twice, perhaps, I caught a glimpse of what might have been. I saw, or thought I saw, a patch of blankness pasted on the busy air. That would be some younger spirit, I surmised, ill-willed enough to taunt me with the possibility of proof or merely clumsy off the mark and caught with one heel still in the doorway.

But it was like the old game of 'Grandmother's Footsteps'. My childish honesty would not allow me to extend in my mind the glimpse I believed I had caught, or would not allow it for long enough to let me shout the magic 'Aha!' that must make me master. Half-disappointed, half-relieved, I would chalk up another failure, aware that as soon as I turned my back the game would whirr into life once more.

And now? Well, I still appear between those walls and step on to that green when the opportunity presents itself or when the fit takes me, and it takes me often enough God knows. (I am truer to the boy I was than the Man I am finds convenient.) But my expectations have a little altered with the passing years and so, therefore, have my findings. Sometimes, when mood and light and season blend in just the right proportions, I feel the numen of the place almost more strongly than I can bear. I know then of a certainty that just around the corner—of my mind at least—are people and their lives, people long gone, and if only I can get round that corner quickly enough I can be one with them.

Sometimes, most times perhaps, the place gives me nothing, or nothing special to me, nothing that John Smith might not be given. And sometimes, also, I come among those ruins as the outsider, the unenlightened one who cannot be forgiven his ignorance till he is admitted and cannot be admitted till he has rid himself of his ignorance. Plocaig then becomes a word perpetually on the tip of my tongue, a huddle of collapsed mean houses brooding, perhaps, a secret. Neither hostility nor kinship emanates from the old walls but only the hugeness of departure: a wisp of smoke on the horizon and the bandsmen packing up their instruments on the empty quay.

November 20th
I never hear of a suicide without feeling a great rush of awe and pity. Nothing except the stars at night could be more amazing or more unfathomable. Three such acts have taken place in this area, to my knowledge, and though all were before my time and all no more to me originally than some childishly-heard anecdote, I have invested each one since with something of my own death. All return to me at intervals with their unsolved and insoluble mystery.

All three were men and all chose to drown. That is a Hebridean form of self-destruction, a kind of acknowledgement or a resumption of origins. The children in Ardnamurchan chant as they play, 'Water to water, for good or ill; if the sea doesn't get you, the river will.'

Of the first of these I know nothing, save that he committed himself to the care of a deep pool in Allt Sanna, where it runs by the crofts. That was a cold death, colder than most, for that stream comes down from the Glendrian Hills and makes one's bones ache on the hottest day in midsummer. The particular pool he selected, too, is always sombre, taking its appearance from something within itself rather than from is surroundings, as lesser pools do.

Yet the purity of the act, it seems to me, had been corrupted. There were occupied houses a hundred yards away and the neighbourhood is a pleasant one. On the far side of the stream at that point a sloping field, once cultivated—cultivated then, I guess—tilts up to the west, as stubbornly green as the pool is black. Sunlight sticks to that field like glue. I could never have killed myself in such a place. I should have glanced up and my eyes would have betrayed my will.

Of the other two local suicides one was a poor madman who lived in Sanna when my grandmother was a girl. And when I say 'madman' I do not mean your licensed fool or your village natural; in the Highlands we take our madness more seriously than that. This was a strange, disturbed fellow who strode about the township stark naked but kept his thoughts veiled and so offended no one in those strict but unpriggish days. He submerged himself in the sea one morning, off a certain rocky ledge that at high water drops down sheer for ten or twelve feet below the surface. He was found when the tide went out, spreadeagled on the rock face like a climber, clinging for dear death to the seaweed.

That was a post-Reformation ending. No Highlander of old could have held on so determinedly. Lightness of spirit would have buoyed him up if lightness of body had not.

The third suicide was the one I like best, the one that best combined the time, the place and the loved one. This man was a gamekeeper who drowned himself by wading into a mountain tarn miles from anywhere, below Meall nan Conn in Glendrian. The setting he chose was a wilderness of grey stone and coarse grass, untainted by bird or beast. Before he went into the water he stuffed his game bag and his pockets with pebbles, with consonance that is to say. On the shore of the tarn—oh supreme artist!—he left a loaded rifle.

November 21st

Several years ago, when I lived and worked in the south of England, I went drinking one evening with my younger brother —a car salesman then—and two male friends of his who were airline stewards. It was very much a 'night out with the boys' occasion. Not my cup of tea. I should not normally have gone; I should not normally have been invited. Only my brother and I were at the time indulging in one of our fitful experiments in togetherness. We were attempting to prove, as we did now and then with indifferent results, that the tag 'blood is thicker than water' could have practical application, that our vastly different ways of life and beliefs could be merged successfully, at least for the brief space of an hour or two.

In the neighbourhood of Slough, then, we toured an indistinguishable series of pubs. I drank little: unable, as always, to let go; unwilling, as always, to abdicate control. The others drank a lot, exchanging many a masculine reminiscence. Innumerable past drunks were re-experienced, innumerable smart deals recounted, innumerable party jokes re-told, innumerable women re-fucked.

I was the ghost at the banquet. I could not make myself companionable, though there may have been moments during the evening when I would have sincerely liked to do so. If such moments came, they soon went. I became bored and embarrassed, depressed and saddened. And the night ended, as such nights do, in a feeling of something missed, something not quite accomplished despite feverish efforts. Amid overflowing ashtrays, the smell of beer and cigarette smoke, fragments of potato crisp awash on some table-top or another, we heard the landlord's sardonic voice call 'Time, gentlemen, please!'

My brother acted as chauffeur. On the way home I was asked by one of the friends—who, like me, were to be dropped off—where I worked.

'Staines Lino,' I replied. This was a local linoleum-producing factory where I was employed as a labourer.

'Hard work?'

'It's a big place,' I said. 'Depends what sort of number you have. But long shifts anyway.'

'What do you mean, long shifts? When do you start?'

'Six o'clock in the morning,' I told my interlocutor.

'Six o'clock in the morning!' he exploded. 'God Almighty! Six o' bloody clock! But normal people just don't start work at that time!'

Perhaps this *was* a conversational set-up. Perhaps his pronounced reaction was partly feigned. Perhaps he knew very well where I worked and what kind of shifts were operated there. Certainly the factory was notorious in the area. And perhaps, too, he did stress the word 'normal' somewhat.

If so, it was all lost on me. I hardly knew these two friends of my brother and I am not, in any event, a suspicious person. But that fragment of talk provided the seeds of a later quarrel. And provided rather more into the bargain.

I forget what I replied, if anything. The conversation languished. Indeed Ian—my brother—went quite silent; ominously so, though I could not know it at the time. Possibly, however, the other two noticed this and sat in quiet trepidation. At any rate, I was the first to be dropped off, at my bed-sitter, and that, as far as I was concerned, was the end of the evening.

On the following day I met my brother for lunch. He told me what had happened next. After my departure, it seemed, there had been a violent argument between him and his friends. It had ended with Ian—always quick-tempered—screeching his car to a halt in the middle of the road and heaving the other two out bodily, to make their own way home as best they could.

My brother, of course, had been quick to resent an insult on my behalf, or an imagined insult; the more so, no doubt, for feeling guiltily that there was some truth in it. He had said nothing while I was still present but had nonetheless seized on what he took to be an over-emphasis on the word 'normal'. After I got out of the car he had made an issue of this.

Now he was resentful, towards me as much as anyone, for he had lost two good friends. 'It was the old herd instinct,' he said, in extenuation of their presumed conduct. 'It was the urge to attack someone different. And let's face it, you're different.'

I made no attempt to defend myself. Argument was not usually my style. But—*different*? How different? In what way different?

I was hurt and bitter. I imagined that in the air, unacknowledged but potent, like a silent fart in polite company, there hung the unspoken and quite false accusation of homosexuality. And perhaps Ian had not even spoken it to himself.

But 'Yes I am different,' I thought at first. 'And thank God for it, too. Different from you and your friends. Different from three little boys trying constantly to outdo one another with booze and status-symbol sex and flash cars and phoned-in bets to a private account and carefully masculine language that goes endlessly fucking this and fucking that.'

'Different!' I thought again. 'My God! In the circles I would like to frequent, the circles I do frequent in my day-dreams, where people read literature and go to art galleries, *you* would be bloody different!'

Yet there was more to it, I knew. There *was* a difference, a difference beyond the obvious one of fashions in life or beyond even simple homosexuality, had that existed. This other difference had always been present. It had set me apart since birth. And I could not erase it by rehearsing in my mind the pointless and boring activities of my brother and his friends, however pathetically juvenile these might be.

For me the incident was the underlining of a something I had perhaps scarcely acknowledged before. It was the final closing of a door beyond which I stood alone. For a long time after it happened I was desolate. Probably I still am. I went home, I remember, and looked in the glass. I looked especially at my brow. I could see nothing but there was a mark there somewhere, I knew.

November 30th
For the past week I have done no work, till this a.m. and these words. I can see my pen moving now as I write, my hand crabbing across the page, very slowly and stiffly.

For, I think, three days and nights I lay on the sofa, not eating or sleeping. Once, I remember—it was dark outside, the house was dark—I heaved myself to my feet and went into the garden. I hoped to see a house-light somewhere or the lights of a passing ship. Some kind of visible proof, that must have been what I was after. But I saw nothing, though I believe I watched for quite a long time.

(On reflection I am not surprised that my vigil went un-rewarded, at least I am not surprised in respect of house-lights. As near as I can now establish by back-tracking this incident must have taken place about three o'clock in the morning.)

It was raining heavily. I had been wearing trousers and a shirt and was shoeless. I returned to the house drenched to the skin and lay down again.

The only other thing I recollect is trying fairly desperately, at one stage, to re-invent myself. I repeated my name over and over. I said it out loud, in an effort to give it body and credence. It came very slowly to begin with but I managed to drag it forth. Then I added my address to it, my occupation, various other scraps of information.

When that ceased to work, when it went from being an invocation to a meaningless and obsessive mumble, I started to enumerate and label the objects on the mantelpiece. I still repeated my name, however, at the end of every listing, thus: firstly, a box of matches and I am Alasdair Maclean; firstly a box of matches and, secondly, a postcard reproduction of Munch's 'The Yellow Boat' and I am Alasdair Maclean; firstly—and so on.

Presently I started to add to this list, too. I tried to be as accurate and as full as possible, though I hardly succeeded in either aim. Thus: fifthly, a French brandy bottle which, I think, I found on the beach here in Sanna and which has perhaps some additional significance for me but if so I do not at the moment quite recall what it is and I am Alasdair Maclean. And so on.

After some further time had gone by—days or years—I became aware that my clothes were dampish and the house was cold. It seemed to be light outside, a light that I took initially for daylight but which I realized at last came from a full moon.

I stood up, took my clothes off, put on a pair of shoes and went outside. It was warmer, almost, than it had been in the house, though still not warm. This time I did find a light, out to sea; the starboard navigational light of a ship. The moon was very bright (or so I thought at first) and all the houses of the village were clearly visible.

I decided to climb Meall Sanna. This took a long time, an hour maybe, for I stumbled about a lot. The light of the moon is never quite as strong as you have thought before you try to do something by it. But at last I stood on top of the ridge and could see both ways, into Sanna and out of it.

It is the particular egoism of the artist to imagine himself unique. Because he is a man and a bit—a bit more and a bit less—he forgets that he is a man. Standing there, I thought that, on the contrary, there must be many like me, alone that night and exposed, on hilltops of various heights and kinds.

It was quiet and very peaceful. The moonlight fell about my body in soft folds. What I did does not matter much but I hallowed the occasion and my surroundings as best as one can by oneself. And when I had finished I came down and wrote this true and faithful account of my adventures, not bowdlerized by above half.

December 5th
I came today to a corner on the seaward edge of the dunes where a mummified thistle, one of last summer's crop, still held its form against rain and gale. It was not a Carline Thistle, so attractive and about here so rare. These commonly survive as husks, sometimes well into the next season. This fellow was an ordinary Spear Thistle, brown and shrunken, like an old man dead in all but will. It might have been nature's master copy, struggling to preserve the idea of a thistle for the next generation of plants.

Two or three of its heads lolled brokenly in the wind, yet its spikes stuck out more prominently than ever from its withered leaves. I thought of a cornered dog, retracting its gums the better to show its teeth. How admirable it was, how puritanically beautiful! I stood beside it for a long time, studying it and trying to fix it in my mind.

December 7th
Another midnight excursion. But I was more circumspect this time. I did not climb any hills but merely walked over to the ruined cottage near here where my grandparents lived. That would have been a five-minute stroll in daylight; it was half an hour to someone whose eyes could not so much as fetch him back a glimpse of his own legs.

How it was dark! With the moon not yet risen ground that had been fifty years my companion turned against me. When I avoided an obstacle I think it was due less to vision than to some deeper and older sense, some proto-receptor long by-passed but stirring once more into life. At last, however, I got to where I was fairly pointlessly going and I sat for a while on the edge of the little 'street' in front of the old walls, my feet dangling into the garden, my mind dangling into the past.

Round that garden once a screen of bushes stood and dotted here and there among those bushes were half a dozen nests where our hens often laid, in preference to their official quarters in the byre. Whenever we heard a hen cackle, in token of duty done, a competition would ensue among us children. We would race round the nests in hope of being the first to locate the one with the egg in it. That would be a still-warm prize to be borne in triumph to my grandmother. Usually there would be a small feather stuck to it or a spot of dung. I looked on such marks as labels when I was a child. I remember them now as symbols of authenticity, the kind of assertion of genuine egginess since vanished from this sterilized world.

In one of those nests our old cat usually had her kittens and was sleepy and contented for a day or two and merely purred the louder when one lifted a kitten to examine it.

But when her allotted brief period of grace had elapsed the purring stopped and the plaintive calling and puzzled searching began. And until I grew older and wiser and a good deal sadder I searched, too, and was just as affected.

I asked questions, of course. At first, I asked a few questions. What had happened to the kittens? I wanted to know.

Well, they were dead.

Had they gone to heaven?

A moment's hesitation here perhaps, then—No, kittens didn't go to heaven.

Where did they go, then?

Oh, don't ask so many questions. Run away and play.

That was the end of my queries but I was not so readily satisfied. Kittens came from the Beyond, I was sure, and must one day go back there, like all living things. I already knew that the world was run on a cyclical basis and that God was the Indian giver to end all Indian givers. The really important questions, it seemed to me, had to do with the sheer arbitrariness of it all. (Needless to say, I never asked about *that*. It was heart-stoppingly daring even to think of it.) Who went and who stayed? For what reasons? Why was span so unfairly allotted? And could not such tiny morsels of life as kittens, such mere fur-covered pulses, be more easily spared than it seemed they were?

It solved nothing to learn, as I did eventually, the secret of the kittens' earthly fate. I discovered that someone came along with an empty sugar bag that had a hole torn in the side and three or four pebbles placed in the bottom. (This was my older brother, usually, and I was slowly to become aware of how some people, apparently, quite liked doing that sort of thing.) In went the kittens and off went the bag to the nearest pond. *Plop!* And that was that.

In due course I was invited to attend one of these executions and, morbidly fascinated by such matters as all children briefly are, I agreed to go. The chosen spot was near the dunes below our house, where a stream had gouged a deep hole in the sandy turf. Toll nan Conn that place was called, in honour of the scores of pups that had been drowned in it. The kittens were not commemorated. In a crofting township dogs are of *some* account, cats of none.

Toll nan Conn is still there and the stream that supplies it with its power still runs. I pass it daily and I think sometimes of the darkness under the surface, a darkness too intense for even the blind eyes of kittens. I am haunted by a hundred bedraggled tiny ghosts.

As a child, I was, I think, less than averagely cruel but I had my moments. Once, in that same garden, I buried alive two or three small crabs that I had brought up from the shore. An hour later, suddenly stricken, I dug them up and rushed them back to the life-giving sea. But as to whether they survived or not I have, perhaps mercifully, forgotten.

There are not many places in the world where the past is as readily available and as cheap as it is in Ardnamurchan. Round every corner a bargain waits.

I have undertaken quite a few night-time expeditions lately. For a week or so I have been sleeping well on into the forenoon and getting up correspondingly late. Maybe the rhythms of my body are changing.

That would be interesting and possibly useful. Better, I reckon, for a writer to be an owl than a hawk. The creature of the night comes closer to being the universal man of the animal kingdom. He can make shift to operate at high noon if need be or if he feels like it. (And round here he often does. How many wildcats and foxes and roe deer have I chanced upon and nodded to in broad sunshine!) His fellow of the day, however, would be dazzled out of his wits at night.

When darkness rises out of the grass, filling the valley bottoms and brimming slowly up the hillsides, a life blossoms that we know too little of (and make too little use of in our art), a life of great richness and strangeness. Imagine yourself a roe deer, with the night at the full and the belly empty, standing on the edge of a meadow, uncertain whether to plunge in. You would be a quivering mass of receptivity. You would be assailed on all sides by a barrage of stimuli, which would have to be registered, decoded and filed for instant retrieval at any time in the next few hours.

If one could undergo such a transformation and somehow retain a human awareness—ah, what an experience that would be! It would be like standing on some canyon floor in the uttermost Pacific, on the far side of silence and blackness, where are born colours and sounds so unimaginably new that one could never be sure, encountering each fresh specimen, whether to watch or to listen.

There would be other advantages, too, in being a night-time creature, though I dare say that not everyone would so regard them. The owl in daylight senses affinities unguessed at by the hawk. See, now, along the join where two fields meet, how darkness races. It is proof that the earth is but pieced together.

But one has to be born to such a life as to the purple. Proletarian senses do not do. When I rise obediently and go to my glass (for one ought to desire belief even if one cannot encompass it) the same old headpiece stares back at me, eyes unwidened, ears unpricked, missing nine-tenths of its signals. The whole ensemble one day older, of course, since my morning shave, so not quite the same headpiece after all. We step and do not step into the same features. Heraclitus said that. At least, that is what he was thinking of.

December 21st
Today is midwinter, the December solstice; a festival on the say-so of the spirit rather than the law. It is a day that harks backwards and forwards, a junction in the calendar. Here the pointsman throws his switch who has never—yet—become absent-minded or bored. A man at such a fork, if he had eyesight enough, might see anything he cared to and much he didn't. There are cold things and old things uncoiling in the earth. In the steading nearby our domesticated marvels kick like billy-oh in their stalls, scenting the possibilities. But in the farmhouse the farmer and his family are being entertained and do not hear or heed the racket.

My father, in his 1960 journal at any rate—at the stage I have coincidentally reached in my editing; good progress!—disappoints me by singling out today only as the shortest day of the year. That is a modern appraisal, conventionally materialistic. It is like remarking of, say, Van Gogh's *Wheatfield with Crows*, that it measures three feet by two.

But Father penned his journal as one beleaguered, aware that his premises might be entered at any time, his writing bundled off for examination. Times were tough and the old gods rampant. Why give hostages, he would have argued, to a Fate that already held nine-tenths of the advantage? He was content to leave a gap between thought and deed that no amount of paper could be used to fill. I am sure that today of all days he heard the scuffling and the squeaking in the bushes and saw the malicious eyes slant and the pointed ears cock towards him. I think he looked at the sky and trembled.

I who write these notes am so far willing to commit myself as to testify that on this particular solstice a westerly gale blew from dawn to dusk, gusting to storm force. It was chilly out of doors when I fetched fresh water in the morning, chilly beyond the poor comfort of gloves or pockets. Showers of hail pocked the windows all day long.

In the afternoon I walked down the croft to the stream that foots it, standing a while on a rise of ground above the bank, propping myself against a cushion of wind and casting my gaze upon the waters below. What my return might be and after how many days, God knows. My nightmares may tell me. The stream looked lovely. It ran dark, almost black, and full and the gale blew straight upstream, flattening and isolating the surface. It was a drumlie deep, superbly menacing; a small drowner of armies.

January 10th
How trusting-hungry are the small birds now! When I scattered crumbs at the garden gate this afternoon (later than usual for it was dusk and town-bred birds would have been well-filled to bed an hour before), a dozen of sparrows hung precariously in the gusts, a bare yard or two from my hand. Though the gale thrust them constantly downwind, away from the source of food, still they persisted, flapping like little machines in an effort to keep

pace with their own lives. At times they took the whirling nourishment on the wing.

I wonder now, sitting over my late journal, in what corner of this many-cornered village do these birds roost? Surely there is no hiding-place here that can so well hug its angles to itself but that the wind pokes a long cold finger in? Yet somewhere they crouch, fluffed out and twittering, and their thin blood slowly crystallizes as the stars wheel overhead.

Not all survive such nights. You find them here and there in the mornings, on their backs, their claws tenaciously gripping air. Even when they live who can tell what transformations may not haunt them as they perch the dark away? When a night like this comes along I think it is a little hibernation that sees these sparrows through. Ghost birds I think they become, for the space of a few hours; approximate creatures. Yet when day appears, or even the appalling masquerade that may substitute for it at this time of year, out from bush or eave they tumble, like toy trumpets from a lucky dip.

January 28th

A sheep, an elderly ewe, was grazing round the perimeter of my garden today, thrusting her grey muzzle through the wire netting (uselessly large in mesh) and plucking away at the sacred herbage. I noticed this from the window where I was working and took violent exception, though I suppose no great harm was being done, if any was being done at all. However, I have been plagued recently by poaching livestock, eyeing my cultivation hungrily and probing its somewhat fragile defences.

So I flew to the door, hurled it open and rushed over to this poor creature. I was on top of her before she was aware of my coming, almost startling the life out of her. She wheeled to bolt, in her terror bending her body more sharply than her old joints could cope with. Away went her legs from under her and down she went, shoulder first to the ground, in an ungainly tangle.

No damage done. She was up immediately and off at a trot. Yet the incident depressed me. I had deprived a fellow creature of pride and dignity and woe to the man who does that! Of all possible sins against creation I believe that to be, in the eyes of nature, among the most serious. I returned to the house chastising myself bitterly and resolving to be more careful and more tolerant in future.

What would Father have done in such circumstances? Opened the garden gate, no doubt, and uttered words of welcome. He to one extreme, I to the other. A pity I do not have a child of my own; a third generation might come at last to something approaching reasonable behaviour.

I have completed my work on the 1960 section of Father's journals and ought to go on now to deal with 1970. But I have not felt too happy lately about what I do. It is not that I do not go on well but that doubts have cropped up again in my mind about my justification for all this. I comment a mere ten years later and who am I, inheritor of a decade's hindsight, to put my father in his place—he into whom so much tribal wisdom flowed? A decade of decades would not suffice.

Yet my father deserves a monument, as a man and as a crofter. That was the first thought to occur to me after his death. Nothing since has changed my mind. On the contrary. And who will rear that monument if I do not?

March 4th
All the pieces of information that in their totality comprised the cultural life of Sanna made their way through the shoals and reaches of time inside human minds. Each piece was passed on carefully before its bearer faltered, transferred live and glowing from consciousness to consciousness, from generation to generation. When the culture was in its prime the onward flow of wisdom was assured. A man would pass his store of knowledge on to his children but if he had none the system allowed for that. He would have siblings or neighbours, whose children would serve to inherit the same riches. So the slack was taken up.

The one essential was people. They were the living channels and as their number dwindled the flow of information, which was really many small streams, began here and there to dry up. Specialized knowledge, the prerogative of perhaps only one family, would suffer first. The sole remaining boatbuilder would die intestate of his skill or the last cobbler. For a while the still necessary boats and boots would come into the village from outside, from some other community not so decayed as yet. But these would not be made in exactly the same way. A local flourish would be lost here, a local adaptation there. Such foreign manufactures would not be shaped to Sanna bodies nor in their blossoming rest so confidently in Sanna eyes.

When numbers became fewer still even the general knowledge that had once been familiar to all the village would begin to perish. For example, small place names; one of the most vital yet least considered areas of cultural erosion. In Sanna such names have fallen away in their scores during my own lifetime and with them have gone a host of associations and meanings and attitudes. That particular rock, let us say, halfway to a certain peat moss, conveniently sited and shaped, where the homeward-bound carriers sat for a moment to ease their burdens, has suffered with the rest. The name that named it, that very likely commemorated its use and value, has disappeared. Indeed you may say that the rock itself has been obliterated for it is no longer significantly there. You could not refer to it now save with a degree of cumbersomeness that would have been utterly inhibiting in a community as primitively urgent as Sanna. You could pass it a hundred times a day and your eye would not light on it with any sense of longing or relief. Deprived of its human attachment it has become one more rock in an anonymously rocky landscape.

What turned that rock into something extraordinary in the history of Sanna was its name rather than its purpose. People might have sat on it before it was so called, or since its return to the wilderness, but they could not talk about it and were therefore indulging a private pleasure instead of participating in a social act. They were not civilized.

Civilization begins with names and must end when they end. It is symptomatic of our slow loss of that gifted state that so many factors today conspire to push us back into the mass. And lacking names we cannot properly embrace for we might as well embrace robots. We must name as we hug; we must bestow the benediction of individuality. When the explorer and the aborigine first inflamed one another's sense of wonder in the outback it was names they required of their respective visions long before they opened the sack of trade goods. Without names for ourselves and our possessions and places we return to the void; we become featureless men interminably and uselessly tracking one another through a vast and featureless desert.

When I was a boy I roamed all over our neighbouring township of Plocaig, which was even then down to its last two inhabitants and was shortly to be abandoned. Often on these expeditions I was accompanied by my grandfather, who had a name for every least hillock, every creek and gully. It was by his side that I first became aware, albeit dimly, how such knowledge set one apart. It was not simply that it gave him material advantage over me, though it did, but that it invested him with a form of spiritual privilege (and, of course, with the comcomitant responsibility). He lived in a different landscape from me, seeing it in a different way and—I came to feel—being seen differently by it. He was accepted, or rejected as the case might be, where I was merely and constantly tolerated. He moved through the mansion of his world as a blood relative where I was but a paying guest.

(I have stepped into his animistic shoes since then, though I may not, out of shame, tell how many sizes too large I find them. For want of a better priest his landscape now relates to me. I feel it, as I walk across it—into it—reaching out to me, however sullenly. We have become reduced to one another. There was for it no other heir in sight; for me no other source of revenue.)

I learned a few of his names, of course, but only a few and of these remembered fewer still. I picked up the names I did pick up as a consequence of some childish whim, being taken with the music in them perhaps; at best as an occasional convenience. He had acquired his as a matter of survival. The gods of place in his young days, the days when one was drawing from a landscape rather than simply walking over it, punished ignorance much more severely.

I dare say that even in his own lifetime my grandfather's knowledge of Plocaig and Glendrian place-names had become unique in its authority. These two townships beyond Sanna, further in and further back, were always his special region; his death has turned most of that huge upland into mere undifferentiated terrain. A land whose moors and bogs and mountains and hollows had submitted or largely submitted—there were always a few pockets of resistance—to the magic inherent in names, coming to heel when called, has been liberated by the grave. Set free, it has reverted to hostile wilderness.

No doubt some of those names linger in the archives or in the care of the Ordnance Survey. If you had a good enough map or were a good enough researcher you would find them. But these are flies in amber. Names preserved in that fashion, the few that are preserved, are preserved scientifically, not culturally; they are perpetuated by means of ink, not semen.

I thought today, as I often think, about my own uniquely-held knowledge of this area. It is not much in quantity and none of it is vital, except in the way that all names are vital. But it fills a small channel flowing through my mind—and flowing no further. In the memory of a middle-aged bachelor, a memory now almost certainly doomed in its genetic future, have by accident come to rest a few facts no longer known to anyone else.

Near the sandy cove on the way to the Glendrian Caves there exists still, though it is slipping away from the world of men and dissolving into wilderness, a fishing rock we patronized, my grandfather and I, a fishing rock long fallen into disuse and no longer, I think, known to anyone but myself. I passed near it the other day and on an impulse tried to find the actual scene of a picture that even yet looms darkly in my mind. (The rock had been one of our favourites.) After some searching and no little hesitation I did find it; not the black steep reef of my memory with the still blacker figure of my grandfather perched atop, but a mildly-stepped platform, sunny and bare and utterly deserted.

For the life of me, however, and for the life of the rock, I could not remember its name and I have not remembered it since. And though it may not matter very much I feel I have betrayed a trust. Because of my carelessness a pleasantly useful place and the row upon row of shadowy earlier fishermen who frequented it have slipped an inch or two more deeply into the great bog that is limbo.

March 25th
There is a type of weather common in Ardnamurchan at the equinoxes and for the past ten days or so, being late March and that time of year, we have endured it. What I mean is a perpetual dry smokiness, accompanied by a stiff breeze of almost trade wind reliability, blowing always from a southerly quarter.

It is not at all, I suppose, bad weather. No doubt other folk would be glad of it, as my mother used to say when I turned my nose up at some dish. But after a while I find it beginning to depress me. The problem, I think, lies in the overcast. I do not generally suffer from claustrophobia but when this weather prevails I feel intensely shut-in. I long to be able to reach up and tear a hole in the cloud cover. I imagine that I could stand at the opening thus created and draw huge gulps of air.

March 26th
I am now well into 1970 with my editing task. Another month, at most, should see me finished. As well, too, for I grow very short of money. I must look to the future now. I must consider what may happen when the last shilling goes and I have to leave here.

If I were sure of being able to support myself with my pen I should not care so much. But freelance writing is such a precarious and at times degrading way of earning a living. Constantly a buttering up of editors, constantly a hinting at commissions. And constantly, too, looking out for the postman, with his good news or his bad news and constantly waiting for a cheque that may or may not be coming or may be coming when someone in an office somewhere gets around to sending it.

I have had my share of all that in the past and am none too keen on going through it again. It is hardly even that the freelance is doing what he wants to do or is doing something at least closely related to his vocation. Very often he isn't.

Yet a small voice inside me says, 'Still it is better than working.' Perhaps so. I have had my share, too, of soul-destroying jobs and know what they can do to one. Nevertheless I have taken the precaution of pulling the one or two gossamery strings I yet hold, to see if I cannot arrange for employment of some kind in Kirkcaldy, where I lived before and where I know people.

I should get on faster if I were better able to transfer my written notes to typescript. The typewriter is a hateful machine. I had rather have the toothache than change a ribbon. And I have coined a new definition of Sod's Law: 'When two typewriter keys are struck at once the one that gets to the paper first is never the one that is wanted.'

March 28th
During a walk this afternoon I witnessed the last act in a miniature drama. Only I don't suppose that 'drama', with its suggestion of portentousness and planned action, is quite the right word for the delicious inconsequentiality of what I saw. As I breasted a hump of ground leading to a small cove I came upon two stoats playing clownish undertakers to the corpse of a full-grown rabbit.

I must say first of all that they were most inappropriately clad for the part. They were so conspicuous, with their red jackets, yellow-white waistcoats and black-tipped tails. Really, to judge from what happened, they ought to have been dressed as the gravediggers in *Hamlet* generally are or as Didi and Gogo in *Waiting for Godot*. Their formality, however, if not its gaiety, may have been suited to their previous role, for I presume they were doubling as funeral directors who had just played executioner.

I came up my rising ground inch by inch till I stood on top. I wanted to be sure that I saw everything. I made myself as still as I could and I watched the final rites unfold. I was that archetypal Charles Addams figure, the mourner with a smile on his face. Indeed once or twice I came close to laughing out loud, which I think would have disrupted proceedings very quickly.

The stoats were trying to drag the corpse away but quite where they were trying to drag it never became clear. There seemed no place in the immediate vicinity that could conceivably have been home to them nor, for that matter, could I discover any reason why they could not have eaten their fill where they were. If eating was their intent the rock on which the rabbit lay could hardly have been more table-like.

At any rate, they were making comically heavy weather of their work. The rabbit, of course—a biggish one—was a good deal larger than both creatures put together. They swarmed round it like tugs round a liner. Sometimes they climbed on top of it and heaved upwards vigorously, as if they hoped to lift both it and themselves into the air. Sometimes, more sensibly, they pulled at it from the ground but then as often as not they pulled from opposite ends of the body.

When that happened the rabbit tautened visibly between them, moving backwards and forwards an inch or two, like the rope in a well-matched tug-of-war.

Sometimes, most farcically of all, they appeared to forget what they were doing and one or both would wander off, pottering about aimlessly for two or three minutes before returning. I had the impression of watching babies, possessed briefly of purpose rather than intelligence.

Once, quite excitingly, one of them became aware of my presence during a wandering-off spell and approached me for a closer look. About ten or twelve feet off he stopped, rearing up on his hind legs, swaying a little from side to side, chattering a bit, peering at me myopically and sniffing. I froze more rigidly than ever, for I wished to see matters through to a conclusion. Presently he decided that I was either a feature of the landscape, or harmless, and he returned to his task.

The end of my play, as one might have expected, was simple anti-climax. As with so many of nature's anecdotes—to change the metaphor a little—the punch line had been given first, before indeed there was an audience to respond to it, and the rest of the joke had followed higgledy-piggledy. After perhaps half an hour, during which the rabbit had been moved some fifteen or twenty feet, though as far as I could tell in no particular direction, the stoats became discouraged or, more likely, bored. They wandered off for the last time, seemingly by some mysteriously mutual and simultaneously arrived at decision, not looking back and showing neither regret nor rancour.

I watched them go and was more than ever reminded of children, older ones this time, loitering along the road on the way to school. They were quite unable to make a straight progression of it but must proceed in sallies, darting hither and yon as this to the right or that to the left claimed their tiny notice. Their world was full of wonder and they moved through it in a series of dots and dashes, alternately busily inquisitive and moonstruck.

When they had vanished from my sight I was loosed and could step down into the cove. Life started up again. Movement and sound flooded back to me and I became aware once more of an ongoing universe. Only the rabbit refused to whirr into motion. When I returned that way an hour later, however, it had gone, though what its fate was I do not know.

March 30th
What, then, of incomers to the Highlands and what, especially, of the much-publicized second-house question, that latter-day Fiery Cross? I can only report what is happening in my own area and try to extrapolate from that.

It is true that cottages offered for sale in Western Ardnamurchan move very briskly indeed. One can easily see them go but it is less easy to discover what sort of prices they fetch. Both sellers and buyers tend to be discreet: the sellers instinctively so, being Highland; the buyers presumably out of a wary anticipation of the sort of reception they might meet in their adopted village. Around the time of my parents' death, however, when I first became interested in this topic, local prices ranged from about £1000 for a somewhat dilapidated but liveable-in two-roomed cottage to something like £4–5000 for a more substantial two-storey six- or seven-roomed one. That was in the early 1970s. Today, less than a decade later, you might pay three or four times those amounts.

Such prices, as with most homes sold now, are considerably in excess of the original cost of building but they are not at all out of line with respect to Britain as a whole. On the contrary. A good West Highland cottage, in fact, can probably still be obtained at—relatively—a bargain price.

In this parish, interest in such houses—as dwellings, I mean, rather than as political footballs—has come almost entirely from outside. Couples setting up in married life here have generally either inherited a house or stay on with parents until they do. To the extent that they show desire for other property it is much more likely to be directed towards the new council houses that are beginning to appear.

As far as I can discover it is not that these couples cannot afford the prices asked or could not obtain assistance to buy (though there may well be some truth in both of these propositions). It is not even that they are, by tradition and perhaps by inclination, renters rather than buyers. It is simply and largely that they are, like working-class people everywhere, more concerned to live in new houses than old cottages. The buying and the renovation of old cottages is, tragically, a middle-class thing almost exclusively.

(One notices the same attitudes being deployed in furnishing. Working-class people go in for new—and often rubbishy—articles, sometimes almost bankrupting themselves in the process. Middle-class couples who cannot easily afford *good* new furniture will happily buy good second-hand stuff instead or may even, indeed, prefer it. Presumably this is a straight reversal of the situation obtaining a hundred or so years ago. It would be interesting to map the how and why of the change in outlook.)

The position in Sanna itself is an extreme one, no doubt. (Though with houses, as in other fields, it is exactly this extremeness that gives Sanna its illustrative and—perhaps—its prophetic power. Terminal situations like ours are easier to read and less open to argument simply because they are terminal.) Of the twenty or so dwellings that comprised this hamlet in its original post-Clearance form only three, as I write, are still occupied by permanently resident natives. The others have all become holiday cottages and all except one are owned by outsiders. The point I want to make is that as far as I know I am the only local person to have bought or even attempted to buy property here.

It is too often forgotten, also, that if strangers are buying up houses in the Highlands it is because Highlanders are selling them. To the best of my knowledge only one local cottage may actually have been sold out of genuine financial need. Yet these properties *were* sold and the sellers generally made handsome profits from something that had cost them nothing, something that had been inherited and was surplus to their own requirements.

I should make it clear, if I have not already done so, that I am not arguing against the sale of houses. I had infinitely rather see a house sold for even occasional use than see it rot, as is happening to one house in Sanna. (It is a sad fact, too, that middle-class incomers are much more vigorous in defence of traditional values and ecological principles than present-day crofters.)

The second-house issue, in short, is being promoted for political gain or simply out of bigotry. It is all a very great pity. The housing shortage is bad enough in all conscience without having that happen to it.

March 31st

For a culture to be worthy of the name, for it to succour natives rather than entertain tourists or entertain those who, in cultural matters, are but tourists in their own land, it must conform to a certain pattern. One might sketch that pattern as follows:–

A culture is the most natural thing in the world. It appears at the same time as its region and is both cause and effect; it cannot be adopted later or manufactured. One might describe the relationship between culture and region as that of foetus and womb, save for the difficulty of deciding which is which. Indeed so coincident are the two, so contingent each upon the other, that if one die the death of the other cannot be long delayed.

Most probably, if a people have begun to talk about preserving their culture—perhaps if they have begun to talk about their culture at all—it is already moribund. While it lives it must be sustained from below rather than from above, kept going by a folk rather than by entrepreneurs or committees. It has nothing to do with scholarship, with benevolence even. You cannot wish it well; to describe it is to help destroy it. It may be reflected in literary magazines and art galleries; it does not originate there. It is certainly not to be found in the popular media of today for these merely represent the pander as cynic, the kind of commercial operation that pleads for excuse the debased taste it has formed and now feeds.

Above all, it must be continuous with the past, have undergone the laying on of hands, breathe air rather than oxygen, be a matter of spirit rather than will, of instinct rather than reason. For a culture revived that was dead, or one whose still-fluttering pulse derives its weak authority from tubes and dials, is no more than a zombie-like husk, a chicken jerking deceitfully in the barnyard dust after its neck has been wrung.

A culture is best confined to that area where it is indigenous, because the further it departs from its centre of energy the more dissipated its strength, the more degenerate its forms. When that happens, those whose birthright it is had best abandon it, for then there's more enterprise in going naked.

Last night, in a house in Kilchoan, I watched, willy-nilly, a 'Highland' programme on television. I was trapped and could not well make my escape. All present but me enjoyed the programme thoroughly; all were Highlanders; all believed themselves to be watching something authentically native. The room was crowded and I was the only scowler there. I was a small oasis of gloom in a desert of delight.

The star performer on this programme was the celebrated Mr X, a singer of popular songs in a pseudo-Gaelic vein and a man, I assure you, more admired in these parts than was the great Maighstir Alasdair in his prime, when he sheltered from the redcoats in the caves of Arisaig, in the desolation that followed Culloden, with his pockets empty and the poetry burning a hole in his mind. My solitary groan when he flashed into view was lost in a chorus of 'oohs' and 'ahs'. He was robed in the full Balmoral fig, the dress that never was on land or sea. He was Tailor-and-Cutter beautiful, an exquisite. O not a *sgian dhu* nor a grouse-foot brooch was out of place about him. His stockings were as unwrinkled as his brow. His hair reflected the studio lights as brightly as his toe-caps.

He sang and he glittered and he clutched his microphone to his mouth like a child with a lollipop. He swayed from the knees. He shimmered and he shimmied.

I thought of my grandfather, in the dungarees and the Burns-and-Laird Line guernsey, the seaboots and the flat cloth cap of all his days. I remember him standing in the peat-bog, in the true Highlands, heaving the newly-cut sods up on to the bank, his palms plated with callouses, an old-master network of ingrained dirt. And round about him the reality of his life sucked and squelched.

I thought, too, of Hotspur:

> But I remember when the fight was done,
> When I was dry with rage and extreme toil,
> Breathless and faint, leaning on my sword,
> Came there a certain lord, neat, and trimly dressed,
> Fresh as a bridegroom, and his chin new reap'd
> Show'd like a stubble-land at harvest-home . . .

My stomach turns. Away with all this tartanry, this obscene and irrelevant clutter of sporrans and gewgaws! Whatever legitimacy it might have had—and it had precious little—has become so tainted a man must needs be lacking in pride and honour and a sense of the absurd to countenance it.

April 5th

It blew hard all day, driving in from the southwest, rain accompanying the wind, long vertical slabs of water following one another endlessly across the landscape, like so many tall grey ghosts. I went nowhere, at least not physically, not even for my morning walk. I wrote and ate and, after lunch, slept on the sofa for an hour, snoring away till I woke myself with the noise I was making.

Who would be a writer? What a frowsty, filthy, half-busy, half-satisfactory life it is. I shall be an old man soon at this rate, existing a little in the spaces between dreams, best pleased to enjoy a painless micturition.

I wrote till daylight faded, till my page got smaller and smaller and my letters larger and larger. The only thing I remember is that at three o'clock—sharp—a pied wagtail came and sat on the garden fence just outside my window, flicking and flirting and bobbing till it caught my eye and I looked up. We stared at each other briefly, pregnantly, then it flew off.

It was obviously a messenger but from whom? From the King of the Birds, I think, who is a great golden eagle eyried in the uttermost Cairngorm and brooding with huge wings over the long injustice of flesh to feather.

I was not in the mood to receive messages and they never try too hard, these envoys from the other kingdoms, the parallel worlds. Only the most delicate tap on your threshold and, no answer vouchsafed, they are gone.

'Put out more food' was perhaps what it came to say. I shall put out more food. It is true that the Cairngorms are a long way off and true also that I am fairly brave for a poet. But I am not foolhardy. I should not care to have one of my innocent walks come to a sudden and knowledge-filled conclusion. I should not care to have my body discovered in the middle of the moor, talon-streaked, with my skin in tatters and my skull crunched like a nut.

April 10th

Tomorrow I shall have to go to Kilchoan for stores and that is not a task I enjoy. The walk itself is pleasant enough; it is the indifference one meets with at the other end that irritates. I began to notice this while my parents were alive and there commenced then a grumble, a pique, that rankles still.

The trouble lies, I am sure, in my too-great expectations. I imagine that I am going to be treated there with a tiny bit of the deference, of the awe even, due to the pioneer. After all, am I not your temporary Crockett, the day's Davy, come back from the frontier for essential supplies? Am I not your Disparate Dan of the high fields and shallow soils?

And I do not swagger it among these soft-living townspeople as I might. No tales of hardship escape my lips, though I could tell them. Moccasin-tongued and sober of mien I brush shoulders with merchants and burghers like an ordinary man.

And so forth. Only I am not quite joking and it is not altogether a matter of self-regard. It would not be me they would be paying homage to so much as those I am the emblem of; not the apprentice but the long-gone masters. When I came to Kilchoan as the representative of my parents, as their assistant, was I not the still-living practitioner of the dead art of crofting? It would be the graveyard they bowed to; their own forebears as well as mine.

It is seemly to respect those among us who have survived great gulfs to transmit something of value. The few black fellows who wander Australia still, how miraculous they are and how precious! How we ought to cherish them and prostrate ourselves before them! The birth of one more ought to bring people singing and dancing into the streets; his death should shock and grieve the world.

It is seemly but it may soon be politic as well. The knowledge borne by such men might one day give life to their persecutors. Honour the aborigine that thy days may be long upon this earth! Yes, all right, but where is he? Why, he was here a moment ago. Too late!

Kilchoan has turned its back on Sanna, on the growing end of its own peculiar culture. What it should have nurtured it has let wither. It has become a fat inland sort of place, dreaming southern dreams. I should excite more interest there as a tourist, even a very ordinary one—a paterfamilias with his followers in a standard Ford. When I go as I am—nothing. 'It is only a crofter,' they say. 'It is only Alasdair from Sanna.' And they yawn and turn their heads away.

April 11th

William Woollett, an engraver contemporary with Blake, used to fire a cannon from the roof of his house whenever he finished an important plate. I have sometimes thought that I might adapt this notion to my own trade. For I finish a poem—a good poem, as I think; an important poem, therefore, since all good poems are important—and I look out of the window to see what has happened to the world. I look in no arrogant fashion but tentatively, shyly almost, as befits one who would pounce on the meanest alteration and treasure it for the rest of his days. I tiptoe to the casement and I stare, combing the view inch by inch in search of nourishment.

Well! It is too bad, really! There are the same old clouds washing backwards and forwards overhead, not lightened or darkened one iota that I can see. There are the same old bodies underneath those clouds and never a hop or a skip do they give in a month of trudging.

But to have a cannon on one's roof! Only think of it! I should like mine to be all of brass, as long-snouted and gleaming as ever cannon left foundry. And when I had done with admiring it I should have the satisfaction of hefting the ball, of feeling the smooth hard roundness of it, of cradling it between my palms. Then the trundling of it down the barrel, a small preliminary growl. Then the fuse, the hiss and the delicious acridity of it. Then—boom!—the slow curving who-o-o-o-osh and the smack of one's own private meteorite thudding into the land-scape.

And then—ah yes, then!—the plume of smoke from the muzzle wreathing one, a new kind of laurel, more visible and no less permanent, and the heads of all the people for miles around jerking suddenly upwards, for once in their lives.

I should whip off my hat next and wave it around me and what a shout I should loose! 'How wrong you all are!' I should cry. 'Dreadfully dreadfully wrong! It does make a difference! It does matter after all!'

How delightful! But at this point in the fantasy a doubt comes swaggering in, as full of bold self-confidence as only an artist's doubts can be. An important plate? A poem that matters? How does one know? Woollett knew but who has heard of Woollett now, who was greater than Blake in his day? *Woollett? Why, he died, sir, and went to heaven or to hell and no man can say whether his cannon or his reputation were rendered down the more quickly.* If art were founded on the artist's intermittent certainties, on those exultant moments when he cuts the new poem or the new painting free of its cord and watches it drift buoyantly off, thinking to himself the while, 'I have fucked the future', how easy it would be! We poets would be trying to hire men with wheel-barrows to carry home our decorations; no such men would be available for all would be at home with pen and paper and rhyming dictionary.

So it goes with those who sit dreaming at desk or at drawing board, waiting for the lightning to strike. On the one hand, humility—and terror, for lightning destroys. On the other, those God-given and all-too-brief moments of ego without which one could not continue.

I *would* have that cannon. I might not bring myself to use it very often but I would hope to have planted a few roundshot in the middle distance before I died.

April 18th

A fine array of washed-in bottles on the shore this morning. I counted fourteen, all of which had contained some form of alcoholic drink. Fourteen bottles is not bad going for a mile of beach. Multiply fourteen by the length of the British coastline and you get a lot of drunken sailors.

I read somewhere once about a beachcomber who lived in the northeast corner of England. He reckoned to keep himself more or less permanently intoxicated from the dregs of bottles he came across on his bit of shore. His collecting method was simple in the extreme. Into the first bottle he picked up on a walk he would empty each succeeding bottle. When his container was full down the hatch it went. *Glug glug glug*.

The mixture could have done little for his palate, I think (except remove it layer by layer) but it must sure as hell have liberated his unconscious.

George Mackay Brown has a poem about a beachcomber who finds a 'half-can of Swedish spirits' on the shore, drinks it and is shortly visited by 'cold mermaids and angels'. Which is to say, I take it—in the language commonly used by men—that he has a vision of sea and sky. That does not seem like much of a tribute to Swedish spirits, when you consider that all this was taking place in the Orkneys. He'd have done as well sober and not had the hangover to worry about.

Despite the legends I think a mortal man could do little for a mermaid except admire her, at least if the old illustrations be true. No wonder such liaisons tend to be unhappy.

And speaking of Mr Brown, one notes that an upbringing is not so easily shaken off, nor an environment, and this holds for the Northern Isles as well as for Ardnamurchan. His world, it seems to me, remains stubbornly Calvinist, for all his fiercely-held conversion to Rome. For the sin of having been born his characters are scourged with a fearsome—albeit somewhat monotonous—regularity. The morrow brings them no relief. If they escape at all it is from the pub to the bedroom, which in Mr Brown's traitorously-Protestant imagination is from the frying-pan to the fire.

This is the post-Knoxian Scottish Kirk paying homage to progress. 'Let's eliminate Purgatory by getting it over while we're still alive.'

But I admit the courage of both men—the English real-life

beachcomber and his Orcadian fictional counterpart. I should
have to be pretty damn thirsty before I would tilt my mouth to
any stray liquid that came along. *Glug glug glug* and Holy Jesus it
isn't vodka as you thought but bloody carbolic.

What it is to believe! To trust your lips to strange girls and
strange bottles and your wits to strange theologies, all with the
same abandon!

But I too have faith and though it doesn't, like Christianity,
make me immune to death, still it lets me partake of immortality.
I have faith in the perfectibility of molten glass. Thirteen of the
bottles I found today were your ordinary boring cylinders but the
fourteenth was a Courvoisier and plumply beautiful, a Renoir
girl among Twiggies. I took it home to stand on my mantel. I can
borrow of its handsomeness whenever melancholy strikes. The
cork came out of it with a juicy squeaky *plop*! and still it smelled of
the south and the distant sun.

It has been a long time since I found a bottle with a note in it. Five
or six years ago, I remember, I went through a period of finding
one almost every week. I do not know why they should be so
scarce now, unless it is that these things go in cycles, in response
perhaps to the fluctuating pressure of history. As world gloom
lightens, it may be, so people are content to stay home and
cultivate their gardens, leaving death to the undertaker (that
house-boy of civilization who sweeps our loved ones under the
carpet). As it deepens so they seal what is most precious and most
fragile of their possessions—their name—into what is most
available and most enduring of their artefacts. Bottle and contents
they cast with a prayer into the sea. *Hear me, mother! It is your son,
John Smith, and I do not wish to die utterly.*

World gloom could hardly be much deeper than it is today. It
would not surprise me, one of these dark mornings, to find the
shore littered with embottled notes.

Casting their names upon the water fascinates a great many
people. I have not gone in for it myself. It is too much like
consulting a ouija board—results are entirely in the hands of fate.
I prefer to retain some control over my medium.

All the notes I ever found were mundane—trawlermen un-
imaginatively pursuing a hobby or holidaymakers having a lark.
Some had their point of origin only yards from where I picked

them up. They had been heaved out in ignorance of an onshore wind and an incoming tide.

How sad! And sad, too, that I have never found the big one, the ultimate note that all red-blooded Highland beachcombers dream about. *Dear Friend, I am a sixteen-year-old Swedish girl and very lonely. If you are an unattached male please write to me.*

Pinned to the note, of course, is a photograph of a beautiful young girl, charmingly naked on some Scandinavian strand.

Dear Ingrid, I found your note today. I am a handsome young poet . . .

Pinned to the reply, of course, is a photograph of Rupert Brooke.

My lovely Ingrid, here is a poem I have written especially for you . . .

Something not too well-known, not too brilliant. No Shakespeare sonnets. No Shelley, Byron, Keats. All's fair in love and war, no doubt, but one ought not to insult the intelligence of one's lover. This might do:

> *Where the thistle lifts a purple crown*
> *Six foot out of the turf,*
> *And the harebell shakes on the windy hill,*
> *O the breath of the distant surf!*
>
> *The hills look over on the south*
> *And southward dreams the sea,*
> *And with the sea-breeze hand-in-hand*
> *Came innocence and she.*
>
> *Where 'mid the gorse the raspberry*
> *Red for the gatherer springs,*
> *Two children did we stray and talk*
> *Wise, idle, childish things . . .*

The lines have a pleasant tinge of *Ubi sunt*. They would make cunning bait for Ingrid, for young girls like to be sadly in love.

Middle-aged poets are sadly in love all the time. That is why the Ingrids of the world and the ageing verse-makers of the world mingle so explosively. There is nothing like an excess of melancholy for reducing everything to rubble. 'Let me see you cry,' the old revolutionary demands of potential recruits. There are tear-stained faces in the committee-rooms, sad hearts at the barricades. A wrinkled bald head and a young blonde one crouch together as the fatal match is struck and the red fuse speeds off on its long short journey. Ten trillion years later, on a distant planet, the astronomers note the disappearance of a distant planet.

And that is why nature generally keeps a North Sea between old poets and young girls, at least in the minds of one party or the other.

April 19th
When I walked through the hills in past years I used occasionally to meet Jack the Shepherd. And though I reckoned myself reasonably good at putting one foot before the other I suppose he covered ten miles for every one I covered. He was nothing much to look at in your Apollo Belvedere line: tall and craggy and more than a little stooped and not at all light of step or clear of eye or any of that kind of thing. Also, he smoked like a chimney. But he could go straight up the side of a hill at a pace that would have left me gasping for mercy.

Now he has retired, lives in Kilchoan and has bought himself a moped. So should I say, 'How are the mighty fallen!'?

I know what he would say. I remember once asking my grandfather, whose seafaring experience went back to the high and holy days of sail and who actually recalled seeing the legendary *Cutty Sark* in Sydney harbour, what he thought of the clipper ships. He spent the next half-hour roundly damning those famous flyers. They were no life for a seaman, he said. On deck at all hours. Shipping water constantly. Never a dry stitch on your back. Give him steamers every time.

Right. There's nothing like a good dose of realism to rid the system of cant. The people who actually lived in the black houses of Ardnamurchan were the first to want out of them.

Perhaps, however, one can earn one's romantic viewpoint. 'The windbelts of the world are deserted now,' lamented Eric Newby, hearing still the melodies of steel rigging and flax canvas. But as a lad Newby had shipped apprentice out of Belfast Lough on the barque *Moshulu*. He had Horned it with the best of them.

Right again. Or if not, God forgive me a pang or two for bygone days. *Honda mobilia*! It is a strange disease to strike the Highlands. From the land of silence and cleanliness it comes. The muscles of the calves it attacks and so enters the nervous system and so at last creeps up to the brain. May every peripatetic saint in the calendar preserve me from that ailment! I hope to walk green hills for a year or two yet.

April 23rd

Coming back in the late afternoon from a walk and passing her house to get to my own—mine being steeper on the same slope—I met my sister. She was out at her coal heap, mining a last pailful in the gathering dusk. She was also exercising her dogs and inquiring of the oncoming night what its intentions were.

That was thrift for you. It had stopped raining momentarily and in the West Highlands we exploit small breaks in the weather as ruthlessly as if they were five minutes borrowed from our final hour.

I spoke to her briefly and as near naturally as makes no difference. Each drew from some inmost recess a small pouch of words, drawstringed against thieving hands and foolish impulses. That is to say, we greeted one another and agreed with infinite goodwill on our estimate of the day's worth. End of conversation.

The tableau held a moment longer, each actor scuffing a toe in the dust, each conscious of being, perhaps, on the verge of great things. But the moment passed safely. I stepped whistling up the hill and where she stepped, if she stepped anywhere at all, I did not look to see.

April 25th

Once upon a time, in the days when I was rich and famous and contributed occasional articles to *The Listener*, I wrote a piece for that organ on the pains and perils of setting up house on the tourist track. 'Woe,' I remarked, in the course of my diatribe, 'to the man who lives in a beauty spot!'—a heartfelt sentence later deleted by the literary editor on the grounds that heartfelt sentences have no place in the smooth ebb and flow of contemporary journalism, being distastefully lifelike.

My article drew the absolute minimum of reaction. One solitary reader wrote in to abuse me for having been unduly severe on motor-borne visitors to Sanna, among whom, it seemed, he had been numbered. 'The likes of us subsidize the likes of you,' he said. 'Our taxes provide your uneconomic services.'

When I had finished with the issue containing this riposte I chucked it into the big cardboard box in the kitchen, where I keep my burnable rubbish. It would help fuel my next bonfire, which would be lit when the rain stopped flowing for an hour or two and the wind stopped hurling cardboard boxes about the land-scape. I thought briefly about my uneconomic services: no electricity (made available since—at a price), no gas; no mains water or sewage; no rubbish collection (my *Listener* reader, during his visit, had noticed the village dump—reasonably well-concealed, actually—and had waxed mightily sarcastic about it in his letter without ever, apparently, guessing the reason for its existence); no nurse within six miles, no doctor within thirty, no hospital or ambulance within sixty; no public transport; no public library (not even a mobile one); a broadcast reception (battery-fed, of course) ranging from poor (Radio Four) to unobtainable (Radio Three).

Some service! With assistance like that who needs enemies?

I didn't reply to my reader. Pointless, I thought, but maybe my attitude was overly-defeatist. Car-owning tourists do not, in my considerable experience, learn easily or gladly but one assumes that they do learn in time. Perhaps I should have offset any bias in my own diagnosis by referring him to a second opinion. Here are some extracts from Gavin Maxwell's account, in *The Rocks Remain*, of his suffering at the hands—and wheels—of unruly car-loads of those same visitors.

With that spring following the publication of 'Ring of Bright Water' *the privacy of Camusfeàrna came abruptly to an end. A great number of people . . . were determined . . . to visit the place; they came by their hundreds . . . As the tourist season reached its height we became desperate . . . . We erected Private notices on the two tracks by which the house may be approached, but these had little effect . . . The number of notices that these* [the uninvited visitors] *had to pass . . . was formidable; at the distance of more than a mile all gates already carried estate notices at the entry to the forestry ground, reading Strictly Private—Young Trees; after a further half mile the hardy encountered the first of my own signboards—This Is A Private Footpath To Camusfeàrna—No Unannounced Visitors Please; then, for those who had penetrated all the outer defences, came an elaborate signboard with a drawing of a beseeching otter and the words:* Visitors: There Are Pet Otters Here—Please Keep Dogs On A Leash; *and finally, at a range of two hundred yards or so from the citadel, the single* word PRIVATE, *in foot-high red letters. Despite all these precautions a steady stream of rubbernecks arrived daily, often with loose and undisciplined dogs, to bang on the single door of the house and demand, as if it were their right, to see the otters and all that had figured in the story.*

And, a little further on in the account

[when], *a few days later I looked out from my window to see a party of five people leaning over the wooden palisade and baiting (I can find no other word) Teko* [one of the otters], *I found the instinct for battle strong in me. I went out and asked them with hostile civility where they came from. Manchester, I was told. 'And in Manchester,' I asked, with what coolness my rage could muster, 'is it the custom to treat your neighbour's house and garden as a public exhibit?' There was a shocked silence; then the paterfamilias said plaintively: 'But this is not Manchester: in Scotland we've been told there's no law of trespass!'*

In his account of this incident Maxwell reluctantly corroborates the assertion about trespass, a point I shall return to. He goes on at fair length in similar vein, other of the tales he tells being distinctly unpleasant. I could cite non-Maxwell sources, too, but enough is enough. Of course there are those who will say that Maxwell at least, as a persistent delineator of the kind of anthropomorphic sentimentality that seems to be ineluctably associated with the taming of certain species of wild creature, generated his own horrors and deserves no sympathy on that account. Perhaps that is true. Yet just as 'Camusfeàrna' had its literary renown, so does this hamlet of mine have its scenic attractions. And anyone who imagines that the raising of otters engenders a specially obnoxious breed of tourist or that Maxwell was unduly sensitive or unduly irascible or even that the discourteous come only from Manchester and not equally, for example, from London or Nether Stowey or Edinburgh or John o' Groats, should be compelled to spend a summer in Sanna. I said in my *Listener* article that a case could be made out for considering the British to be among the dirtiest and rudest people in the world. A decade more of life in these islands has but made me the less inclined to hedge that opinion.

As for Maxwell's comment that the law of trespass does not

obtain in Scotland, this would appear to be more or less correct. (Legal experts, however, say that the position here is nothing like as clear-cut and simple as the common notion would have it. There is astonishingly little Scottish case law on the subject; the idea of a public right of unlimited and unqualified access has scarcely been challenged. Indeed to some extent at least the concept of a totally no-trespass Scotland partakes of popular myth. And what price, also, those rolling miles of Scotland comprehensively barred to all and sundry by the military? Does the law of Scotland not apply to them?) I have often heard my fellow-countrymen boast of the absence of such a provision. The point almost joins with 'James Watt' and 'Bannockburn' and 'penicillin' and 'Clyde-built' as one of the 'facts' that Scotsmen love to club Englishmen with in bar-room disputes. No doubt it is pleasant to wander over moor and mountain at will and no doubt a bluntly-worded noticeboard can provide a brutal and discouraging end to a day's tramping. But one does not have to be a fine lord with vast acres at one's disposal nor yet one who loves a lord to be affected by the lack of a trespass law. I consider myself as egalitarian as any and about as acreless as it is possible to be but I have regretted such a lack, and with good reason, on more than one occasion.

However, it is not only frontally-directed arrows that one has to fear in a place like Sanna; those that thump into one's back can be just as deadly. They may not be alloy-shafted, computer-controlled and all the rest of it but they are tipped with a particularly virulent Highland poison.

The nub of the difficulty here is that Sanna happens to be the Ardnamurchan peninsula's supreme tourist attraction: quaint little cottages, green *machair*, golden dunes, long and unspoilt white-sand beaches, clear blue water, all the stuff of the brochures. And scarcely a restriction worth speaking of. Though the place is communally-operated croft land from hilltop to sea, and private estate to boot, there is never a fence in sight. You can just about go where you please and do what you please and this is a situation which goes to the heads of a depressing number of people.

Contrast this with the circumstances prevailing in Kilchoan, say—the larger village and shopping-cum-tourist centre five miles up the road. Kilchoan is fenced-off from end to end; it is more than your life is worth, almost, to step off the highway. (So much for no-trespass!) Even little Achnaha, Sanna's neighbour-ing hamlet a mile away, is a-bristle with barbed wire. But not Sanna. Because of its decay as a crofting township, with the resulting absence of able-bodied men, the fences they erect and keep in repair and the deterrent effect on mischief-making their visible presence imposes and because, too, of the nature of its terrain, Sanna is wide open. A considerable number of people in Ardnamurchan are determined to keep it that way and are prepared to be utterly ruthless in pursuit of that aim.

If it were not for Sanna, in other words, most of those engaged in the Ardnamurchan tourist trade could put up their shutters tomorrow. Even those who tap tourism only as a sideline, such as bed-and-breakfast people, or those who benefit from it indirectly through the general nature of their business, such as local shop-keepers, would be hard hit. Sanna is a small gold-mine but it is not the Sanna folk who swing the pick-axes. (To us merely the slag heaps and the noise.) It is the hinterland that benefits and it is the hinterland that resents and fears even the mildest attempt to regulate the numbers of feet and wheels. The long and sorry tale of visits to Sanna on dark nights after pub hours by car-loads of boozed-up Kilchoanites intent on tearing down or painting out notice-boards and generally intimidating our handful of pen-sioners; the intrusion of nationalist politics into what ought to be purely an ecological issue, so that anyone who—for instance —ropes off an eroded footpath becomes thereby 'English' or 'a landlord' or 'a bloody outsider trying to deprive native-born Highlanders of their inalienable rights'; the indignant letters to the *Oban Times* about restrictions placed on Sanna, letters written by people who do not live in Sanna but nonetheless benefit from it; all this indicates the power of self-interest in human affairs. And while some of it may be peculiar to Sanna now, it may also suggest, *mutatis mutandis*, an evolving pattern for the Highlands as a whole.

Add to this the commercial interests of local graziers who see Sanna not admittedly or not exclusively as a tourist bonanza but as an exploitable area of—relatively—rich grass and you have some idea of the strength of feeling to be overcome by anyone attempting to convince both those who visit the West Highlands and those who receive them that the long term matters just as much as the short term, that indeed the one merges imperceptibly into the other and that he who endeavours to separate them does so at his peril. (Our forefathers knew that and shaped their lives and their works accordingly; we have forgotten it or choose to ignore it.)

My concern in these pages has been to commemorate a vanishing and vanished people: the crofters of the West Highlands, their ways and their means. I have not busied myself greatly with the future. Whatever form that may take it will be as little willing to take the form I should predict for it as the form I should wish for it. I am not a believer in progress, which I find not merely incompatible with the contents of my daily newspaper but an inherently unlikely notion. At best there are tides, great comings and goings, scourings arbitrary on any scale we can conceive. Or, to put it another way, there is an ocean of history, by now fairly thoroughly polluted, wallowing about the world in search of a beach to crash on.

Beware of calculation, I would say; fear and despise the putting of a two below a two. As well put a red queen below a black king. I have the same horror of solutions as Yeats had of opinion. Indeed opinion in masquerade is what they all too often are.

Yet I suppose that even a poet, who finds the world a frosty place and too clear-cut by half for his purposes, who allows his every exhalation, in consequence, to settle about his shoulders in a little cloud of ambiguity, even he must shuffle forward to the mark at last. If what I write here, in this my final entry, is minute in length compared to what has gone before, it is not so much that I am reluctant to break my own rules or to make a fool of myself as that I do not care to prolong the latter process at least, for my reader's sake equally with my own.

What the Highlands needs before anything else is a decision. Is it to continue living on the remnants of its own history, boosted by tourism, the visitors tripping round the exhibits once a year and with luck putting a shilling in the collecting box on the way out? Or is something less frivolous envisaged, something more rooted and more vigorous, so that the land with its resources is used fundamentally and organically, as land ought to be used (and as it ought to be used before it is quite taken away from us, as a toy is taken away from a spoiled child)?

If the former, little needs to be done save by way of regulation and advertisement. You must publicize your museum; you must see to it that the visitors are supplied with brochures and tea rooms while dissuading them from leaning too heavily on the glass cases. The natives, too, must be reminded that if they are to perform a service for people and wish to make an honourable profession of it (as they should if they select that option and as the profession of service can be) they should go to work pleasantly and thoroughly, remembering while they have their crofting hats on that the balance between man and land in the Highlands is a particularly delicate one, maintainable only by a conscientious process of putting back what is taken out. Our descendants may one day have to decide whether the desert that confronts them came from the hand of nature or from those who exploited her. It will be small consolation to them to reach a verdict, whatever it is.

Of all likely futures for the Highlands that is the most likely, if only because it is the cheapest and simplest, being largely in force already. Of all *likely* futures it is the one I should most prefer myself, since it comes closest to the ideal of my forefathers, closest to my own ideal insofar as I am, for the brief present, a Highlander in the Highlands: the ideal of non-interference, the ideal—at whatever terrible price—of being left alone.

If, however, the decision is taken to attempt a reinvigoration of the Highlands it follows that a very considerable commitment must accompany that decision. The required investment of re-sources would be formidable, though by the standards applying today (by comparison, say, with the investment in nuclear power) it need not be outrageous (and would be much more likely to yield dividends, I believe, even financial dividends, than that fabulously capacious drain that for two or three decades now has been swallowing so much of our country's money so efficiently while demonstrating efficiency in so little else). Im-agination, effort and capital, those are the three requirements and though all are important the first is the most so. Ten years of wholehearted devotion to transport problems would in itself effect a transformation both in reality and in prospect. The immediate removal of any subsidies, hidden or overt, on hill sheep would do as much or more.

It will not happen. None of that will happen.

'Dark and true and tender is the north.' So Tennyson advised his swallow. 'Bright and fierce and fickle is the south.' The older I grow the more highly do I esteem the great Victorians, and Tennyson especially. Surely he is the supreme artist among the

English poets; no one else wrote so much so finely. I suspect that by the time I become an old man I shall have done with modern poetry and shall have come out on the other side of that dark tunnel, among the school anthology pieces of my boyhood, in the fair fields of my youth. The more one's taste evolves, it seems to me now, the more of a slant it takes, so that at last one walks back along one's own earlier tracks, into the limbo from whence one came, one's smart new luggage—so hard won, so much a matter of pride!—discarded casually by the wayside and fingering for all comfort, in the uttermost depth of one's pocket, a marble or two, a lump of putty, a length of tarry string.

North and south are relative concepts, to men if not to birds, but hunger is a universal absolute. Tomorrow morning, in the grey of what I should call a northern dawn, I leave Sanna for an uncertain but presumably well-fed future in that same fickle south, as so many have left before me. They went on foot mostly, for the initial stage of their journey at least; a hired car will come for me. That's progress. The generations go down like grain to the reaper; so thick they stood and so tall, yet now their very dwelling-places bow to the brambles. A day's hacking and clearing will scarcely allow you to distinguish door from window and no man living can tell you on which slope of the hill their corn patch lay. But we go into exile on sprung cushions.

I take up a job which I shall not greatly care for, which I should not greatly care for were it the softest and best-paid little occupation in the world, every hour of it larded with as much of knowledge and interest as a twelvemonth of ordinary work. I want to write; I need to write. Unfortunately I also need my three or four necessities, my two or three comforts, or I say that I do. I shall have a full belly and an empty scrotum, which are the symptoms of a disease much afflicting twentieth-century poets.

I am resigned to going rather than downhearted. My Ardnamurchan visit has not been useless. I have completed the editing of my father's old log books and shall, I think, include both that work and my own later jottings in a book. That is to the good. I have written, or have overseen the production of, a handful of poems: respectably clad rustics, the cut of the clothes rough, perhaps, un-Tennysonian in the extreme, but the material of the best and with a leaf or two of something daft—docken maybe —in the bonnet for gaiety; lads of parts, I trust, diffidently determined to make their way in the world. And that is to the good. I have overcome an obstacle or two and have crawled, as little muddied as may be, out of a pit I had dug with my own horny hands. So, better and better.

I have not, it is true, found a home for my soul. The thread picked up on my arrival here and followed into the ancestral maze has led to no particular niche or treasure, no familiar voices bidding me 'welcome!' but has directed me to a hall of mirrors and a plenitude of puzzled men with threads in their fists. That, too, may be no bad thing. Who knows? I think that few poems bear a home address for a letter-head.

Earlier this evening, before writing these words, I climbed the hill behind my house and sat for an hour, looking and thinking, until these occupations blended and faded, as they always do with me at last, giving place to a state of mind that the cynical would call a daydream but which I like to think of as a dialectical synthesis. It is not necessarily a pleasant state to achieve, though it may be a productive one. It is a time when visions come. Nothing then is where it ought to be. Abstractions lumber about a convoluted grey landscape; grass grows on the surface of the brain and vast herds browse there.

Ardnamurchan is a magnifying glass, a device for observing reality a little more closely. To live here is to live with one skin the less. I pray God that when I leave I shall not grow too hide-bound.

It was a fine evening on my hilltop after our recent rain. I sat on till it grew dark, watching, when I watched anything at all, the beach far below me and the old waves of the world, that visit Sanna perhaps once in ten thousand years of wandering, falling on the sand and renewing themselves in the moment of dissolution.

EPILOGUE

[Looking across Sanna Bay towards the hamlet of Portuairk. The ruins of
the 'big house' (since restored) in middle distance on right]

EPILOGUE

Kirkcaldy, 1980:
the periwinkle and the dog-fish

The periwinkle, and the tough dog-fish
At eventide have got into my dish!
The great, where are they now! the great had said—
This is not seemly, bring to him instead
That which serves his and serves our dignity—
And that was done.

I am O Rahilly:
Here in a distant place I hold my tongue
Who once said all his say, when he was young!

From the Irish of Egan O Rahilly,
translated by James Stephens

For the first two more-or-less adult decades of my life I was a
wild rover. I rambled and tumbled so convincingly that I became
an honorary dishonourable citizen of three or four countries in
two or three continents. Yet in terms of my surroundings I seem
to have spent those years walking in a great circle. Where I
thought I was striding out boldly I have in fact so bent my steps as
to arrive back at something very close to my starting point. The
streets and houses I see about me now are much the same as those
I saw when I set out on my travels. Indeed I could be said to have
lost by the change for if I have succeeded to a smaller scale and a
measure of comprehension with it I have also inherited from my
wanderings a neighbourhood characterized by a sort of dispirited
shabbiness rather than the dynamic horror of the Glasgow slum
that bore me. It is a neighbourhood, too, entirely lacking in the
comradeship of the tenements, in the experience of clannishness.
The people here go in ones and twos, survivors of a fragmented

tribe, keeping themselves to themselves. Their old demons have been missionized away and what need now to link hands against the terrors of the night? They have retreated from the kraal to the hut and take their fulfilment out of trade goods. Mirrors and beads they cherish who once kept lions at bay. In shininess lies the new security.

This was not how it was meant to be, of course, back in the opening act when our servant heroine set about showing her masters that she was capable of replacing them. Who would have thought in those brave days that she would fall for the first greasy pimp to cross her path and speak her smoothly?

It is a post-coital sadness that afflicts the working class. The affair with progress has ended, only the messy results are with us still. All animals are tristful after love, says the tag, but especially when the subsequent accouchement can spawn only wall-to-wall carpeting and a mechanical voice in the corner of the room endlessly mouthing insults.

When I put to my own glass the question that one puts to glasses it tells me that I grow old. That is what glasses are for. Our being allowed to build houses rather than inhabit caves was conditional upon our acceptance of these instruments on our walls. To make it clear to us that we are men and not gods is their one function and however inexpertly they may perform it when first we hang them up they grow skilful by and by. Our progress through life is real as well as apparent.

So it goes in the out and beyond, I think, or so at least it goes in my corner. How I came to be where I am and why, when the world is wide, I remain in place would be the story of my life and I am not here embarking on a full-scale autobiography. I mean this concluding section of my book to serve as a traditional tailpiece, an account of the fate of the narrator. It is enough for now to note that I sometimes wonder if there does not lie a good deal of one's own design behind an end as seemingly inconsequential as this. It may be—or I feel that it may be in my more despondent moments—that our unconscious chooses neighbourhoods for us as it chooses marriage partners, matching people to bricks with a merciless accuracy no computer could rival. That is to say, we get the surroundings we deserve and in our deep hearts want. Our attempts to wrestle free are foredoomed, for we do not really mean them to succeed. If by chance they did succeed we should be the worse for it.

*   *   *

Kirkcaldy, where I write these final words, is a small manufacturing town in Lowland Scotland, one of many in these parts to flourish with the Industrial Revolution and decay with its passing. The chief characteristic of such towns is that their centres are hollow; whatever of life one still meets in them is confined to the outskirts. Driving into them one's first awareness is not of city dwelling as such but of undirected sprawl (which is strange given the numbers and activity of the planners). One comes across the town's extruded guts spilled out on to the land, digesting acres as they go. Here is a housing scheme, there is an industrial estate, on either side of the highway. And so such towns progress, moving over the face of Britain like so many Crown-of-Thorns starfish. What they leave behind is ruin.

It goes without saying that the new houses are lived in. Indeed there are long and never-diminishing waiting-lists for them. People must have shelter and when your home starts to crumble and its official owners will not rebuild it for you, having decided in your name that you ought to live several miles away, what can you do but agree? Agree, then settle back in despair, counting the years till the agreement should materialize in the shape of bricks and mortar.

What it means to have a basic human need made the sport of longevity only those who have undergone the experience can tell. And telling is something they become less and less capable of. That, of course, is good tactics on the part of their masters. Rob your victim, then hamper his pursuit; first the watch and chain, then the trousers.

With the speculative new factories it is different: all the world over capacity chases product, satiety outstrips even twentieth-century greed, the automated assembly lines stutter to a halt. These quite often remain unsold, despite the keenness of the rates they are offered at and the junketing assiduity with which they are touted. They stand empty, eerily stranded in green fields, like those churches one sometimes comes across in rural England where the motivating village has long since gone under grass and where the unwary visitor, chancing on all that devotion leaking quietly away into the wide landscape, blinks and rubs his eyes and for a moment thinks himself come amid stone-loving madmen.

The destruction of land is a continuing process and, it would seem, an irreversible one. 'Gobble gobble' go the municipal bulldozers or the Ministry bulldozers or even, one sometimes feels, bulldozers themselves, keeping in practice in an idle hour. Farms—precious, miraculous farms—are turned into factory sites but if there is a project anywhere afoot to turn factory sites into farms I have not heard of it. The toll of poisoned and concreted acres mounts. We live richly the while, maybe, but at what a cost! We are the ultimate cannibals at the last great banquet, each man disappearing slowly and bloodily while he dribbles and crunches.

Occasionally a town rich enough and mad enough tries to disguise the hollowness at its heart. It does not do so, unfortunately, by creating new growing land out of the central waste. That would be the poor and sensible device and the economic difficulties of this country have not yet—not quite—become severe enough to force sense on her inhabitants. The cure attempted, rather, is to pour in concrete: the Glasgow Solution. And the concrete, as always, sets hard, far beyond the wit and courage of man to unset it.

Kirkcaldy has never been able to afford such fillings. The itch to tear down is equally here but the vacancy remains vacancy, festering with tins and bottles and hundreds of old mattresses that have ceased to fulfil their duty and rest their owners. I look on it all with a mixture of sadness and delight. One may see a beauty in dereliction only deepened by the knowledge that it is dereliction. No scene in the countryside is capable of stopping the heart as a ruined cottage might stop it and if a vacant city lot does not often affect one in such a fashion still it may.

Gallatown, the old and time-worn suburb where I live, perches on the northern rim of the town, where Kirkcaldy slopes inland and upward. My flat, on one side, looks out over the coast and it used to be that I could partially anaesthetize myself to the horrors on the other side by staring from that window. I positioned my writing table accordingly and a draught of Berwick Law or the Bass Rock would sustain me through five hundred words and fifty revving lorries. Moreover, between me and the coast was a further stay in the shape of a farm, with wide fields and placid creatures.

No more. Since those spacious days Kirkcaldy has gone past me on its way north. 'Gobble gobble' said the bulldozers and they swallowed my farm. What they gave me in exchange was a couple of large factories, half a dozen of smaller ones and about the same number of scrapyards.

The scrapyards would more accurately be termed graveyards. They do a little recycling, yes, but mainly they act as dumps. That is their physical function, I mean; their social function is to enable those citizens who live in daintier areas to delay a while their cognizance of where we are all going.

Every scrapyard is under the dominion of a pair or more of huge and woolly Alsatians. It is an appropriate comment on us that we should go to greater length and expense to guard our excrement than to protect our wild flowers. And who, I wonder, guards the guardians? You cannot so much as walk through that jungle without finding yourself menaced on all sides by these donkey-sized creatures. They hurl themselves at the chain-link fencing in a perfect fury of frustrated rage. Or perhaps it is only hunger.

The thing about guard-dogs is that they bark. They bark at passers-by, at domestic dogs being walked, at teasing and foolhardy schoolboys. They bark at courting couples in cars who find the ill-lit lanes of the night-time industrial estate ideal, it seems, for parking. And how astonishing that is! To choose to make love amid such an uproar! To have one's tiniest murmurings and thrustings so hugely underlined! Though perhaps, after all, it lends a sense of urgency to the occasion. *But at my back I always hear Shane and Sheba loud and clear.*

When I first came here I used, naïvely, to try and discuss the astonishing cacophony that is Gallatown with my fellow-residents. One could still manage outdoor conversation then, though barely. And when I did my shopping I soon got on to nodding terms with some of the neighbourhood housewives who were similarly employed. And from nodding we proceeded, by the usual local progression, to greeting. They were mostly elderly enough to absorb me into their midst without inhibitory coyness. So after a month of small talk on the weather and the cost of living I found myself looked on, not as fully female quite, not altogether as a member of that great and secret sisterhood, but at least as a harmless neuter with a shopping basket, ambiguous enough to be gossiped with.

'Tell me, ladies,' I used to ask, 'is it not frightful this continual noise, this appalling thunder ever about our ears?'

'What?'

'The noise!'

'Can't hear you!'

'I SAID WHAT ABOUT THE NOISE?'

'WHAT NOISE?'

I should like, before I go into that final silence, grass-sealed and absolute, to live in a cleaner and quieter Britain. But I do not allow myself much hope of achieving that goal. It is a matter very low on the list of priorities drawn up by our political masters, if indeed it is on the list at all. They do everything backwards. 'Let us take care of the economy first,' they say. 'Time enough for the environment later when we can afford it.'

How foolish! Take care of the environment and the economy will take care of itself.

I do not gossip with my ladies now, even on the rare occasions when traffic noise permits conversation. In ten years I have passed beyond simple acceptance and have become as the pillar box on the corner, a piece of local furniture. That is how it should be. One who sets up as a watcher and a listener ought to be as unobtrusive as possible.

I follow my trade and day comes and night comes. I fall eventually, if I am lucky, into my usual troubled sleep. If I wake then it is only after my private scourge, apnoea, has held me in its cold grasp; after I have, one more time, fought my yearly-more-laboured way back from the crossroads. Or when instinct warns me to kick fresh life into the campfire.

My fellow-citizens sleep soundly enough, both day and night. It is not coal they keep in their bathtubs but dross in their minds. On the one hand the District Council argues about vandalized bus shelters, like a terminal cancer patient peering into his mirror for blackheads; on the other, the common man sits playing with his government-issue console, watching the pretty lights wink on and off and the tinny robots glide in and out with the armfuls of gift-wrapped empty boxes. If he is aware, this common man, that on all sides impudence and indifference conspire to rob him of the uncountable part of his wages you would never by the least squawk know it.

When I first came to Kirkcaldy a row of terraced houses stood opposite the house where I live, on the other side of a narrow lane. They reared up just across the way without so much as a fringe of pavement for modesty's sake. I could have shaken hands, through our respective windows, with the family whose position in the row corresponded to my flat. I never did, of course; it would have embarrassed both of us. I watched their comings and goings intently. I spied on them, though trying hard to strike a balance between their right to privacy and my need to penetrate it.

Where, I wonder, does loneliness end and voyeurism begin? Is it true that a stiff poem knows no conscience? Who winds up the philosophers when they rise of a morning? I think other philosophers. What hung from the trees in the Academy? I think mirrors.

I had houses and people about me then, to brace me up whenever sorrow struck. It was contact without consummation, true; the immemorial diet of the writer. But I am used to that. It has kept body and soul together for me through the years and I should gag now, I suspect, at richer fare. The Muse sets a scanty table, being a lean bitch herself.

One knows nothing of a man till one knows the secrets of his water closet, how he comports himself at stool. My lavatory is a small lean-to at the back of the house. To reach it I have to go down my outside stairs and across the yard, which is a nuisance at times. Yet there may be compensations. Standing in a draughty privy at two o'clock on a January morning, ballooning shirt-tail sustained around one's ears, may peculiarly suit one's mood. There is a pleasant feeling of being on duty while the world sleeps.

The outside of my lavatory door is painted Buckingham Green; my landlord's all-purpose colour, his one solution to life's problems and not a bad answer at that. Inside is as plain as can be. Function rules, as it ought to in lighthouses and lavatories. There is room to sit but not to stretch your legs. This is a cool white-washed little cell, devoid of ornament. It is a very northern lavatory, a very Protestant lavatory if you like, your windswept Iona rather than your encrusted Rome. Here is no plaster mediator simpering in a niche but a man alone with his god.

And not altogether without delight of artefact. Over one's head, as one sits, is a water-tank of Victorian solidity and generosity of content, designed to flush away the confident empire-building turds of the nineteenth century. Pendant from the tank, on the end of a brass chain, is a beautiful porcelain pull-handle bearing a message from the maker amid intertwined red roses: *Shanks' Supreme* it says, name and boast combined in two short words, an epic in miniature. It is a pleasure to pull such a handle. I often sit with my hand resting on it, ready to call down a modest benediction on my twentieth-century efforts. The Victorians were proud of their technology, not ashamed of it; things were seen to work—and heard. *Flush*! goes my lavatory, with lovely onomatopoeia. And one rises, lightened in mind and body. Every morning a fresh start in life.

I am proud of my lavatory but I do not allow myself to become too proprietorial about it, for I am by no means its sole user. Others indeed are residential rather than merely casual. Among them is a colony of woodlice, those ancient humble creatures. I am very fond of woodlice. They are inoffensive and engaging little animals, troubling no one and of a lineage going back in a direct line to the primal seas. They watched Gondwanaland disperse. I come across them often in my lavatory, sometimes halfway up a wall, on a fantastic and perilous journey in search of food and dampness. If you touch them they curl up like plated hedgehogs but I do not touch them if I can help it, except perhaps now and then out of friendship; every creature has a right not to be poked and prodded.

Woodlice are common in Ardnamurchan, as one might expect given the climate, and are tolerated more than they are here, where every man's foot is against them. My landlady calls them 'slaters' and stamps on them very firmly, pivoting her shoe backwards and forwards on the ball of her foot. X million years of evolution are reduced to a smear on the ground. Some day, I think, the pendulum will reach the end of its tether and the development process will go into reverse, if indeed it has not done so already. *Pithecanthropus* will swing in and out of our window spaces, puzzled a little as to why he should have chosen such uncomfortable quarters, loping off one evening into the wilderness without a backward glance, unconsoled by grass-grown pavements and the arboreality of drainpipes and television antennas.

Besides woodlice my lavatory is the haunt of spiders, who spread their webs in every corner. God knows what they find to eat, for there is no way that I can see for insects to enter, save when I open the door to go in and out and that is a period of no more than a second or two. Perhaps half a dozen gnats come in and one juicy housefly. Perhaps not. It is frugal fare yet the spider is patient. I look on her as an analogue. Poets, too, wait for the door to open and are troubled by the preponderance of gnats.

Opposite my lavatory and not very far away at that—forty or fifty feet it may be—is the back of a row of council houses. The second-floor back bedrooms of these overlook our garden and my lavatory door. Sometimes dusting housewives with knowing half-smiles watch my progress to and fro. One imagines oneself being timed and the frequency of one's visits noted. 'Four times already this morning, poor man! I suppose the bladder is starting to go.' But it is not the bladder, housewives, so much as the gallons of bitter tea. And if you knew what that does to the imagination, believe me, you would not stand there half so lightly.

There is no lock on the inside of my lavatory. Merely one holds the door closed and there is not very much to grasp. Neighbour-hood cats sometimes hook an investigative paw around the door-edge, velvetly inquisitive, or a mischievous wind whips both door and dignity from one's clutch.

On occasion, if it is a calm day and there are no cats about, I sit with my door ajar a trifle. There is a lovely and acutely truthful scene in an Erskine Caldwell novel where three men loll in a shack in a field, taking turns at a jug of liquor and turns, too, at peering through a knothole in the side of the shack. The view through the hole is quite unremarkable; there is nothing to be seen—and everything. In the end the men become more concerned about the hole than the jug, elbowing one another out of the way to get at it. It becomes almost hypnotic in its effect on them; a drug or perhaps a substitute. So I loll at my six feet by one inch knot-hole. Indeed, to tell the truth I sometimes go down there when I have no physical need, just to sit and stare through the crack at my narrow world. It is the smallest of gaps and, lacking the magnet-ism of the Hebrides, I do not feel any great power drawing me out through it. I think I have become an *habitué* of my own mind, a loiterer without intent.

Et in Arcadia ego. When I was a child in Sanna I loved best to lie on my back in the summer hayfield, where I could be a secret of the grass, where I could stare at the sky, watching the clouds form and re-form over Ardnamurchan. To me that was a long slow ecstasy, such a consummation as one might expect at nature's hands. Yet, as I discovered, it was a finite ecstasy, as all human emotions must be. Lying so, one's position became at last unbearable. One's sense of the turning globe beneath grew so pervasive that one found oneself clutching the ground lest one be spun off into space.

Somewhere north and west of here the clouds whirl and alter still and the mountains thrust up nakedly, shedding their rags of mist on the way, and the waves break and re-break on my beloved beach. Who will visit the hill lochans now, those remote and reed-fringed sanctuaries whose margins sometimes do not feel a human footfall from one year's end to another? How will they know they are beautiful if I do not tell them so? The red deer graze there but have no need of speech. And who of the blood royal will stand in the doorways of the ruined houses with tears on his cheeks? Who will mourn Ardnamurchan and its dead?

Outside my house in Kirkcaldy the road runs by. Like all roads it is controlled by small gods, lesser Fates, one at every fork, directing traffic with a keen eye to confusion and disadvantage. Yet that road goes to Ardnamurchan as surely as any highway does. If the driver be cunning enough and determined enough he will drive at last on to the green *machair* at Sanna, where driving ends and helmsmanship begins. I do not think I will take that way again, except once.

One dare not be self-conscious in Eden. All perversions are allowed save that. Acquire that faculty and you find yourself, with a sudden and brutal magic—your last experience of magic —transported beyond the gates. That is the Maker's protection against imitation. That is the heavenly jest at the heart of all earthly paradises: you have to leave them to recognize them.

> The farms of home lie lost in even,
>   I see far off the steeple stand;
> West and away from here to heaven
>   Still is the land.
>
> There if I go no girl will greet me,
>   No comrade hollo from the hill,
> No dog run down the yard to meet me:
>   The land is still.

The land is still by farm and steeple,
   And still for me the land may stay:
There I was friends with perished people,
   And there lie they.

A. E. HOUSMAN